Writing Strategies
for
Mathematics
Second Edition

Authors

Trisha Brummer

Sarah Kartchner Clark

Contributing Author

Jessica Hathaway, M.S.Ed.

Publishing Credits

Robin Erickson, *Production Director;* Lee Aucoin, *Creative Director;*
Timothy J. Bradley, *Illustration Manager;* Sara Johnson, M.S.Ed., *Editorial Director;*
Leah Quillian, *Assistant Editor;* Grace Alba, *Designer;*
Corinne Burton, M.A.Ed., *Publisher*

Image Credits

All images Shutterstock

Standards

© 2010 National Governors Association Center for Best Practices and Council of Chief State School Officers (CCSS)
© 2004 Mid-continent Research for Education and Learning (McREL)
© 2007 Teachers of English to Speakers of Other Languages, Inc. (TESOL)
© 2007 Board of Regents of the University of Wisconsin System. World-Class Instructional Design and Assessment
  (WIDA). For more information on using the WIDA ELP Standards, please visit the WIDA website at www.wida.us.

Shell Education

5301 Oceanus Drive
Huntington Beach, CA 92649-1030
http://www.shelleducation.com
ISBN 978-1-4258-1153-2
© 2014 Shell Education Publishing, Inc.

Table of Contents

Table of Contents (cont.)

What Is Writing?

For thousands of years, humans have been communicating by writing down characters, symbols, numbers, or letters with implied meaning. Being able to write and to write well is more important today than ever before, given the complex world in which we live. Writing is the making of letters or characters that constitute readable matter with the intent to convey meaning. Writing demands that one not only knows how to read what one has written but also knows the rules of writing that dictate how characters or letters are to be written and therefore understood.

What is writing? Is it brainstorming? Is it spelling? Is it scribbling words and phrases? Is it a report? Is it a simple paragraph? Writing in the classroom can be simply defined as any symbolic representation (Hefflin and Hartman 2002). As Bena Hefflin and Douglas Hartman explain, the definition of writing includes representations that are "linguistic, graphic, pictorial, or otherwise." This broad definition of writing welcomes a wide variety of writing formats.

Everyone Should Teach Writing

Because educators understand the need for improved reading and writing skills in students, there has been a renewed focus on teaching literacy skills within the Common Core State Standards (National Governors Association Center for Best Practices, Council of Chief State School Officers 2010) as emphasis is placed on the shared responsibility of teachers across disciplines and content areas to help students develop the necessary reading and writing skills to succeed in that particular subject, including mathematics. Pam Allyn supports this claim, making her argument for the shared responsibility of teachers to teach literacy skills as she closely analyzes the word *core* itself, noting that "the word *core* is a homonym: *core* and *corps*…[The Common Core] is at once about the *core* of why you teach and how you can enhance every aspect of your work…[It] is also about building a true *corps* of teachers, parents, and communities working together to ensure that *every* child has the certainty of gaining college- and career-ready outcomes," shifting the responsibility from a single classroom teacher to a body of teachers, parents, and community members who are collectively responsible for ensuring the academic success of the children in their community (Allyn 2013, 4–5).

Most educators agree on the need for writing instruction in the content areas but differ on where instruction should occur. Because of curriculum demands, many teachers feel there is not enough time to teach writing in the content areas; adding one more component is just too much strain on the time and quality of lessons. However, researchers claim that most writing assignments do not need to be graded, which eliminates a major concern about the teacher workload (Worsley and Mayer 1989; Hightshue et al. 1988; Self 1987). And writing assignments can serve as ongoing assessments of students' understanding of content knowledge, which informs future instruction and helps "teachers determine what students need and then design an appropriate instructional response" (Harvey 1998, 203). In this sense, writing instruction across the content areas cannot be overlooked as it is a powerful tool for assessing students' content mastery.

What Is Writing? *(cont.)*

Writing is an instrument of thinking that allows students to express their thoughts and helps them understand and share their perceptions of the world around them. Teachers can give students power in their world by teaching them to write and to write well. The written word "enables the writer, perhaps for the first time, to sense the power of…language to affect another. Through using, selecting and rejecting, arranging and rearranging language, the student comes to understand how language is used" (Greenberg and Rath 1985, 12).

Literacy Demands

The literacy needs for the 21st century are tremendous. Literacy was defined a century ago as one's ability to write one's name. A literate person could write his or her name; an illiterate person could not. In 1940, more than "half of the U.S. population had completed no more than an eighth grade education," which is an evolving statistic as education continues to change and develop into the 21st century (National Center for Education Statistics 2013).

Education as an institution is similarly evolving to meet the demands of what it means to be considered literate in the 21st century. With the advent of the Common Core State Standards (National Governors Association Center for Best Practices, Council of Chief State School Officers 2010), students are considered literate individuals when:

1. They demonstrate independence.

2. They build strong content knowledge.

3. They respond to the varying demands of audience, task, purpose, and discipline.

4. They comprehend as well as critique.

5. They value evidence.

6. They use technology and digital media strategically and capably.

7. They come to understand other perspectives and cultures.

Furthermore, students who meet the standards outlined in the Common Core State Standards by the time they leave high school are "prepared to enter college and workforce training programs" with success (National Governors Association Center for Best Practices, Council of Chief State School Officers 2010). There is a clear movement toward fostering the skills necessary for students to succeed in real-world contexts and thrive as productive citizens and workers. This need to develop productive members of the workforce is in line with alarming findings related to dropout rates and the U.S. economy (Wolk 2011, 75):

> *An analysis by the Alliance for Excellent Education (2010) shows that the U.S. economy would grow significantly if the number of high school dropouts were cut in half. If just half of these students had graduated, research shows, they would have generated more than $4.1 billion in additional earning every year, and states and localities would have received additional taxes of more than $535 million. If the nation continues to lose students at the present rate, about 13 million students will drop out in the next 10 years at a financial loss of $3 trillion (Alliance for Excellent Education, 2009).*

What Is Writing? *(cont.)*

The cost of high school dropouts to the economy is clear and an unfortunate statistic that cannot be ignored in the midst of today's economic state. But what can classroom teachers do to remedy these findings? Why are students dropping out of high school at such an alarming rate? Does the desire to drop out begin in high school or long before? Research suggests that the reasons behind student-dropout rates take root long before students make the active choice to drop out. In fact, experts in the field claim that to make a lasting difference in high school dropout rates, "[w]e must understand and focus on why students choose to leave school. Dropping out is not an impulsive decision. The process begins long before high school, often by the 4th or 5th grade. More often than not *it is rooted in the failure of students to learn to read*—not just decode the English language, but to read and understand what they read" (Wolk 2011, 77; italics added). Teachers need to develop in students the *desire* to read, to actively read, to habitually read, and to read with comprehension and purpose. When students read an extensive amount of literature and informational texts, they absorb the variety of language being used and apply it to their written work. Students are experiencing failure in reading at an early age, which significantly impacts their motivation to read, write, and develop the skills necessary to be considered college and career ready. We must examine how to effectively motivate students to read and write and instill the lifelong love for reading that goes hand-in-hand with reading independence, comprehension, and deep learning expressed through writing. But to understand how to instill this thirst for reading and writing, teachers must first understand *who* their students are and how 21st-century learners have very different learning needs from previous generations during a time when technology and digital learning played a small role in students' lives both in and out of the classroom.

Technology and 21st-Century Learning

It is no secret that technology is changing education like never before and consequently the lives of young people growing up in the "Net Generation." As such, what it means to be literate in the context of advanced technology is not the same definition from even a decade ago. In "Comprehending and Learning From Internet Sources: Processing Patterns of Better and Poorer Learners," Susan Goldman et al. (2012) note that technology is "changing the face of literacy," stating that people of all ages look to the Internet to resolve a variety of problems that "arise in academic, personal, interpersonal, and occupational contexts" (356–357). Students are looking to the Web for their schoolwork, marking the development of 21st-century skills crucial to students' ability to strategically navigate and "critically evaluate information sources for their relevance, reliability, and consistency" as nearly anyone can post information—regardless of its validity—to the Internet.

Having said that, it is no wonder that the strategic use and navigation of technology and digital media is included in the Common Core State Standards definition of literacy in the 21st century. Students must learn to integrate and evaluate the information they encounter on a daily basis from diverse media, including both print and digital resources, whether in school or at home. We have entered a new era in education, and this era is deeply tied to the technological advances that now permeate our modern lives. Today, children can use a cell phone to take a picture before they can speak. A typical three-year-old can turn on a computer and begin a game program without assistance from an adult. Students in school can use the Internet and online libraries to access information from remote locations. They can interview experts in faraway locations through email.

What Is Writing? *(cont.)*

According to Susan Metros, Professor of Clinical Education at the University of Southern California, college students today are "media-stimulated, but not necessarily media-literate" (quoted in Wagner 2008, 183–184). But today's college students are not the same learners who are presently immersed in today's elementary and secondary education system. Bearing this in mind, the Common Core State Standards emphasize the development of those skills in preparation for college and careers beyond the classroom. The hope is that students become media-literate as they meet the standards outlined by the Common Core and are able to navigate the complexities of the digital realm. Now, more than ever, it is each content area teacher's responsibility and duty to prepare students for the reading and writing demands of our technological age. In order to become effective and efficient readers and writers, students need to use comprehension strategies automatically and independently. Students need teacher guidance to help them become independent readers, writers, and learners so they not only understand what they read but can also question it and write about it.

The Reading/Writing Connection

According to Gay Su Pinnell (1988), "As children read and write they make the connections that form their basic understandings about both. Learning in one area enhances learning in the other. There is ample evidence to suggest that the processes are inseparable and that we should examine pedagogy in the light of these interrelationships. Hence, the two activities should be integrated in instructional settings. Teachers need to create supportive situations in which children have opportunities to explore the whole range of literacy learning, and they need to design instruction that helps children make connections between reading and writing." Additionally, "a considerable mismatch between reading phases and writing phases is a red flag to indicate that instruction is not balanced," so providing students with opportunities to read and write will help to remedy this imbalance and work towards building students' overall literacy skills (Gentry 2006, 35). Moreover, J. Richard Gentry goes on to say that "[c]hildren who receive little opportunity to write in school…and too little appropriate writing instruction sometimes excel as readers but struggle as writers and spellers" (35).

Writing is the expression of ideas and thoughts gathered while reading. Mathematics texts are often heavily loaded with difficult vocabulary words and complex concepts that are challenging for students to understand. Encouraging students to both read and write about mathematics topics helps them understand the information presented. When students read content without writing about it, they miss a crucial step in the process of understanding the information because "writing serves as a vehicle for learning both content standards and standards of written expression" (Combs 2012, 12).

The connection between reading and writing is complex and intricate, placing the act of reading as a necessary and crucial counterpart to writing: "Reading cannot be separated from writing. It's neither research-based, practicable, nor sensible to read first without writing. Students must connect reading and writing everyday (Routman 2005). It has to be writing *and* reading first" (Gentry 2006, 145). In fact, this notion is especially true for young writers as nearly "half of the time that beginning readers invest in a piece of writing is spent on reading rather than writing. Many children reread multiple times as they write even a single word!" (Calkins, Hartman, and White 2005, 87). Essentially, the skills one uses to write are the same skills one uses to read (2005).

What Is Writing? *(cont.)*

· ·

However, that is not to say that the reading/writing connection should be simplified to have you believe that reading is only involved in writing when students reread drafts for revising and editing. As noted by Stephanie Harvey (1998, 60), "Samuel Johnson once said, 'The greatest part of a writer's time is spent reading, in order to write; a writer will turn over a half library to make one book.'" Reading and writing cannot be examined in isolation; both modes of literacy complement each other, similarly building the skills necessary for college and careers beyond the classroom.

Motivating Students to Write

Today's students are radically different learners from those of us who Marc Prensky rightfully terms "digital immigrants" in today's digital age (quoted in Wolk 2011, 166). Bearing this in mind, teachers must be prepared to identify the evolving motivational needs of their students in order to spark the desire to write in the content areas.

Intrinsic and Extrinsic Motivation

To provide students with a motive to write is to provide them with relevant and real reasons to write, instilling within them a desire or a need for writing. In order to motivate today's 21st-century learners who are, according to John Seely, "growing up digital," teachers must explore new motivational strategies to adapt to the changing needs of today's students (quoted in Wagner 2008, 170).

There is no doubt that today's world is drastically different from the world 100 years ago. So, why is it often the case that educators implement motivational strategies that are similarly outdated and no longer relevant to the students they seek to motivate? In Bob Sullo's *Activating the Desire to Learn*, he makes the argument that teachers' instruction should be evolving to meet the motivational needs of their students instead of rigidly adhering to ineffective strategies of the past (2007, 5):

> *Given that we've spent a century or so believing that external stimuli explain human behavior, teacher training programs typically require educators to learn how to systematically reward and punish students. Many educators thus see themselves as responsible for shaping the behavior of students by extrinsically rewarding them for compliance. Yet ironically, our system of rewarding students for academic achievement devalues the very thing we say we want: learning. 'If it weren't for the reward we are offering, what we are teaching you would not be worth learning.' In short, a system of education based on rewards and punishment is fundamentally anti-educational.*

In this sense, *extrinsic* motivation is a form of motivation external to students, a form in which rewards and punishments are tangible and concrete. But as Sullo (2007) argues, extrinsic motivation does not seek to instill the lasting desire or need to write.

Intrinsic motivation is the alternative to extrinsic motivation and a form of motivation that has long-term, lasting results. Educators need to demonstrate the value of writing by making the writing process relevant to students' lives and important to their success both in and out of the classroom.

Motivating Students to Write *(cont.)*

Interests

Many motivational strategies exist to help generate student interest in particular writing tasks, but one strategy to promote interest in writing focuses on fostering the lifelong love for *reading* that extends beyond the day-to-day reading tasks of classroom life. As aforementioned, intrinsic motivation has long-term results, which makes intrinsically motivating students to write the preferred method of motivation. To do this, teachers should become familiar with students' interests as early in the school year as possible, provide students with reading materials throughout the year that are specific to their interests, and tailor writing assignments to students' needs and interests. Once these high-interest texts are made available, students are more likely to be self-motivated to read because they *want* to discover more about the topics that interest them, oftentimes inspiring them to write extensively on nonfiction topics that interest them most. Reading texts of interest allows students to fine-tune their literacy skills in the context of reading experiences that are interesting, familiar, and comfortable for them, in turn providing them with the confidence and practice needed to effectively navigate and write about texts that are more advanced, unfamiliar, or unexciting. Additionally, reading from a variety of informational texts allows students to use them as mentor texts for writing assignments by absorbing the structure, language, and style of the nonfiction writing they read, which students can apply in their own nonfiction writing.

Unfortunately, many students do very little reading and writing, and some do not read or write at all outside of school, which makes the act of writing a difficult skill to teach: How can you teach students to write when they have limited exposure to good models of informational writing? It is for this reason that teachers, especially mathematics teachers, must encourage and provide many opportunities for students to read and write about engaging materials. According to Rosalie Fink, "[r]eading interest inventories are easy to administer and modify to fit each student's age or developmental stage" (2006, 18). Distributing surveys is a quick and confidential way to ask questions of your students that are geared toward discovering interests that may otherwise be overlooked. These surveys may also help you assign writing tasks that are specific to students' interests, which motivates students to first read a variety of informational texts on their topic of interest before delving into expressing their understanding through writing. As we all know, interests can take many shapes, so ask questions that are purposeful in determining your students' interests and helpful in locating texts about these interests, such as categorical topics related to family, sports, friends, hobbies, books, movies, dream careers, food, music, or any other subject. There are a variety of student-interest surveys available online you can use to inspire your own survey, or you can create a survey of entirely your own making.

Motivating Students to Write (cont.)

An Authentic Audience

Students today must "respond to the varying demands of audience, task, purpose, and discipline," according to the Common Core State Standards (2010). The mere act of publishing students' polished pieces of writing is motivating in and of itself: "Recognizing students' writing by publishing it may be the single most powerful task of the writing process" (Combs 2012, 167). What better way to show students that their writing is valued and taken seriously than to publish their work for all to see, thus providing students with an authentic audience to view and constructively critique their work? The act of publishing student writing—on the classroom walls, in the school hallways, or even on a classroom website or blog—prompts students to write with purpose in mind as they tailor their written work for public display. Additionally, the structure of the writing process—prewriting, drafting, revising/editing, and publishing—is inherently interactive and engaging for students as they collaborate and work together to workshop their writing and improve their literacy skills (Peregoy and Boyle 2005, 215):

> *When you use the process writing approach, writing ceases to be a solitary activity and becomes a highly interactive group endeavor. Of course, individuals ultimately own their work. However, throughout the phases of the writing process, they have worked with the whole class, in pairs, and in small groups, brainstorming ideas, focusing on their topics, considering ways to express themselves, revising their papers, getting ready for publication, and, finally, sharing their polished pieces with the entire class. Thus, the process approach calls for group collaboration and support at every phase: prewriting, writing (drafting), revising, editing, and publishing.*

The writing process is collaborative and active, which is highly motivating for 21st-century learners. Moreover, "In *Growing Up Digital* (1998), Don Tapscott said that this 'Net Generation' watches much less television than did its parents. The television is not interactive, and this generation prefers to be active participants in all that they do," which marks the writing process as highly engaging for today's active learners (Tileston 2004, 3). In addition to having students be active participants throughout the writing process, the mere act of collaborating with one another is an authentic experience with an audience: the students' peers. This collaboration serves to motivate students to produce writing that takes into account the demands of their peers (audience) while also helping students to develop the Speaking & Listening skills outlined in the Common Core State Standards (National Governors Association Center for Best Practices, Council of Chief State School Officers 2010).

The Classroom Library

Given the connection between reading and writing, providing students with access to high-interest, engaging texts is critical to their success in developing proficiency in writing. One of the easiest and most effective ways to improve literacy is to allow time for students to read during class. Students who frequently read a wide variety of materials have better vocabularies and better reading comprehension skills that can be applied in their written work. As Randall Ryder and Michael Graves (2003) point out, wide reading fosters automaticity in students because it exposes them to more words in different contexts, provides them with knowledge on a variety of topics, and promotes lifelong reading habits.

Motivating Students to Write *(cont.)*

Teachers can create a mathematics library corner in their classroom libraries by collecting and providing high-interest mathematics texts for students to read. Mathematics teachers have an intimate knowledge of mathematics-based reading materials for a wide range of reading abilities, so they can recommend books to any student to read outside of class. Lesley Mandel Morrow, president of the International Reading Association (2003–04), explains that research indicates children in classrooms with literature collections read 50 percent more books than children in classrooms without such collections. As such, this percentage likely translates into the sheer volume of writing students are able to produce. According to Harvey (1998, 4), "the best nonfiction writing emerges from topics the writer knows, cares, and wonders about and wants to pursue," which makes the availability of high-interest texts critical to the development of students' written abilities. With the availability of high-interest texts, students are able to identify their interests and pursue topics that they find highly engaging to write about.

High-Interest Texts

Working with the school librarian or media specialist and parent organizations is a great way to build a sizeable collection of texts for their classrooms, which can be a mixture of informational and fictional books from which students can choose to read based on their interests. Bear in mind that this library may serve to generate the interest to read and write about a variety of texts on many different subjects, so providing students with a wide range of texts from which to choose will be beneficial in fostering students' desire and motivation to read and write. In addition to simply providing students with informational and fictional texts, be sure to provide texts that are at your students' readiness levels and also texts that may present more of a challenge. The rich diversity of language students will encounter from immersing themselves in high-interest texts will serve as models of good mathematics writing around which students can mirror their own writing, allowing them to express their understanding and comprehension of mathematical concepts coherently and purposefully. Especially with interest-based texts, students can build their prior knowledge about a given topic at a less challenging reading level, in turn preparing them to apply their understanding through writing. "Michael Pressley and his colleagues (2003)…found high-motivational and high-performing classrooms were, above all, filled with books at different levels of text difficulty. Conversely, on their list of the characteristics of classroom practices that undermine motivation and achievement is: 'The teacher does not give students opportunities to have power over their own learning. Students do not have choice in their work'" (Calkins, Ehrenworth, and Lehman 2012, 50), which is counterproductive to what we as teachers aim to achieve in the context of the Common Core: fostering the literacy skills students need to be "college and career ready." Furthermore, according to Fink, "the more a student reads in one content area, the 'richer' or better that student's reading becomes in that content area," which in turn will translate into students' success with writing in the content areas as they absorb the academic language of the informational texts available to them (2006, 79). This notion is in line with Fink's other findings regarding the language acquisition of English language learners, which is applicable to all students' language acquisition: "to encourage striving readers…to read [and write] about their interests, teachers should create their own content area libraries full of enticing materials at all readability levels" (81).

Motivating Students to Write *(cont.)*

Oftentimes students are unaware they have interest in a particular topic until they encounter it for the first time, so providing a variety of interest-based texts can only serve to offer students a wide variety of texts from which to read and topics about which to write. Additionally, research suggests that the most influential factor in motivating students to read is "ensuring the students [have] easy access to high-interest texts," so making these high-interest texts available to your students is an important factor to consider when developing your classroom library (Calkins, Ehrenworth, and Lehman 2012, 50). To support students' nonfiction writing, it is important to provide them with a variety of high-interest mathematics reading materials that both motivate and inspire them throughout the writing process:

- **Number and Operations** (counting, addition, subtraction, multiplication, division, skip counting, place value, etc.)
- **Measurement and Data** (length, width, perimeter, area; graphing, table making, chart making)
- **Geometry** (shape recognition, polygons, etc.)
- **Operations and Algebraic Thinking** (patterning, functions, etc.)
- biographies of famous mathematicians (Archimedes, Isaac Newton, George Cantor, Leonardo Fibonacci, René Descartes, etc.)

Differentiation

Below-level students will benefit from scaffolding as well. They may need to be constantly reminded to refer to their rubric—which should be adapted to address their individual needs—to meet the expectations of the assignment. Teachers can provide graphic organizers during the prewriting phase to help these students get started in an organized fashion. When revising and editing, teachers can model how to identify errors and make changes so that these students have a clear understanding of this difficult stage of the writing process.

Above-level students can be challenged at each step of the writing process to work more independently, create longer or more elaborate pieces, use multiple sources, write from different points of view, incorporate richer vocabulary, or write with a greater variety of sentence structures. Teachers should also adapt rubrics to challenge these students.

The English language learner should not be left out of this discussion. Second language acquisition for English language learners is strikingly similar for native English speakers and non-native English speakers: *"English reading and writing development processes are essentially similar for both English learners and native English speakers*…That is, in reading, all learners gradually come to use their developing English language knowledge, their world knowledge, and their understanding of print conventions to make sense of written text. Similarly, in writing, they use their developing English language knowledge, world knowledge, and understanding of print conventions to put their ideas on paper" (Peregoy and Boyle 2005, 159). In looking at this statement, it is clear that the relationship between reading and writing is not exclusively reserved for native English speakers; language acquisition—whether first or second language acquisition—is largely similar for all students, so the explicit instruction of both reading *and* writing strategies will help to remedy any imbalances in reading and writing skills you identify in your English language learners.

Motivating Students to Write *(cont.)*

The demographics of students in our classrooms today is becoming increasingly more diverse, prompting teachers to differentiate their instruction to allow for students of all backgrounds and languages to develop the skills necessary to succeed. And with this growing diversity, it is important to note that English language learners often struggle with more than just accessing content but also with developing literacy skills in the context of unfamiliar cultural references, tales, and legends that native English speakers are naturally more familiar with. Because the Common Core State Standards emphasize the shared responsibility of teachers across content areas to help students learn to read and write critically, providing English language learners with access to texts that will help develop their overall reading ability is also essential to developing their writing skills. English language learners "will benefit from actively seeking exposure to language and social interaction with others who can provide meaningful input in the second language. Furthermore, they—and you, the teacher—can enhance students' English language skills by placing language learning in meaningful and interesting contexts" (Dunlap and Weisman 2006, 11).

It is our responsibility to provide students with meaningful and interesting contexts to learn language and build their literacy skills. The ability to access content and demonstrate mastery of particular skills and knowledge through writing hinges on each student's ability to dissect and interact with texts, unquestionably marking the act of reading as a necessary skill to succeed with informational academic writing. When implementing the writing strategies in this book, discuss the importance of using a variety of writing strategies to express their understanding of the new information they glean from their reading of informational texts so that the importance of reading, writing, and developing fine-tuned literacy skills is effectively communicated and made known. The explicit instruction of the writing strategies provides English language learners with meaningful contexts for learning language, so this discussion is of the utmost importance in establishing a reason for writing in the content areas, not only for your English language learners, but for all of your students. In doing so, teachers simultaneously aid in the development of students' collaborative, communicative, and group-based skills emphasized in the Common Core State Standards' Speaking & Listening skills, subsequently helping all students to strategically communicate and interact with those around them within the context of the English language.

The Writing Process

"A writer," say James Britton et al. (1975, 47), "draws on the whole store of his experience, and his whole social being, so that in the act of writing he imposes his own individuality." The most complex form of writing is the college-level argumentative essay. Taking notes is the least complex form of writing. Writing for meaning and expressing oneself to others is intricate and complex work. Using the writing process helps the writer take a piece of writing from the beginning, or brainstorming, to the end, or the published piece. This process is especially important to follow as students write mathematics reports and other writing assignments. The writing process at the emergent writing level is usually conducted as a group, though on occasion it is done individually. Students in higher grades who have more familiarity with the writing process can complete it individually.

What is the writing process? It includes prewriting, drafting, revising/editing, publishing, and reflection. Read the description of the writing process steps below. There are different points to consider at each step of the writing process.

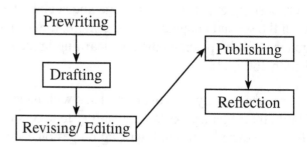

Prewriting

This is the phase where all writing begins. At this stage, writers generate ideas, brainstorm topics, web ideas together, or talk and think about ideas. Teachers explain that students may get writing ideas from personal experiences, stories, pictures, magazines, newspapers, television, and a variety of other sources.

This phase sets the foundation for a specific piece of writing. Before brainstorming or prewriting can begin, students need instruction on the genre or format (data report, journal entry, visual presentation, etc.), audience (the teacher, fellow classmates, mathematics competition judges, etc.), and purpose (to explain, to persuade, to inform, etc.). These elements impact the types of information to brainstorm.

Students need to have a clear understanding of a mathematics topic before they are expected to write or report on it. Teachers can provide resources for research and model note-taking strategies. Mathematics topics are often complex and difficult to understand, so discussion will help prepare students to write. Such strategies as Note-Taking (pages 123–136) and Using Diagrams and Maps (pages 137–172) can help students organize the major points in their writing.

What does prewriting look like?

- researching a chosen topic, using print and digital sources
- analyzing the characteristics of the intended genre
- examining sample writing pieces
- discussing the topic with the teacher, a partner, or the class
- brainstorming ideas about the topic
- using webbing or other graphics to organize information
- discussing the assessment tool

The Writing Process *(cont.)*

Drafting

At the drafting stage of the writing process, students begin to put their ideas on paper. Students need to keep in mind the genre or format, audience, and purpose. For beginning writers, pictures and drawings may very well be part of the composition. Teachers should encourage students to write as much as they can on their own throughout the writing process.

Another area that students struggle with is writing in an orderly manner. Students should already have graphic organizers, notes, or outlines from the prewriting stage that can help them sequence and organize their writing.

What does drafting look like?

- working fairly quickly
- leaving blank spaces for missing words
- guessing at spelling
- focusing on simply putting ideas on paper
- using notes or graphic organizers to stay focused
- drafting a preliminary version of the writing assignment (story, letter, report, essay, etc.)

Revising/Editing

This phase of writing consists of two parts: revising looks at the organization and the structure of the writing while editing looks at the mechanics of the writing. Students must understand how to do both. When revising, students analyze their writing for the required traits: sequencing words in a data report, descriptive language in a mathematics fiction story, topic sentences and supporting details in a persuasive essay. They also ask questions of their writing: *Does it make sense? Is anything out of order? Should anything be added or deleted?* Use the Self-Assessment strategy (pages 239–241) to give students an opportunity to evaluate their own writing. Use the Teacher Conference strategy (pages 244–245) to give students feedback throughout the writing process.

What does revising and editing look like?

- reading the writing aloud to make sure that it makes sense
- adding missing information
- deleting unnecessary, incorrect, or duplicate information
- proofreading for spelling, capitalization, grammar, and punctuation
- self-analysis by students
- conferences with peers or the teacher

The Writing Process *(cont.)*

Publishing

Publishing allows students to write for an authentic audience and celebrate their hard work. It occurs after the other steps are completed and students are ready to produce the final copy, which can be handwritten or typed on a computer. Teachers should consider the abilities of their students. The goal is to present the written information attractively so others can enjoy it.

What does publishing look like?

- creating a final copy
- adding illustrations, borders, a cover, etc.
- sharing orally
- publishing "in-house" in a class book
- posting on a classroom website, blog, social media site, or other digital platform

Reflection

Reflection is a key element in the writing process. It encourages the writer to think about his or her writing, look at the writing from a different point of view, and see progress in the writing effort. Reflection also allows the writer to look back at brainstorming and the beginning of a writing project to see if the original goals were met.

What does reflection look like?

- Reading what has been written and asking the following questions:

  Is that what I wanted to say?

  Is there more I should have written?

  Which is my favorite part in this writing?

  Did I write this piece the way I planned?

  What can I learn from this assignment?

  How can I continue to improve my writing?

The Writing Process *(cont.)*

The Writing Process Center

As previously stated, the writing process involves the different stages from developing an idea to publishing a piece of written work. Students need support to create a finished product. Teachers can set up permanent stations throughout their classrooms for each stage of the writing process. This not only motivates students at each stage of the writing process but also makes it easier to incorporate all stages of the process. This way, students will have access to all the materials needed to work through the writing process. Here are some ideas for each station of the writing process:

- **prewriting**—texts with writing suggestions and ideas, story starters, writing samples, pieces of writing about mathematics, blank graphic organizers, books and magazines about mathematics topics, and encyclopedias
- **drafting**—established rubrics and criteria, music available for students who need a relaxing environment as they write, resources, pencils, erasers, floor pillows, and comfortable places to sit and write
- **revising**—peer editing checklists, samples of quality writing, rubrics, and word lists (such as a list of vivid verbs to replace more overly used verbs)
- **editing**—dictionaries, thesauruses, writing reference books, colored pens or pencils, and proofreading checklists
- **publishing**—computers, pens, bookbinding materials, sample finished products, a printer, colored pencils for illustrations and diagrams, rulers, a variety of lined and unlined paper, and access to the Internet for digital publication

Bulletin Board Writing Display

Student exposure to writing is often limited. Therefore, it is imperative for the teacher to provide students with a wide variety of writing samples relating to mathematics (Ryder and Graves 2003). These samples should be available for students to look at and use as models. Designate a bulletin board in the classroom to display these writing samples or devote a page on the classroom website that showcases exemplary writing samples. Be sure to add to the collection frequently so that students remain interested and curious about the new additions. Encourage students to bring in samples of writing that are related to mathematics. This will also help them locate and identify mathematics-related writing samples.

Writing Across the Curriculum

Mathematics teachers may wonder where writing fits in the mathematics curriculum. What do run-on sentences have to do with fractions and exponents? The answer lies in the fact that writing is the means through which students are able to articulate complex mathematical terms and synthesize concepts. Writing is a tool that students can use to understand and dissect the subject of mathematics. It is a tool that allows students to translate complex ideas into words and language they understand.

There is an overemphasis on the process of writing instead of using writing to assist comprehension and understanding (Fisher and Frey 2004). In general, writing assignments in mathematics mainly consist of asking students to write the answers to the questions at the end of the textbook chapter, with an occasional mathematics journal response with little direction from the teacher. Evidence shows mathematics achievement increases when students are actively engaged in reading, thinking, and writing about what they are learning.

Research shows that there are two forms of writing that need to take place across all subject matters being taught. One form is called *writing to learn*, and the other form is *learning to write*. Anne Walker (1988) explains that the two forms are parts of a virtual circle. Writing allows students to become active in their learning. Active learning requires active thinking. In order to write, students need to be actively thinking (Steffens 1988; Walker 1988). A teacher who works as a facilitator of knowledge will encourage deeper thinking, therefore increasing student understanding (Self 1987; Hamilton-Wieler 1989).

Does Writing Across the Curriculum Work?

Research studies (Gere 1985; Barr and Healy 1988) seem to suggest that writing in the content areas does make a difference. Mary Barr and Mary Healy state that "schools succeed when the emphasis by both teachers and students is on writing and thinking about relevant and significant ideas within the subject areas." The encouragement of writing across the curriculum leads to higher-order thinking skills (Gere 1985), especially in consideration of the fact that "colleges are consistently reporting that incoming students have weaker reading and writing skills than the freshman classes before them…and findings also show that our children are not demonstrating writing skills that will allow them to eventually perform well in the workplace" (Allyn 2013, 10). Writing across the curriculum will aid students in developing the literacy skills they need to communicate their understanding for college and beyond. Additionally, shifts in student attitudes have been documented as a great benefit to writing across the curriculum (Winchester School District 1987). And with the evolving needs of today's learners and the variety of multigenre, multimodal texts they will encounter, "the ability and propensity to read and understand nonfiction is a necessary skill for students involved in inquiry and research," marking the act of writing across the curriculum as a necessity to students' success outside the classroom (Harvey 1998, 69).

Writing Across the Curriculum (cont.)

Is there enough time to write and cover all the objectives and demands of the mathematics curriculum? Research shows that writing can help meet those objectives and demands. Here are three time-saving advantages to consider (Worsley and Mayer 1989; Hightshue et al. 1988; Self 1987):

- Mathematics teachers find that they need less review time if students write about the concepts.
- Mathematics teachers spend less time reteaching content after testing if they have incorporated writing strategies in the curriculum.
- Most writing in mathematics classrooms does not need to be heavily graded, so the teacher's workload is decreased.

Ideas and Questions to Consider

The emphasis on literacy is not enough. The new emphasis is on *content literacy* (Fisher and Ivey 2005). Content literacy supports the view that students construct knowledge through activities such as reading, discussion, and writing. Students must begin to personally connect with the content information they are learning and gathering as they study mathematics.

Douglas Fisher and Nancy Frey (2004) explain that learning is language-based. Telling students information is not sufficient. Students must think about, read about, talk about, and write about information in order to synthesize it and to retain it. Reading and writing are critical to all learning. Questions to ask about how to incorporate reading and writing into content area learning are suggested by Hefflin and Hartman (2002):

- How do you determine what to write about?
- What is the goal and the purpose of the writing?
- How will the writing be assessed?
- What is being activated or constructed by the writing?
- What supports the bridge between what students write and read?
- Who does the writing in mathematics class?
- What role does discussion play in preparing to write?
- What role does discussion play during writing?
- How will you know the writing activity or assignment is successful?
- How will you know when to use which writing strategy?

Writing to Learn

Writing helps create the bridge between the content knowledge and understanding. Reading from the textbook and answering the questions is a very passive way to learn and not engaging for today's learners. A wide variety of writing assignments and activities can help students become actively engaged in mathematics. Examples include mathematics journals, free writes, vocabulary journals, observation reports, topic analyses, diagrams, and charts. All of these writing formats encourage students to think about mathematics and connect prior knowledge or experiences with new learning.

Writing Across the Curriculum *(cont.)*

Writing to learn is expressive writing that encourages students to write about what they are thinking and learning. Examples of this type of writing are journal entries, reflections, reading responses, question-answering, personal notations, etc.

Not all writing-to-learn activities must be graded. Teachers should offer feedback and comments but should not feel compelled to grade the spelling, grammar, organization, and content of these writing activities. The purpose of writing-to-learn activities is to promote active learning, encourage discussion, engage all students, and encourage thinking. There is usually a required time set aside to complete the writing. These less formal writing assignments may be expanded into more formal assignments.

Writing to Apply

When students use their new knowledge in mathematics to write in a more formal manner, they are writing to apply. In these activities, students are asked to analyze and synthesize information and then communicate their thoughts in a coherent, organized manner. This type of writing can be more challenging for students because they need to not only understand the content and be able to process it at a higher level but also communicate it using the strategies of the writing process, the features of the chosen genre, and the conventions of the grade level. Teachers are most likely comfortable with this type of writing in mathematics class, as it may have been what they were exposed to in school.

One familiar example of this type of writing is a research report. However, there are many other options to consider: microthemes, friendly letters, business letters, fictional stories, and more. Unlike writing-to-learn activities, writing-to-apply activities are meant to be graded. With these assignments, students are showing what they have learned, demonstrating their capability to communicate in a formal writing format. A variety of assessment options are described in Part 3 of this book.

Assessing Student Writing

To be effective in communicating their learning through writing, students need ongoing feedback throughout the writing process in order to develop their ideas and revise their written work. And in the same way that the writing process occurs in phases, assessment of written work should similarly occur in phases as an ongoing, collaborative process with students. Assessment of student writing can take many different shapes, including providing students with clear, straightforward rubrics to assess and guide their final work, and more informal feedback in the form of conferring with students and comments on written work.

Writing Across the Curriculum *(cont.)*

Rubrics

Students' writing should be formally assessed at the end of the writing process as students submit final, polished pieces that demonstrate their understanding of mathematics concepts and topics. Providing students with straightforward rubrics that clearly lay out your expectations is effective in sharing which components of students' writing will be evaluated and each component's quantifiable importance. In doing so, you inform students which pieces of their writing hold the greatest significance for that particular assignment and which skills they should focus on most. However, in order to create a well-crafted rubric, you must first identify the learning objectives of the assignment and how much weight to give to each component on the rubric.

Consider evaluating students' mastery of content knowledge and students' writing skills in different categories, allowing for you to both evaluate how well they understand the concept being investigated through writing and how well they articulate their understanding through their written work. As appropriate to the assignment, assign each category (e.g., Ideas, Audience, Structure, Mathematical Understanding) a quantifiable value (e.g., 1–10 or A–F) that students understand and skills that students are prepared to demonstrate (e.g., *Strong audience awareness; Engages the reader throughout*). Distribute rubrics to students to support them as they set out to begin a writing task, continuing to refer to your expectations throughout the writing process as they work toward completing the assignment. This way, you reiterate your expectations and support students' growth as writers in a very clear and straightforward manner where skills and expectations are both attainable and quantifiable.

Informal Feedback

After distributing rubrics and thoroughly discussing your expectations for a particular assignment, confer with your student writers during the writing process to provide them with an informal setting to workshop their writing and to improve their written communication prior to evaluating their final work.

Conferring

Conferring with students is a form of assessment that is interactive, and the immediacy of your verbal feedback is invaluable to students' development as writers. Ask students about their work, their ideas, their understanding of mathematics concepts, and their grasp of the conventions of writing, among other questions. Model for students the best strategies for editing and revising their work. Whether conferring with students individually or in small groups, constructively critique students' writing by acknowledging areas where students have met or are working toward meeting your expectations and areas that need improvement, being mindful to not overload students with excessive, unfocused comments. Your informal feedback should guide students in the direction of meeting the criteria for the assignment but not to the point where revising their work seems like an impossible task. Allow students to maintain ownership of their work by suggesting "options or open-ended alternatives students can choose for their revision path" (University of Nebraska–Lincoln Writing Center 2013). In doing so, students learn both to assess their own writing and to revise accordingly. Conferring with the young writers in your classroom is crucial to their development and growth as writers.

Writing Across the Curriculum (cont.)

Written Comments

As students work toward meeting the expectations for a particular writing assignment, reviewing their drafts and providing them with specific and focused feedback is vital to their success in conveying their mathematics knowledge through writing. When reviewing students' drafts, making notes on their work may prove effective in identifying specific areas in need of improvement (e.g., marking misspelled words, grammatical errors, or unclear and unfinished thoughts). Identifying these areas of improvement will inform your instruction, allowing you to modify your explicit teaching of the writing strategies in order to help students become better writers. Apart from specific feedback, you can evaluate the written work as a whole (e.g., writing comments at the end of a paper), with less focus on particulars and more emphasis on the overall success of the written piece in meeting the expectations identified in the rubric.

Spotlight Reading

Providing students with informal feedback can be an enjoyable moment as well where students are excited to share their work with the class. Set aside a time each week for students to read aloud and share the writing they have accomplished or are working on. These writings may be less formal pieces such as journals, free writes, or feature analyses, or they may be formal writing pieces like observation reports. This practice keeps students focused and aware of an audience as they write, and it allows them the opportunity to give and receive feedback. It is an effective way to validate the hard work and effort of students and may even eliminate the need for the teacher to formally assess a piece of writing. Finally, this spotlight reading also provides an opportunity for students to hear their writing aloud. They will automatically think of things they are learning about mathematics objectives and they will become more aware of what they need to change to improve their writing.

Writing Instruction

What Great Teachers Do to Encourage Writing

1. **Share vocabulary-rich books and reading materials about the subjects you are studying in mathematics class.** Megan Sloan (1996) explains that the best source of learning about mathematics vocabulary is reading good books that use the words. This allows the teacher to introduce them, allows the opportunity for students to hear them in context, and provides an opportunity to discuss the mathematics vocabulary words.

2. **Provide plenty of time for students to experience the writing process** (Corona, Spangenberger, and Venet 1998). It takes time to teach the writing process, but it is worth it. Taking a writing project from planning to publication is very meaningful to students because it validates their efforts and understanding of mathematics concepts.

3. **Allow time for students to evaluate others' writing and receive teacher feedback** (Corona, Spangenberger, and Venet 1998). Writing is communication. Students need to share their writing with others, both giving and receiving feedback from peers and teachers. This helps to cement students' understanding of mathematics concepts. The process also provides teachers with the opportunity to clarify and reteach concepts as needed.

4. **Offer daily writing opportunities to your students.** "A writer-centered classroom emphasizes using written expression to communicate ideas. Writing is an important part of all areas of the curriculum" (Corona, Spangenberger, and Venet 1998, 29). Be sure to include a wide variety of assignments. Some assignments might be more formal while others may be more casual. Also include a range of different types of writing such as journal entries, outlines, poetry, reports, short stories, etc. Students usually benefit from having a choice regarding what they are asked to write about. Encourage students to use mathematics vocabulary when they write.

5. **Encourage students to be aware of and look for new and interesting mathematics words.** Students can browse through books looking for words that catch their attention and add them to their vocabulary journals. They may also be assigned to look for specific mathematics words that are being studied in class. Finally, create a Word Wall in your classroom (see pages 34–38).

6. **Incorporate practice and repetition as a way for students to become familiar with vocabulary words and how they are to be used** (Laflamme 1997). Students can be exposed through writing, discussions, modeling, classroom exercises, and reading.

7. **Teach students the strategies to read, understand, and write about increasingly complex text.** These same strategies can help students work through difficult concepts to arrive at deep learning. Students who can recognize text patterns will be better prepared to use those patterns in their own writing (Fisher and Ivey 2005).

8. **Focus students' reading and writing on big ideas. Don't get caught up in the details.** Rote learning does not lend itself to lifelong learning. Focusing on themes, concepts, and big ideas lends itself to linking new information to prior knowledge as well as life experiences and events that are happening in the world today.

Writing Instruction (cont.)

Writing Venues in the Mathematics Classroom

Mathematics teachers can easily incorporate the same techniques that language arts teachers have used for years to help students become more strategic and skilled writers and to help them comprehend and write about the mathematics materials they encounter. There are a variety of ways to teach students new ideas and to incorporate writing into the mathematics curriculum. The first is to consider changing class configurations to use writing in mathematics. Content-area teachers often lecture to the whole class and seldom pair students together or assign small groups to work together for reading and writing. Following are suggestions for the types of configurations a mathematics teacher can consider:

Large groups are best for:

- introducing a new writing strategy
- modeling think-alouds to show how good writers work through a piece of writing
- practicing think-alouds to apply a strategy to students' own writing and allowing students to share their experiences and ideas using the strategy

Small groups are best for:

- providing more intensive instruction for students who need it
- introducing above-level students to a new writing piece or strategy so that they can apply it independently to more challenging writing assignments
- preteaching new strategies and vocabulary to English language learners or below-level students

Conferences are best for:

- checking students' understanding of mathematics concepts and the writing strategies being used
- providing intensive writing strategy instruction for students who may need extra attention
- coaching students in how they might reveal their thinking by writing to others
- pushing students to use a strategy to think more deeply than they might have imagined possible
- individually editing and correcting student writing

Pair students with partners:

- to discuss free writes, dialogue journals, think-pair-share, etc.
- to edit and gather input on product writing pieces

Writing Instruction (cont.)

Habits of Highly Effective Writers

Nell Duke and P. David Pearson (2001) have established that good readers read and write a lot. They also set goals, make predictions, and read selectively. Many of the same practices of good readers are also done by good writers. Here are some more specific suggestions for highly effective writers:

- **Good writers write all the time.** The more experience one has writing, the better writer he or she becomes. Learning to write takes practice and more practice!

- **Good writers read a lot.** Reading provides a great model for writers as to what the finished product looks like (Fisher and Ivey 2005). Students who read will know how to write better than those who do not.

- **Good writers are aware of correct spelling.** There are no excuses for poor spelling. Commit to learning and using correct spelling in writing—even in the rough draft, if possible. Good writers use all the resources available and understand the limitations of computer spell-check programs.

- **Good writers appreciate critiques and feedback.** Good writers have a "thick skin" and ask for input and suggestions from many different sources.

- **Good writers keep a learning log handy.** The learning log can be used to store good writing ideas, to document what is being learned, to activate prior knowledge, and to question what is being learned (Brozo and Simpson 2003; Fisher and Frey 2004). Using this learning log also helps cement learning and helps students avoid writer's block.

- **Good writers write for a variety of purposes.** Learning to write in a variety of formats makes for a well-rounded, experienced writer. Teachers should expose students to different types of mathematics writing formats.

- **Good writers read and edit other people's writing.** Good writers look for opportunities to work with others to improve their writing. Peer editing groups are an excellent way to get feedback and reinforcement from peers. This feedback is important for the self-image of the writer (Gahn 1989). Editing others' work will also help students recognize writing errors, such as an off-topic response, a weak topic sentence, a lack of supporting detail, weak vocabulary, and errors in spelling or grammar.

- **Good writers think objectively.** Good writers need to be able to step back and really look at their writing. Some writers are so happy to be done with their writing that they never really look at it again.

- **Good writers read it out loud!** Teachers can encourage students to give their writing a voice. Many errors or additions are discovered when a student listens to the writing being read aloud.

- **Good writers use and create rubrics and checklists.** Mary Huba and Jann Freed (2000) reiterate the importance of using and creating rubrics and checklists, which help to clarify the expectations for writing assignments. Rubrics and checklists also enable students to become self-directed in mastering the content learning.

How to Use This Book

The focus of this research-based book is to demonstrate how to incorporate more writing in the mathematics classroom. Increasing the use of writing is a key way to promote stronger literacy in the content areas. Research shows that using writing in mathematics is the best way to help students understand the complex concepts and terms introduced in the content areas. This book provides mathematics teachers with the information needed to implement writing activities and assignments that correlate with mathematics objectives and goals. The strong research connection in this book helps tie together what teachers actually do in the classroom with the most current research available.

We also know that students come into our classrooms at varying reading and readiness levels to access the content at hand and express their understanding through writing. As such, this resource provides suggestions for differentiating the writing strategies for different groups of students so that they can benefit from the writing strategy being implemented, whether those groups are English language learners or below-, on-, or above-level students.

Part 1: Writing to Learn

This section is composed of strategies for using writing to learn in mathematics. These include developing vocabulary, previewing and reviewing, journal writing, note-taking, and using diagrams and maps. These strategies use writing as a tool for students to process and personalize what they learn so that they are able to synthesize and break down the complex mathematics terms and concepts.

Part 2: Writing to Apply

This section offers strategies for using writing to apply new knowledge in mathematics: authoring, summarizing, and applying knowledge in all genres. These strategies provide opportunities to utilize the entire writing process to compose a piece of writing that incorporates their mathematics knowledge. Teachers may wish to use strategies from Part 1 as building blocks for working toward these application assignments.

Part 3: Assessing Writing

This section describes several holistic assessment options for writing in the mathematics classroom. Each strategy listed in the book includes the purpose for and benefits of the strategy and its connection to writing and mathematics, the grade levels for which it is appropriate, and the McREL and Common Core standards that it meets. A step-by-step activity description follows, along with variations, if appropriate, and differentiated instruction to accommodate all types of students. These alterations and suggestions are written for English language learners, above-level students, and below-level students.

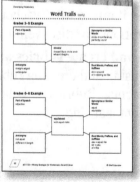
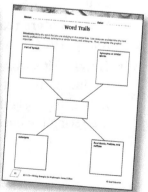

Correlation to Standards

Shell Education is committed to producing educational materials that are research and standards based. In this effort, we have correlated all of our products to the academic standards of all 50 United States, the District of Columbia, the Department of Defense Dependent Schools, and all Canadian provinces.

How to Find Standards Correlations

To print a customized correlation report of this product for your state, visit our website at http://www. shelleducation.com and follow the on-screen directions. If you require assistance in printing correlation reports, please contact Customer Service at 1-877-777-3450.

Purpose and Intent of Standards

Legislation mandates that all states adopt academic standards that identify the skills students will learn in kindergarten through grade twelve. Many states also have standards for Pre–K. This same legislation sets requirements to ensure the standards are detailed and comprehensive.

Standards are designed to focus instruction and guide adoption of curricula. Standards are statements that describe the criteria necessary for students to meet specific academic goals. They define the knowledge, skills, and content students should acquire at each level. Standards are also used to develop standardized tests to evaluate students' academic progress. Teachers are required to demonstrate how their lessons meet state standards. State standards are used in the development of all of our products, so educators can be assured they meet the academic requirements of each state.

Common Core State Standards

The lessons in this book are aligned to the Common Core State Standards (CCSS). The standards support the objectives presented throughout the lessons and are provided on the Digital Resource CD (standards.pdf).

McREL Compendium

We use the Mid-continent Research for Education and Learning (McREL) Compendium to create standards correlations. Each year, McREL analyzes state standards and revises the compendium. By following this procedure, McREL is able to produce a general compilation of national standards. Each lesson in this product is based on one or more McREL standards, which are provided on the Digital Resource CD (standards.pdf).

TESOL and WIDA Standards

The lessons in this book promote English language development for English language learners. The standards correlations can be found on the Digital Resource CD (standards.pdf).

Correlation to Standards *(cont.)*

The main focus of the strategies presented in this book is to promote the implementation of explicit writing instruction in the mathematics classroom. The correlating standards for the strategies in this resource are provided on the Digital Resource CD (standards.pdf).

Common Core State Standards

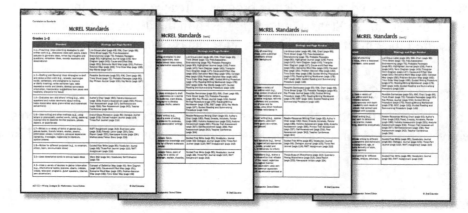

McREL Standards

TESOL and WIDA Standards

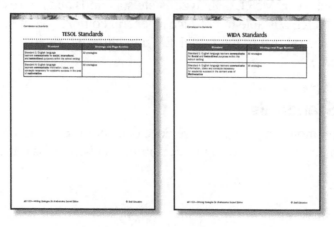

Developing Vocabulary Overview

Mathematics Vocabulary and Writing

Extensive research shows that the size of a student's vocabulary is directly related to a student's ability to read (Laflamme 1997). The larger the vocabulary, the easier it is for students to read. The connection between vocabulary and writing is even stronger. One's ability to write is directly tied to one's ability to understand and use vocabulary words. Unlike with reading, students do not have the benefit of using context clues to determine the meaning of words. As writers, they are creating the context clues!

Wesley Becker (1977) has determined that the deficiencies a student may have in vocabulary may lead to poor academic achievement. With the pressure to increase the science, technology, and mathematical skills of students, there is no room to fail. Enriching the vocabulary of students is a necessity if we want students to continue to build and learn mathematics terms.

Because students are exposed to a large number of mathematics vocabulary words in the mathematics classroom, they need opportunities to interact with these words to become familiar with them and build them into their background knowledge. Students will not internalize and remember these words by reading alone. They must learn to know and understand these words well enough to write about them. Their writing and comprehension skills depend upon it. According to Cathy Corona, Sandra Spangenberger, and Iris Venet (1998, 26), "At any level, written communication is more effective when a depth of vocabulary and command of language is evident." Research about vocabulary demonstrates the need for an emphasis on writing for students to understand new terms. Writing is the way a student can personalize unfamiliar terms and incorporate them into his or her vocabulary.

Students should be engaged in activities where they discuss and write about mathematics terms and concepts, as well as generate questions, predict answers, and evaluate evidence. Building students' vocabulary will assist teachers in accomplishing this task. The following strategies provide teachers with vocabulary exercises and activities to help build students' vocabulary in the subject of mathematics.

So how do students increase their vocabulary in order to incorporate it into their writing? Research suggests that we learn the meaning of words by using them in the context of "old" words we already know and understand (Adams 1990). New learning is continually building on old or previous learning. The same is true for old and new vocabulary words. New vocabulary words are learned by building on known words. We use these "old" words to describe and define new vocabulary. Most of learning is acquired through language (Adams 1990). The learning occurs through accessing prior language and connecting it to new language.

Developing Vocabulary Overview *(cont.)*

Standards Addressed

The following chart shows the correlating standards for each strategy in this section. Refer to the Digital Resource CD (standards.pdf) to read the correlating standards in their entirety.

Strategy	McREL Standards	Common Core State Standards
Word Wall	Grades 1–2 (2.1) Grades 3–5 (2.1) Grades 6–8 (2.1) Grades 9–12 (2.1)	Grade 1 (L.1.6) Grade 2 (L.2.6) Grade 3 (L.3.6) Grade 4 (L.4.6) Grade 5 (L.5.6) Grade 6 (L.6.6) Grade 7 (L.7.6) Grade 8 (L.8.6) Grades 9–10 (L.9-10.6) Grades 11–12 (L.11-12.6)
Frayer Model	Grades 3–5 (4.7) Grades 6–8 (4.3) Grades 9–12 (4.6)	Grade 3 (W.3.7, W.3.8) Grade 4 (W.4.7, W.4.8) Grade 5 (W.5.7, W.5.8) Grade 6 (W.6.7, W.6.8) Grade 7 (W.7.7, W.7.8) Grade 8 (W.8.7, W.8.8) Grades 9–10 (W.9-10.7) Grades 11–12 (W.11-12.7)
Concept of Definition Map	Grades 1–2 (4.2) Grades 3–5 (4.7) Grades 6–8 (4.3) Grades 9–12 (4.6)	Grade 1 (CCRA.W.7, W.1.8) Grade 2 (CCRA.W.7, W.2.8) Grade 3 (CCRA.W.7, W.3.8) Grade 4 (CCRA.W.7, W.4.8) Grade 5 (CCRA.W.7, W.5.8) Grade 6 (W.6.7) Grade 7 (W.7.7) Grade 8 (W.8.7) Grades 9–10 (W.9-10.7) Grades 11–12 (W.11-12.7)

Developing Vocabulary Overview *(cont.)*

Strategy	McREL Standards	Common Core State Standards
List-Group-Label	Grades 1–2 (1.1) Grades 3–5 (1.1) Grades 6–8 (1.1) Grades 9–12 (1.1)	Grade 1 (CCRA.W.4) Grade 2 (CCRA.W.4) Grade 3 (W.3.4) Grade 4 (W.4.4) Grade 5 (W.5.4) Grade 6 (W.6.4) Grade 7 (W.7.4) Grade 8 (W.8.4) Grades 9–10 (W.9-10.4) Grades 11–12 (W.11-12.4)
Vocabulary Self-Collection	Grades 1–2 (2.1) Grades 3–5 (2.1) Grades 6–8 (2.1) Grades 9–12 (2.1)	Grade 1 (L.1.6) Grade 2 (L.2.6) Grade 3 (L.3.6) Grade 4 (L.4.6) Grade 5 (L.5.6) Grade 6 (L.6.6) Grade 7 (L.7.6) Grade 8 (L.8.6) Grades 9–10 (L.9-10.6) Grades 11–12 (L.11-12.6)
Possible Sentences	Grades 1–2 (1.2) Grades 3–5 (1.2) Grades 6–8 (1.2) Grades 9–12 (1.2)	Grade 1 (W.1.5) Grade 2 (W.2.5) Grade 3 (W.3.5) Grade 4 (W.4.5) Grade 5 (W.5.5) Grade 6 (W.6.5) Grade 7 (W.7.5) Grade 8 (W.8.5) Grades 9–10 (W.9-10.5) Grades 11–12 (W.11-12.5)
Word Trails	Grades 3–5 (4.3, 4.7) Grades 6–8 (4.3) Grades 9–12 (4.2, 4.6)	Grade 3 (W.3.8, L.3.6) Grade 4 (W.4.8, L.4.6) Grade 5 (W.5.8, L.5.6) Grade 6 (W.6.8, L.6.6) Grade 7 (W.7.8, L.7.6) Grade 8 (W.8.8, L.8.6) Grades 9–10 (W.9-10.8, L.9-10.6) Grades 11–12 (W.11-12.8, L.11-12.6)

Word Wall

Background Information

A Word Wall is a display of key vocabulary or concept words. It can be created on a bulletin board or on a large sheet of paper taped to the wall. A Word Wall is an effective way to keep track of new grade-appropriate words students are learning and an easy reference for them during class to develop oral and written language as they demonstrate their understanding of the new vocabulary. Students will be more apt to use the Word Wall if they are involved with the creation and the upkeep of the wall.

Grade Levels/Standards Addressed

See page 32 for the standards this strategy addresses, or refer to the Digital Resource CD (standards.pdf) to read the correlating standards in their entirety.

Genres

Expository, Summary, Narrative, Persuasive

Stages of Writing Process

Prewrite, Draft, Revise

Activity

Prepare strips of cardstock that are large enough to be read easily from a distance and ask students to neatly print the vocabulary words. Encourage students to include illustrations for each word, if possible. Designate a spot in the classroom for the Word Wall, and reserve a specific area for new vocabulary words. Remind students to use this resource as they write about or learn new concepts. There are many activities that can be incorporated with the Word Wall. Select from the activities listed or create activities to best meet the needs of your students to help them acquire and use accurately the new vocabulary:

- **Make a List**—Have students classify the Word Wall words by part of speech, roots, affixes, etc.

- **Defining Sentence**—Assign each student a word. Students must create a sentence for the assigned word that gives the definition of the word.

- **What's at the End?**—Identify and discuss words with similar endings.

- **See It, Say It, Chant It, Sing It, and Clap It!**—Find as many different ways as possible to read and spell the words on the Word Wall.

- **Be a Mind Reader**—Have a student give clues about a selected word while class members try to guess the word. Clues can include the beginning or ending letter, rhyme clues, the definition of its roots, prefixes, or suffixes, number of letters in the word, etc.

- **Guess the Covered Word**—Write sentences on the board using the Word Wall words, being mindful to cover the vocabulary word of focus, and challenge students to guess which word belongs in each sentence.

- **Find It First!**—Call two students up to the Word Wall at a time. Call out a word; see which student can find it first and use it in a sentence.

Word Wall *(cont.)*

- **Seek and Find**—Challenge students to search newspapers, brochures, letters, business cards, etc., to highlight Word Wall words.

- **Crossword Puzzles**—Have students use the words on the Word Wall to make crossword puzzles, exchange crossword puzzles, and then solve them.

Differentiation

For English language learners, the Word Wall is particularly helpful because it exposes students to important vocabulary words and is an easy reference for students during the lesson. Give English language learners a list of the words to keep at their desks and take home for assignments, if necessary. Encourage above-level students to add more challenging words to the Word Wall. These students can generate a list of words they have an interest in learning. Give below-level students a copy of the words to place in their notebooks. They may need repeated explanation of the meanings and use of each word.

Word Wall (cont.)

Grades 1–2 Example

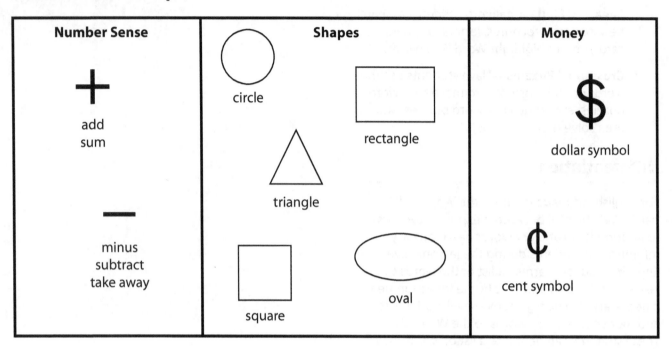

Grades 3–5 Example

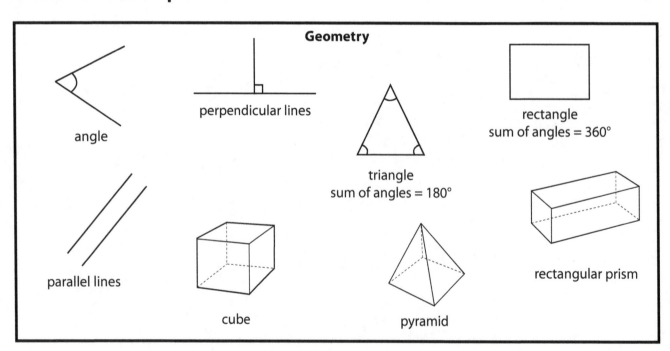

Word Wall *(cont.)*

· ·

Grades 6–8 Example

Order of Operations

PEMDAS

Parentheses
Exponents
Multiplication
Division
Addition
Subtraction

$+$

addition

$(\ )$

parentheses

exponent

$6^2 \qquad (x + 7)^2$

$-$

subtraction

$[\ ]$

brackets

$\bullet$

$\times$

$*$

multiplication symbols

$\div$

$^\#/_\#$

$\dfrac{\#}{\#}$

division symbols

$6 + 7 - 8 + 2$

solve left to right

Word Wall (cont.)

Grades 9–12 Example

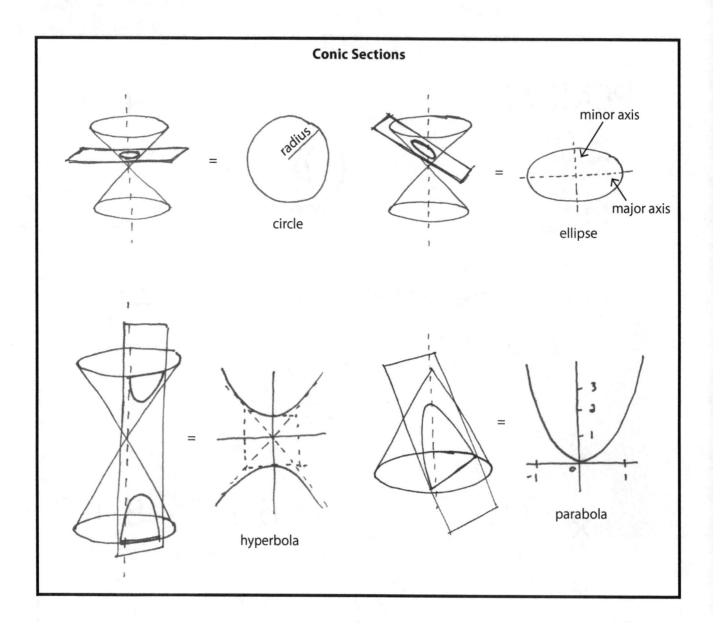

Conic Sections

circle

ellipse

minor axis

major axis

hyperbola

parabola

Frayer Model

Background Information

The Frayer Model (Frayer, Fredrick, and Klausmeier 1969), also known as a word map (Schwartz and Raphael 1985), is a strategy designed to help students understand relationships and similarities between concepts by gathering information from print and digital resources and categorizing that information in a graphic organizer. This strategy uses a graphic organizer to help students understand a concept and recognize similarities and differences between that concept and other concepts being discussed. The framework of the Frayer Model consists of the concept word, the definition, characteristics of the concept word, examples of the concept word, and nonexamples of the concept word. A key element of this model is providing an example of what the concept is and what it is not. The Frayer Model is often used when teaching vocabulary, but it can be used to teach and reinforce mathematics concepts as well.

Grade Levels/Standards Addressed

See page 32 for the standards this strategy addresses, or refer to the Digital Resource CD (standards.pdf) to read the correlating standards in their entirety.

Genre

Expository

Stage of Writing Process

Prewrite

Activity

Distribute the *Frayer Model* activity sheet (page 42, frayermodel.pdf). Have students write the concept of the lesson at the center. This may be a concept phrase or a single word, depending on the needs of students and the lesson objective. As a class, determine the definition of this concept. Students can briefly conduct research to gather relevant information from informational texts or a variety of resources to develop a definition that is clear, concise, and easy to understand. Next, help students determine the characteristics or attributes of this concept. Finally, determine as a class what the concept is and what it is not. Encourage students to generate their own examples and nonexamples, and allow time for students to discuss their findings with the class. Once students are comfortable using this strategy, they can work in small groups, in pairs, or independently to research different concepts relating to mathematics. When the graphic organizer has been completed, students then write a paragraph about the concept using the *Frayer Model* activity sheet as a guide.

Differentiation

Place English language learners in groups or pair them with partners to complete the activity. Working with a partner will help them learn how to complete the activity sheet, and they will also benefit greatly from the discussions. Call on above-level students to model how to complete the organizer for the class. Above-level students can work with two or three classmates to show the class how to complete the *Frayer Model*. The class can learn from watching this discussion, and it encourages above-level students to think through their reasoning. Provide one-on-one instruction during the small-group work for below-level students and select an appropriate concept word.

Frayer Model *(cont.)*

· ·

Grades 3–5 Example

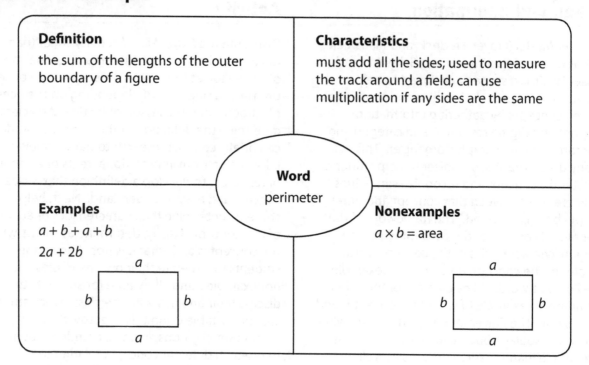

Definition
the sum of the lengths of the outer boundary of a figure

Characteristics
must add all the sides; used to measure the track around a field; can use multiplication if any sides are the same

Word
perimeter

Examples
$a + b + a + b$
$2a + 2b$

Nonexamples
$a \times b = $ area

Grades 6–8 Example

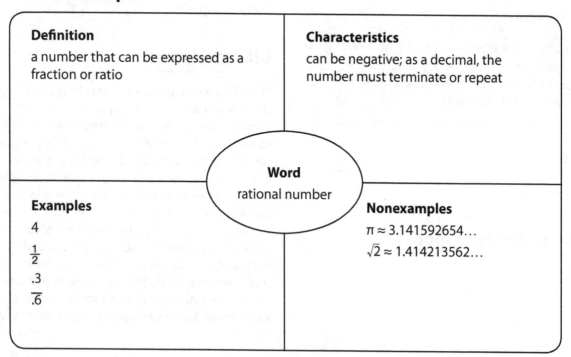

Definition
a number that can be expressed as a fraction or ratio

Characteristics
can be negative; as a decimal, the number must terminate or repeat

Word
rational number

Examples
4
$\frac{1}{2}$
.3
$.\overline{6}$

Nonexamples
$\pi \approx 3.141592654\ldots$
$\sqrt{2} \approx 1.414213562\ldots$

Frayer Model *(cont.)*

Grades 9–12 Example

Definition
a mathematical expression with two or more terms

Characteristics
polynomials can contain a combination of coefficients, variables, and positive exponents

Word
polynomial

Examples

$a^2 + 2ab + b^2$

$4x^2 + 3x - 5$

$a^2 - b^2$

$3a^2 - 2b^5 + c^4 + 8$

Nonexamples

$6x^{-3}$

$\dfrac{1}{x^2}$

$\sqrt{x}$

Frayer Model

Definition	Characteristics

Word

Examples	Nonexamples

#51153—*Writing Strategies for Mathematics Second Edition*

Concept of Definition Map

Background Information

Using the Concept of Definition Map graphic organizer (Schwartz and Raphael 1985) helps teach definitions of vocabulary words used in mathematics. There are many different ways to learn the definition of a term other than looking up the dictionary definition in reference sources. The Concept of Definition Map outlines a variety of ways for students to learn the meaning of a word. Looking at words in a variety of settings helps students make connections with words, including briefly conducting research to deepen understanding and gathering relevant information from print and digital resources. The Concept of Definition Map makes use of students' senses and their prior knowledge to help them learn new word meanings. The characteristics of the new term are analyzed, including the simple definition (*What is it?*), comparative descriptions (*What is it like?*), and examples of the new term (*What is it an example of?*). These strategies promote long-term memory because students have had an opportunity to personally connect with the word.

Grade Levels/Standards Addressed

See page 32 for the standards this strategy addresses, or refer to the Digital Resource CD (standards.pdf) to read the correlating standards in their entirety.

Genre

Expository

Stage of Writing Process

Prewrite

Activity

Prior to assigning a reading selection, determine the words that students may not understand or that may be new to them. Select one of these words and write it on the board. Use a document camera to display the *Concept of Definition Map* activity sheet (page 47, conceptdefinition.pdf) and write the word at the center of the map. Work as a class to complete the map. Students should be encouraged to use all of their senses to understand the new word. Ask the following questions:

- What is it?
- What are some things you know about it?
- What is it like?
- What is it an example of?

Assign students a passage of mathematics text that incorporates the new word. Encourage them to add any new information to their maps. Allow time for students to share their maps. Write examples on the board of good definitions and analogies that students have generated.

Differentiation

Pair English language learners with partners to assist them in completing the map. These students will also need reinforcement from the teacher to ensure that they understand the definition(s). Challenge above-level students to complete more than one map using a variety of words. Ask these students to do further research on these words and use a variety of sources other than the textbook. Require older students to cite references used. Below-level students can complete a map that includes some of the answers already filled in.

Concept of Definition Map *(cont.)*

Grades 1–2 Example

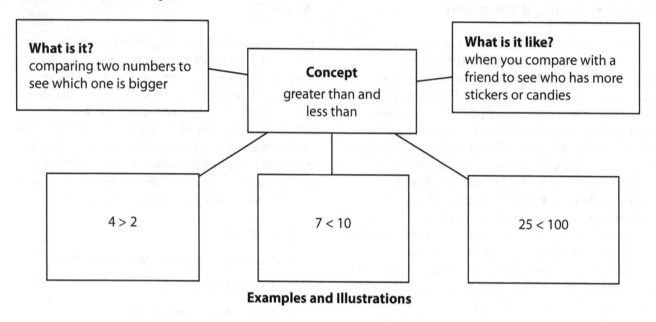

What is it?
comparing two numbers to
see which one is bigger

Concept
greater than and
less than

What is it like?
when you compare with a
friend to see who has more
stickers or candies

4 > 2

7 < 10

25 < 100

Examples and Illustrations

Grades 3–5 Example

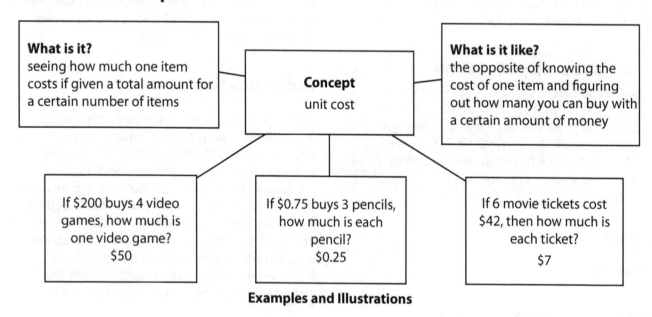

What is it?
seeing how much one item
costs if given a total amount for
a certain number of items

Concept
unit cost

What is it like?
the opposite of knowing the
cost of one item and figuring
out how many you can buy with
a certain amount of money

If $200 buys 4 video
games, how much is
one video game?
$50

If $0.75 buys 3 pencils,
how much is each
pencil?
$0.25

If 6 movie tickets cost
$42, then how much is
each ticket?
$7

Examples and Illustrations

Concept of Definition Map *(cont.)*

Grades 6–8 Example

What is it?
seeing how far you can travel in a certain amount of time

Concept
distance, rate, and time

What is it like?
going on a road trip with your family and seeing how far away it is and figuring out how long it will take you to get there

$D = rt$, so how far could you travel if you drove 60 mph for 3 hours?
$D = (60)(3)$
$D = 180$ miles
You could travel 180 miles.

If $D = rt$, then $r = \dfrac{D}{t}$, so how fast would you be driving if you drove for 2 hours and went 30 miles?
$r = \dfrac{30}{2}$
$r = 15$
You would be driving 15 mph.

If $D = rt$, then $t = \dfrac{D}{r}$, so how long would it take you to go 500 miles if you were driving 50 mph?
$t = \dfrac{500}{50}$
$t = 10$
It would take you 10 hours.

Examples and Illustrations

Concept of Definition Map *(cont.)*

Grades 9–12 Example

What is it?

an exponential function that illustrates growth over time

Amount $= P(1 + r)^t$ where P is the principal amount, r is the growth rate (as a decimal), and t is the time

Concept

exponential growth function

What is it like?

figuring out the projected population of a city given its current population and growth rate

What would the population of a town of 5,000 residents be after 5 years if it is growing at the rate of 2.5% per year (round to the nearest whole number)?

$A = 5000(1 + .025)^5$

$A = 5,657$

What would the balance of a bank account be after two years if the starting balance is $300 and it has a 6% growth rate (round to the nearest dollar)?

$A = 300(1 + .06)^2$

$A = \$337$

How many bacteria would have grown in a culture by noon if the culture started with 100 bacteria at 9:00 and was growing by 100% an hour?

$A = 100(1 + 1)^3$

$A = 800$

Examples and Illustrations

Concept of Definition Map

Directions: Fill out the different categories for the selected word. Use a dictionary or a thesaurus if necessary.

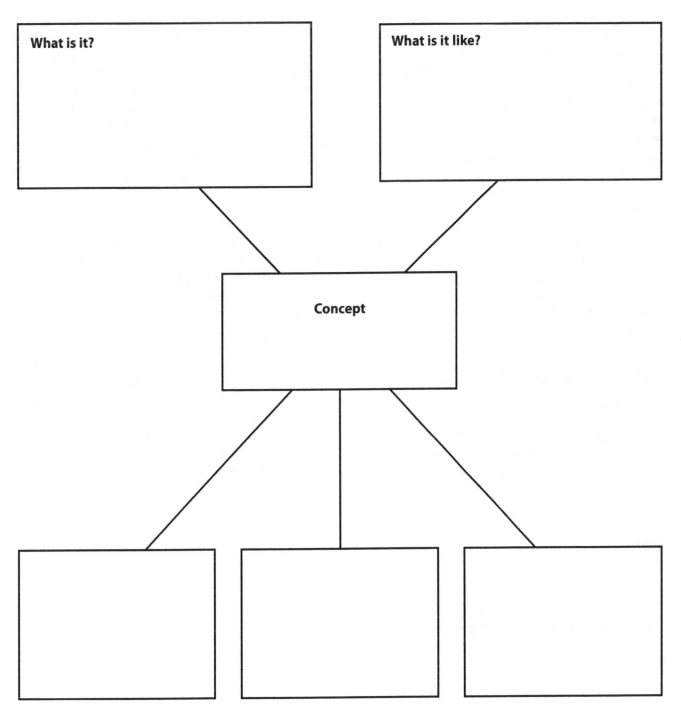

| What is it? | What is it like? |

Concept

Examples and Illustrations

List-Group-Label

Background Information

The List-Group-Label (Taba 1967) classification strategy encourages brainstorming to categorize and organize mathematics vocabulary in relation to the text. Students combine their prior knowledge about concepts as appropriate to the task and then organize the information into categories. This activity can be done at the beginning of a lesson to introduce students to new words and concepts, or following a lesson as a review of concepts. Most words are associated with other words, and grouping these words in meaningful ways clarifies understanding of words and their meanings. Students can also see hierarchical relationships between words, as well as word parts and word associations. This activity is the bridge between students' background knowledge and the new mathematics vocabulary being introduced as they organize new vocabulary into clear, coherent categories.

Grade Levels/Standards Addressed

See page 33 for the standards this strategy addresses, or refer to the Digital Resource CD (standards.pdf) to read the correlating standards in their entirety.

Genre

Expository

Stage of Writing Process

Prewrite

Activity

Prior to the lesson, select a word or phrase that describes the topic of the lesson. Write this word or phrase on the center of the board or display it for students using a document camera. Ask students to think of words that are associated with this word and list them on the board. As students suggest words, encourage them to explain the connection to the focus word. This will help eliminate words that are unrelated to the focus word. Allow students to receive assistance from other students to justify their words.

After students have generated a list of 20–30 words, distribute the *List-Group-Label* activity sheet (page 52, listgrouplabel.pdf) to individual students, partners, or small groups. Ask students to group the words into categories based on attributes, characteristics, or features that the words have in common, and assign each category a label. Students may need to generate further categories to group all of the words. Some words may need to be eliminated if they do not fit into the categories. Students should continue explaining and justifying their decisions for the selected categories and labels and placement of words in the categories. Remind them to add any additional vocabulary words to the categories if possible.

List-Group-Label (cont.)

After categorizing and grouping the words, meet back together as a class. Invite each group to share its version of categorizing and organizing the vocabulary words. Engage the class in a discussion until an agreement can be reached on the categories, labels, and the respective words included in each category. Again, students can continue to add words to the map as they think of them. Students may need to reorganize or relabel categories and relocate words before they reach a consensus. Students must continue justifying the categories they have selected by presenting a rationale.

Keep students focused on words and categories that are directly related to the lesson objectives. The more students describe and explain their rationales for the categories and words selected, the more they will make associations to new words.

Variation

Present the class with a list of words (rather than having students generate the words), and ask students to individually, or in small groups, determine how to classify the words and select the labels for those categories. Or conduct the brainstorming session and then scaffold the remainder of the lesson by providing the group labels.

Differentiation

Provide English language learners with resource books or pictures during the brainstorming process so that they can locate words. Use several words to explain each word associated with the topic so that English language learners can better understand. Take extra care to make sure all of the words and phrases on the board are clearly defined and understood by below-level students. Both English language learners and below-level students will benefit from working in mixed-ability groups. Encourage above-level students to work on generating a list independently or to reclassify the words into alternate categories.

List-Group-Label (cont.)

Grades 1–2 Example

Topic: Addition vs. Subtraction

List

4 + 9	4 + 5	9 − 7	7 − 4	22 − 14	2 + 4	856 − 266
2 + 4	9 − 4	6 + 4	11 + 22	94 − 6	745 + 698	

Categories

Addition		Subtraction	
4 + 9	11 + 22	9 − 4	22 − 14
2 + 4	2 + 4	9 − 7	94 − 6
4 + 5	745 + 698	7 − 4	856 − 266
6 + 4			

Grades 3–5 Example

Topic: Multiplication vs. Division

List

6 × 4	21 ÷ 3	63 ÷ 7	12 × 3
12 ÷ 4	8 × 8	6 × 5	5 × 4
24 ÷ 6	54 ÷ 9	7 × 9	

Categories

Multiplication	Division
6 × 4	12 ÷ 4
8 × 8	24 ÷ 6
6 × 5	21 ÷ 3
7 × 9	54 ÷ 9
12 × 3	63 ÷ 7
5 × 4	

List-Group-Label (cont.)

Grades 6–8 Example

Topic: <u>Upward slope vs. downward slope</u>

List

$y = 6x + 8$

$y = -5x + 5$

$y = -6x - 7$

$3y = -9x + 12$

$2y + 6x = 12$

$y = 4x + 6$

$2x = 3y + 8$

$9y = -7x + 2$

Categories

Slopes upward

$y = 6x + 8$

$y = 4x + 6$

$2x = 3y + 8$

Slopes downward

$y = -5x + 5$

$y = -6x - 7$

$3y = -9x + 12$

$2y + 6x = 12$

$9y = -7x + 2$

Grades 9–12 Example

Topic: <u>Parabolas in standard form vs. vertex form</u>

List

$y = -(x - 4)^2 + 6$

$y = x^2 + 2x + 1$

$y - 4 = (x + 3)^2$

$y = x^2 - 10x + 21$

$y = x^2 + 6x - 10$

$y = 2(x - 1)^2 + 7$

$y = x^2 + 6x + 8$

$y = (x - 2)^2$

Categories

Standard Form

$y = x^2 + 2x + 1$

$y = x^2 - 10x + 21$

$y = x^2 + 6x - 10$

$y = x^2 + 6x + 8$

Vertex Form

$y = -(x - 4)^2 + 6$

$y = (x + 3)^2 + 4$

$y = 2(x - 1)^2 + 7$

$y = (x - 2)^2$

List-Group-Label

Directions: Write in the topic, then make a list of words about the topic. Look at the list and create categories of related words. Be sure to label each category.

Topic: _____

List

_____ _____ _____

_____ _____ _____

_____ _____ _____

_____ _____ _____

_____ _____ _____

_____ _____ _____

_____ _____ _____

Categories

_____ _____ _____

_____ _____ _____

_____ _____ _____

_____ _____ _____

_____ _____ _____

_____ _____ _____

_____ _____ _____

Vocabulary Self-Collection

Background Information

Martha Haggard (1982, 1986) designed the Vocabulary Self-Collection strategy to help students create a list of vocabulary words they would be interested in learning and researching. The strategy is meant to stimulate vocabulary growth so students can acquire and use accurately academic and domain-specific vocabulary. Research shows that the more exposure students have to the written word, the more their vocabulary increases. By generating lists of words to study, students become more sensitive to and aware of words and their meanings.

Grade Levels/Standards Addressed

See page 33 for the standards this strategy addresses, or refer to the Digital Resource CD (standards.pdf) to read the correlating standards in their entirety.

Genre

Expository

Stage of Writing Process

Prewrite

Activity

Instruct students to create a list of words from their mathematics reading materials that they are interested in studying. The words should be of interest to them. Have students review their lists and nominate one of the words to be studied by the class. As you write these words on the board or display them with a document camera, ask students to define them and justify the selection of each word. Clarify the meaning of each word and clear up any misunderstandings, consulting a dictionary if needed. Students may ask one another questions about the words and their definitions. After the discussion, challenge the class to decide which words should make the final cut. For example, delete words that most students already know, duplicates of words, and words of little interest to students. Have students write down the selected words and their meanings in their Vocabulary Journal (see pages 99–102), and post them on the Word Wall (see pages 34–38). Incorporate these words into lessons and writing activities that will reinforce definitions and understanding. Encourage students to accurately use these words as often as possible in their own writing to move the new vocabulary words into their expressive languages.

Differentiation

During the discussion, clarify and elaborate further on some definitions if necessary to ensure that English language learners understand the meanings. Use visuals as well as thorough descriptions. Challenge above-level students to document the use of the vocabulary words in their personal writing assignments. Below-level students may need assistance articulating the meanings of difficult words, so encourage them to use visuals or drawings, if needed.

Vocabulary Self-Collection *(cont.)*

Grades 1–2 Example

Text:	Jane's newspaper route is on one street in her neighborhood. The addresses are numbered 24 through 56. She delivers a newspaper to all of her neighbors that have even address numbers, including numbers 24 and 56. How many newspapers does she deliver in her neighborhood?
Nominated Words:	numbered, even address number, including

Grades 3–5 Example

Text:	The 6 fifth-grade classes at your school are going to the Museum of Natural History for a class field trip. That is a total of 150 students who need to travel on the buses. Each bus will accommodate 35 students. There are 80 boys and 70 girls in the fifth grade. How many buses will the school need to reserve in order for all of the fifth graders to attend the field trip?
Nominated Words:	total, each, all

Grades 6–8 Example

Text:	Danny needs a total of 425 pickets to make his vibrant new fence. He wants equal quantities of each shade in an alternating sequence. He already has 35 white pickets, 29 black pickets, 12 yellow pickets, and no red pickets. How many more of each color does Danny need to purchase? The pickets cost 25 cents each, and Danny gets 25% off if he buys 50 or more of the same color and 30% off if he purchases 60 or more of one color. How much does Danny need to spend? Create a pictorial representation of your answer and how you determined it.
Nominated Words:	equal, quantities, alternating, sequence, pictorial representation, determined

Grades 9–12 Example

Text:	A circle with the center point (3, 4) is graphed on the same plane as a line with the equation $y = 5$. The circle and line intersect at the point where $x = 6$. What is the radius of the circle?
Nominated Words:	center point, plane, equation, intersect, radius

Possible Sentences

Background Information

David Moore and Sharon Moore (1986) designed the Possible Sentences strategy as a way to teach vocabulary words introduced in a text. Other benefits of this strategy include making predictions about reading, providing a purpose for reading, and encouraging interest in text. Students learn to make predictions about new words, check their predictions, and use the text to rewrite and refine their predictions, developing and strengthening their writing as needed with support from the teacher.

Grade Levels/Standards Addressed

See page 33 for the standards this strategy addresses, or refer to the Digital Resource CD (standards.pdf) to read the correlating standards in their entirety.

Genre

Expository

Stages of Writing Process

Draft, Revise

Activity

Make a list of important vocabulary words from the mathematics text and write them on the board or display them using a document camera. Read each word aloud to model correct pronunciation. Guide students in selecting two words from the list to use in one sentence that might appear in a mathematics text. Record sentences on the board and underline each vocabulary word. Encourage students to generate sentences until all the vocabulary words have been used in at least one sentence. Remind students that good writers edit and revise their work to develop and strengthen their writing, and have them read through the sentences again to make any needed changes.

Next, ask students to read the selected text and compare the class sentences with the actual sentences in the text. Students should take notes (or draw pictures for younger students) on meanings of words. After reading the text, carefully examine the sentences to see if they are written accurately. Have students explain how to edit and revise sentences as needed. Call on students to write revised sentences independently using their new knowledge and understanding of these vocabulary words.

Differentiation

Preview the meanings of the vocabulary words with English language learners to ensure understanding. Encourage English language learners to draw pictures or write short phrases if they are not yet ready to write sentences. Encourage above-level students to write multiple sentences using various forms of the words and more complicated sentence structures. Scaffold the strategy for below-level students by providing sentence frames. Also, encourage these students to extend their sentences by adding additional information.

Possible Sentences (cont.)

Grades 1–2 Example

Vocabulary Words:

diamond, oval, circle, rectangle, square, triangle

Possible Sentences/Before Reading:

My mom has a <u>diamond</u> ring.
An <u>oval</u> and a <u>circle</u> look the same.
A <u>square</u> and a <u>rectangle</u> look the same.
A <u>triangle</u> has three sides.

Revised Sentences/After Reading:

My mom has a <u>diamond</u> ring, but that is different from what we call a diamond shape.
An <u>oval</u> and a <u>circle</u> look similar, but an oval looks more like a stretched circle.
A <u>square</u> and a <u>rectangle</u> look similar, except that all of the sides of a square are equal, and a rectangle has two short sides and two long sides.
A <u>triangle</u> has three sides and three corners.

Grades 3–5 Example

Vocabulary Words:

cone, cube, cylinder, pyramid, rectangular prism, sphere

Possible Sentences/Before Reading:

I ate my ice cream from an ice cream <u>cone</u>.
I put a lot of ice <u>cubes</u> in my drink.
A <u>cylinder</u> is long and round.
The <u>pyramids</u> are in Egypt.
A <u>rectangular prism</u> has rectangles in it.
A <u>sphere</u> is a ball.

Revised Sentences/After Reading:

A sugar cone for ice cream is shaped like an open <u>cone</u>.
I think of ice <u>cubes</u> to remind me what a cube looks like.
A <u>cylinder</u> is long and round, with two flat circles at each end.
The <u>pyramids</u> are in Egypt and are a good way to remember what a <u>pyramid</u> looks like.
A <u>rectangular</u> prism looks like a cube that has been stretched.
A <u>sphere</u> is a circular shape, like a ball.

Possible Sentences *(cont.)*

Grades 6–8 Example

Vocabulary Words:

multiple, factor, least common multiple, greatest common factor, numerator, denominator

Possible Sentences/Before Reading:

A <u>multiple</u> is a number that can be multiplied.
A <u>factor</u> of 42 is 7.
The <u>least common multiple</u> of two numbers is the lowest number that can be divided into both.
The <u>greatest common factor</u> of two numbers is the biggest number that both can be multiplied into.
A <u>numerator</u> is the top of a fraction.
The <u>denominator</u> is the bottom of a fraction.

Revised Sentences/After Reading:

A <u>multiple</u> is a number that can be divided exactly by a particular smaller number.
A <u>factor</u> is one of two or more numbers or quantities that can be multiplied together to give a particular number or quantity. The numbers 3 and 5 are factors of 15.
The <u>least common multiple</u> is the lowest whole number that is divisible without a remainder by all of the members of a set of numbers.
The <u>greatest common factor</u> is the highest number that can be exactly divided into each member of a set of numbers. The greatest common factor of 60 and 84 is 12.
A fraction is made of a <u>numerator</u> on top and a <u>denominator</u> on the bottom.

Possible Sentences *(cont.)*

Grades 9–12 Example

Vocabulary Words:

coefficient, like terms, monomial, binomial, polynomial

Possible Sentences/Before Reading:

A <u>coefficient</u> is a number with a variable.

<u>Like terms</u> means the variables are the same.

A <u>monomial</u> is a single variable or a single term.

A <u>binomial</u> is an expression with two variables or two terms.

A <u>polynomial</u> is an expression with many variables or terms.

Revised Sentences/After Reading

A <u>coefficient</u> is the number that precedes the variable. In the expression $2x^2 + 3x + 5$, 2 and 3 are coefficients because they come before the variable x.

<u>Like terms</u> refers to expressions containing the same variable, even if the variables have different coefficients.

A <u>monomial</u> is an expression with only one term, such as $3xy^2$. The term may have multiple variables.

A <u>binomial</u> is an expression with two terms, such as $3xy^2 + 2x$.

A <u>polynomial</u> has multiple terms, such as $3xy^2 + 2x + y$. Binomials are a type of polynomial.

Word Trails

Background Information

A strong relationship exists between word knowledge and reading comprehension. Without word knowledge, readers read less and are more apt to be poor readers (Anderson and Freebody 1985). Seldom do words stand alone, isolated from and unrelated to other words. The Word Trails strategy helps students build connections or "trails" from unknown words to familiar ones so they can ultimately acquire and use accurately academic and domain-specific vocabulary. This strategy asks that students gather relevant information about the word of study by looking to print and digital resources for more information. Students need to have a repertoire of strategies to use when they face unknown words in their reading. The Word Trails strategy offers a way to build those bridges.

Grade Levels/Standards Addressed

See page 33 for the standards this strategy addresses, or refer to the Digital Resource CD (standards.pdf) to read the correlating standards in their entirety.

Genre

Expository

Stage of Writing Process

Prewrite

Activity

Introduce a new domain-specific word and then build "trails" and connections from other words to the new word. Have students use both print and digital resources to locate and connect relevant information about the word.

The following are the main trails that connect words:

- **root words**—Many mathematics words have similar root words. Knowing these can help students determine meaning.

- **prefixes and suffixes**—Recognizing and identifying prefixes or suffixes in a word can help determine its meaning.

- **synonyms or similar words**—Words become "friends" and can help students remember definitions. What are other words that have the same or similar meaning to the new word? What are examples of this word?

- **antonyms**—Identifying opposites is an effective way to clarify word meaning. What are the words that mean the opposite of this new word? What are nonexamples of the word?

Distribute the *Word Trails* activity sheet (page 62, wordtrails.pdf), and have students identify the trails from this word to other words. When finished, discuss students' findings. Primary grade teachers may want to complete the *Word Trails* activity sheet as a class, and then post it on the Word Wall (pages 34–38). Students can add these words and their trails to their Vocabulary Journal (pages 99–102).

Differentiation

Preteach English language learners how to use the *Word Trails* activity sheet so they understand the format. Consider also preteaching the roots, prefixes, and suffixes that will be addressed during the whole-class lesson so these students will be able to recognize them and apply meaning to the unknown vocabulary word. Use visuals whenever possible. Encourage above-level students to study additional or related vocabulary words and present and explain their maps to the class. Limit the number of vocabulary words for below-level students to allow them to focus on a few words.

Word Trails *(cont.)*

Grades 3–5 Example

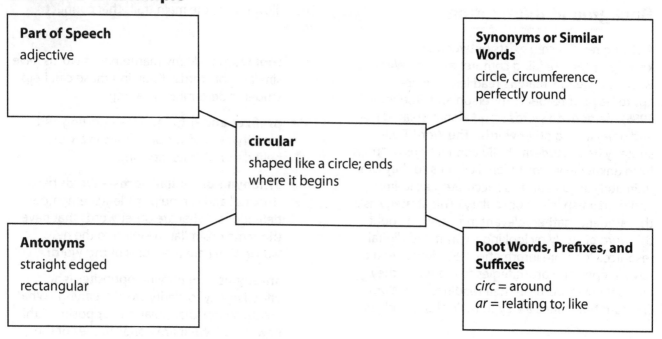

Part of Speech
adjective

Synonyms or Similar Words
circle, circumference, perfectly round

circular
shaped like a circle; ends where it begins

Antonyms
straight edged
rectangular

Root Words, Prefixes, and Suffixes
circ = around
ar = relating to; like

Grades 6–8 Example

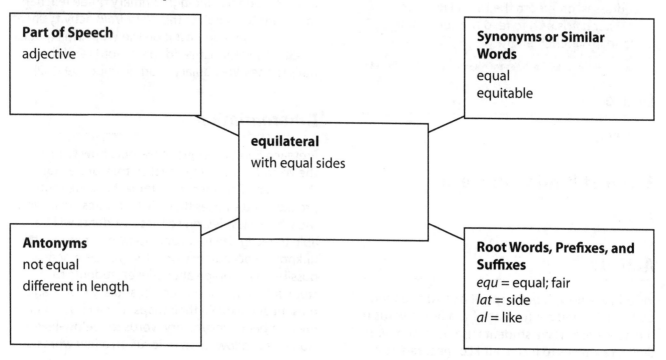

Part of Speech
adjective

Synonyms or Similar Words
equal
equitable

equilateral
with equal sides

Antonyms
not equal
different in length

Root Words, Prefixes, and Suffixes
equ = equal; fair
lat = side
al = like

Word Trails *(cont.)*

Grades 9–12 Example

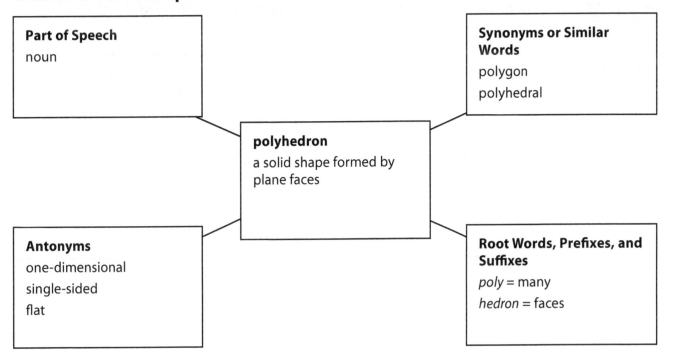

Part of Speech
noun

Synonyms or Similar Words
polygon
polyhedral

polyhedron
a solid shape formed by plane faces

Antonyms
one-dimensional
single-sided
flat

Root Words, Prefixes, and Suffixes
poly = many
hedron = faces

Word Trails

Directions: Write the word that you are studying in the center box. Use resources to determine the root words, prefixes and suffixes, synonyms or similar words, and antonyms. Then, complete the graphic organizer.

Part of Speech

Synonyms or Similar Words

Antonyms

Root Words, Prefixes, and Suffixes

Previewing and Reviewing Overview

Activating Prior Knowledge in Mathematics

Research shows that activating background knowledge increases the comprehension that students have (Christen and Murphy 1991). Accessing students' prior knowledge opens the doors for the new knowledge to find a place. Teachers who link new information to students' background knowledge encourage curiosity and provide a purpose for the new information. This enables the teacher to build on this knowledge. Students are able to make personal connections and incorporate these new thoughts and ideas into what they read and write about. Prior knowledge can be defined as any information that we know on a given topic before we begin learning new information.

Reviewing and Spiral Knowledge

We all use scripts and categorical rules to interpret the world. When new information arises, our brains work to see how it fits with our predetermined ideas and scripts (Widmayer et al. 2004). Throughout our lives we add to our knowledge base, and it continues to grow. This is known as spiral knowledge (Poplin 1988, as cited by Dechant 1991).

Using Expressive Writing

Expressive writing leads to the discovery and reinforcement of concepts being taught, so it is appropriate for reviewing in mathematics. Toby Fulwiler (1980, 16) states, "Every time students write, they individualize instruction; the act of silent writing, even for five minutes, generates ideas, observations, emotions…regular writing makes it harder for students to remain passive." In the mathematics classroom, expressive writing enables students to turn quantitative information into qualitative information. Students put the information in their own words and begin to own it. Writing is another way for the brain to make sense of information and learning (Emig 1977).

When students use writing as a strategy to help them make sense of what they are reading and learning, they are writing to learn. This is often called expressive writing in the content areas. It is a vital piece of the content area curriculum because it allows students the opportunity to express their ideas about and respond to what they are learning.

There is a variety of expressive writing activities: journals, KWL (Ogle 1986), T-List, free writes, dialogue journals (Atwell 1984; Harste, Short, and Burke 1988), problem analyses, learning logs, peer dialogues, and many more. Many of these strategies will be explained and described in this section of the book. With expressive writing, students are encouraged to use their own vocabulary, and the emphasis is on the content and students' understanding, not on the writing mechanics. Sharon Hamilton-Wieler (1988) explains that this kind of writing is "a way into or means of learning, a way into understanding through articulating."

Previewing and Reviewing Overview (cont.)

. . . .

Standards Addressed

The following chart shows the correlating standards for each strategy in this section. Refer to the Digital Resource CD (standards.pdf) to read the correlating standards in their entirety.

Strategy	McREL Standards	Common Core State Standards
KWL Chart	Grades 1–2 (1.1, 1.2) Grades 3–5 (1.1, 1.2) Grades 6–8 (1.1, 1.2) Grades 9–12 (1.1, 1.2)	Grade 1 (W.1.5) Grade 2 (W.2.5) Grade 3 (W.3.5) Grade 4 (W.4.5) Grade 5 (W.5.5) Grade 6 (W.6.5) Grade 7 (W.7.5) Grade 8 (W.8.5) Grades 9–10 (W.9-10.5) Grades 11–12 (W.11-12.5)
Think Sheet	Grades 1–2 (1.1, 1.2) Grades 3–5 (1.1, 1.2) Grades 6–8 (1.1, 1.2) Grades 9–12 (1.1, 1.2)	Grade 1 (W.1.5) Grade 2 (W.2.5) Grade 3 (W.3.5) Grade 4 (W.4.5) Grade 5 (W.5.5) Grade 6 (W.6.5) Grade 7 (W.7.5) Grade 8 (W.8.5) Grades 9–10 (W.9-10.5) Grades 11–12 (W.11-12.5)
Free-Association Brainstorming	Grades 1–2 (1.1) Grades 3–5 (1.1) Grades 6–8 (1.1) Grades 9–12 (1.1)	Grade 1 (W.1.5) Grade 2 (W.2.5) Grade 3 (W.3.5) Grade 4 (W.4.5) Grade 5 (W.5.5) Grade 6 (W.6.5) Grade 7 (W.7.5) Grade 8 (W.8.5) Grades 9–10 (W.9-10.5) Grades 11–12 (W.11-12.5)
Probable Passages	Grades 1–2 (1.1, 1.2) Grades 3–5 (1.1, 1.2) Grades 6–8 (1.1, 1.2) Grades 9–12 (1.1, 1.2)	Grade 1 (W.1.2, L.1.5) Grade 2 (W.2.2, L.2.5) Grade 3 (W.3.2, L.3.5) Grade 4 (W.4.2, L.4.5) Grade 5 (W.5.2, L.5.5) Grade 6 (W.6.2, L.6.5) Grade 7 (W.7.2, L.7.5) Grade 8 (W.8.2, L.8.5) Grades 9–10 (W.9-10.2, L.9-10.5) Grades 11–12 (W.11-12.2, L.11-12.5)

Previewing and Reviewing Overview (cont.)

Strategy	McREL Standards	Common Core State Standards
Guided Free Write	Grades 1–2 (1.8) Grades 3–5 (1.5, 1.6, 1.10) Grades 6–8 (1.5) Grades 9–12 (1.5, 1.6)	Grade 1 (CCRA.W.10, W.1.5) Grade 2 (CCRA.W.10, W.2.5) Grade 3 (W.3.5, W.3.10) Grade 4 (W.4.5, W.4.10) Grade 5 (W.5.5, W.5.10) Grade 6 (W.6.5, W.6.10) Grade 7 (W.7.5, W.7.10) Grade 8 (W.8.5, W.8.10) Grades 9–10 (W.9-10.5, W.9-10.10) Grades 11–12 (W.11-12.5, W.11-12.10)
End-of-Class Reflection	Grades 1–2 (1.6) Grades 3–5 (1.11) Grades 6–8 (1.12) Grades 9–12 (1.12)	Grade 1 (CCRA.W.4) Grade 2 (CCRA.W.4) Grade 3 (W.3.4) Grade 4 (W.4.4) Grade 5 (W.5.4) Grade 6 (W.6.4) Grade 7 (W.7.4) Grade 8 (W.8.4) Grades 9–10 (W.9-10.4) Grades 11–12 (W.11-12.4)
Reader-Response Writing Chart	Grades 3–5 (1.4, 1.10, 1.11) Grades 6–8 (1.4, 1.12) Grades 9–12 (1.4, 1.12)	Grade 3 (W.3.4) Grade 4 (W.4.4) Grade 5 (W.5.4) Grade 6 (W.6.4) Grade 7 (W.7.4) Grade 8 (W.8.4) Grades 9–10 (W.9-10.4) Grades 11–12 (W.11-12.4)

KWL Chart

Background Information

The KWL Chart is a three part strategy introduced by Donna Ogle (1986) to activate student knowledge and encourage active thinking in mathematics in order to develop and strengthen writing. A KWL Chart is divided into three columns: K (What I Know); W (What I Want to Know); and L (What I Learned). This interactive study approach also shows students how reading, writing, research, and observation further develop their knowledge of a particular subject.

The KWL Chart is used prior to a mathematics unit or lesson to engage students in writing about what they already know about the topic. Students also write any questions they have about the topic. After the reading, hands-on lesson, or activity, students write what they learned. They also review their information in the first column to see if it needs to be revised and check to see if all their questions were answered in the lesson. In this way, students engage in the prewriting process of gathering information and use the skill of editing and revising information when necessary.

Grade Levels/Standards Addressed

See page 64 for the standards this strategy addresses, or refer to the Digital Resource CD (standards.pdf) to read the correlating standards in their entirety.

Genre

Expository

Stage of Writing Process

Prewrite

Activity

Distribute the *KWL Chart* activity sheet (page 71, kwlchart.pdf), and have students write the topic at the top. Before reading, researching, or observing, ask students to list in the K column all the information that they *Know*—even if it may not be correct—about the topic. Next, have them list in the W column what they *Want to know* about the subject. Encourage them to think of interesting and pertinent questions, just as good researchers do. After reading the text or completing a mathematics activity, instruct students to review their charts. Guide students by having them look at the K column to see if the information they listed as prior knowledge was correct. With your support, have students delete or rewrite statements so that they are accurate. Students may need to use more description or more words to share accurate information. Next, have students look at the W column to see if all the questions were answered in the text. If not, students may need to find an alternate source to find the answer. After the discussion, have students write in the L column what they *Learned*.

Variation

For primary grade students, re-create the *KWL Chart* activity sheet on a large sheet of butcher paper and complete it as a class. Invite students to dictate a sentence or question for you to write on the chart, or allow individual students the opportunity to write on the chart.

KWL Chart (cont.)

The KWL Chart can be extended to include other categories or columns:

- **Categories of Information We Expect to See**—This addition directs students to anticipate the categories of information the author may provide in the reading selection. Students can use this same strategy of matching information with a topic when planning a writing assignment.

- **Still Want to Learn (KWLS)**—This extension encourages students to articulate any other questions they might wish to explore, and these ideas may provide a springboard for independent research or future writing activities.

- **How to Find Out (KWLSH)**—This category requires students to think about how they might investigate their questions, thereby developing research skills. See grades 6–8 and 9–12 examples on pages 69–70.

Differentiation

Pair English language learners with partners who can help discuss and articulate thoughts and ideas on the subject before completing the *KWL Chart* activity sheet. This will eliminate confusion resulting from the differences in language and the learning of new mathematics vocabulary. Consider providing sentence stems to assist these students in formulating their contributions: *I know that, What is…?,* and *I wonder.* Encourage above-level students to add new categories and conduct research independently or in groups. If time allows, these students can present their research findings to the class to enhance the lesson topic. Prior to introducing a new unit of study, inform below-level students of the next topic of study. Provide them with additional time to access their prior knowledge on the topic to assist them in the reading task. Have resources available for students to read before completing the *KWL Chart* activity sheet.

KWL Chart *(cont.)*

Grades 1–2 Example (before reading)

Topic: <u>Time</u>

K	W	L
There are numbers 1–12 on the clock. When the big hand is on the 6, that means 30. When the big hand is on the 12, then the hour is whatever the little hand is on.	What is the little red hand that moves around so fast? Why don't people say 4, 2 when the little hand is on the 4 and the big hand is on the 2? What should I say if the little hand is on the 4 and the big hand is on the 2?	

Grades 3–5 Example (after reading)

Topic: <u>Polygons</u>

K	W	L
The prefix *poly* means a lot or more than one. We will be talking about shapes. A triangle is a polygon. A square is a polygon.	I wonder how many kinds of polygons there are. Is a circle a polygon?	Polygons are organized by the number of sides they have. A triangle has 3 sides. A square, trapezoid, diamond, and rectangle are polygons with 4 sides. A pentagon has 5 sides. A hexagon has 6 sides. A heptagon has 7 sides. An octagon has 8 sides. A nonagon has 9 sides. A decagon has 10 sides.

KWL Chart *(cont.)*

Grades 6–8 Example (after reading)

Topic: <u>Percentages</u>

K	W	L	S	H
75% off is a great sale at the store. Percent has something to do with 100 because cent means 100. 50% is the same as $\frac{1}{2}$.	How do you calculate a percent off of something? What is meant by a percent markup? How do you convert a decimal to a percent?	To calculate the percent off, you multiply the original amount by the decimal value of the percent. For example, 35% off $200 is $200 \times .35 = \$70$ off. So, the final cost is $200 – $70 = $130. Percent markup means that a value is marked up by a certain percent. To convert a decimal to a percent, you just move the decimal to the right 2 places.	I have heard that jewelry is marked up by about 500%. I wonder what the actual markup is for diamonds or gold.	I could look it up on the Internet. I could also visit a local jewelry store and explain to them that I am learning about percents and markups and see if they could tell me the average markup amount.

KWL Chart *(cont.)*

Grades 9–12 Example (after reading)

Topic: Pyramids

K	W	L	S	H
A pyramid is a three-dimensional shape. The bottom is called the base. All of the faces meet at a single point at the top.	How many sides can a pyramid have? How do you figure out the volume of a pyramid? Are the sides of a pyramid always triangles?	The base of a pyramid is a polygon, and the number of sides of the polygon determines the number of faces of the pyramid. Each side of the base extends up to meet at a single point, so all faces of a pyramid are triangles. You can find the volume using the formula $\frac{1}{3} \times$ area of the base $\times$ height (altitude).	How many sides do the Egyptian pyramids have? Are they all four-sided? How tall are the Egyptian pyramids? What are their volumes?	I could research Egyptian pyramids on the Internet or in a book on Egypt. I could also visit a natural history museum with exhibits on ancient Egypt.

Name: _____ **Date:** _____

KWL Chart

Topic: _____

K	W	L

Think Sheet

Background Information

The Think Sheet strategy enables students to examine their knowledge on a mathematics topic with your support and guidance before reading about it, and then compare that to what they learn after reading or discussion. This strategy provides practice in generating information related to a topic, which students need to learn for the prewriting phase. Students also use the revising skill of analyzing existing notes for missing or incorrect information in order to strengthen their writing. Both skills are keys to successful writing.

Grade Levels/Standards Addressed

See page 64 for the standards this strategy addresses, or refer to the Digital Resource CD (standards.pdf) to read the correlating standards in their entirety.

Genre

Expository

Stages of Writing Process

Prewrite, Revise

Preparation

Prior to a reading, lesson, or observation, formulate some questions about the topic that will activate prior knowledge, generate thinking, and promote curiosity. Then, add the questions to the *Think Sheet* activity sheet (page 75, thinksheet.pdf).

Activity

Distribute the prepared *Think Sheet* activity sheet, display it using a document camera, or re-create it on the board. Present the main issue to the class, and ask students to answer the questions and write down what they know. Be sure to encourage them to write any questions that they have about the topic. Collect students' activity sheets, and then teach the lesson or complete the activity as planned. Redistribute the activity sheets so that students can use their new knowledge to edit their original answers. Ask questions such as, "How did your knowledge change after this activity? Can you add any additional information? Do you have any questions that were not answered? Were any of your original thoughts inaccurate?" Encourage students to write additional questions they have on the topic. Allow students to share what they have learned from the reading and encourage them to make connections between their questions, their thoughts, and the information presented in the text.

Variation

Complete this activity as a class with primary grade students. Lead a brief discussion about each question, and ask students to help develop an answer. You may choose specific students to help write some or all of the sentences on the board.

Differentiation

For English language learners, spend time clarifying the questions that are being asked. Remind students that these are new questions and they are not expected to know the answers. Encourage above-level students to conduct further research to answer the questions left unanswered and share their findings with the class. Scaffold the activity with some completed responses for below-level students. If the level is too high, read aloud to them or have them do a paired reading.

Think Sheet (cont.)

Grades 1–2 Example (before reading)

Main Issue: Money

Teacher Questions	My Questions/Thoughts
1. What are the names of all the coins that are used in the United States? *penny, nickel, dime, quarter, half dollar* **2.** How much is each coin worth? *A penny is worth 1 cent. A nickel is worth 5 cents. A dime is worth 10 cents. A quarter is worth 25 cents. A half dollar is worth 50 cents.* **3.** How many of each equals a dollar? *A dollar equals 100 pennies. A dollar equals 20 nickels. A dollar equals 10 dimes. A dollar equals 4 quarters. A dollar equals 2 half dollars.*	I know there is a penny, a nickel, a dime, and a quarter. I know that a penny is 1 cent. A nickel is 5 cents. A dime is 10 cents. I don't know how many cents a quarter is, but 4 of them make a dollar. How many pennies, nickels, and dimes make a dollar? Are there any other coins?

Grades 3–5 Example (after reading)

Main Issue: Probability

Teacher Questions	My Questions/Thoughts
1. If you toss a quarter in the air 100 times, how often would it land on heads? *It would land on heads about half the time.* **2.** How could you illustrate the results of flipping the coin 100 times? *I could create a bar graph or a line graph.* **3.** If you flipped the coin 200 times, does that raise or lower your chances of getting heads? *It would still be about half.*	It seems that most people pick heads. I wonder why that is, when the odds are 50/50. Does it matter which coin is used? Would you get the same results with a penny or a nickel?

Think Sheet (cont.)

Grades 6–8 Example (after reading)

Main Issue: Statistical Measurements

Teacher Questions	My Questions/Thoughts
1. What is the mean? *The mean is the average of a group of numbers.* **2.** What is the median? *The median is the number that is in the middle of a list of numbers in order of value.* **3.** What is the mode? *The mode is the number that occurs most often in the list.*	What kind of situations would this type of information be useful in? I know in baseball, they calculate batting average, and I have used my grades to figure out my average grade. When would you use median and mode?

Grades 9–12 Example (after reading)

Main Issue: Roots

Teacher Questions	My Questions/Thoughts
1. What is a root? *You can think of a root as a fractional exponent. The square root of a number is a number that when multiplied by itself equals the desired product. $\sqrt{9} = 3$ because $3 \times 3 = 9$.* **2.** Are there other roots besides square roots? *Yes, there are many other types of roots like cube roots, for example $\sqrt[3]{8} = 2$, or fourth roots, such as $\sqrt[4]{16} = 2$.* **3.** Can negative numbers be square roots? *Positive numbers have both a positive and negative square root (because a negative number times itself always equals a positive number), but the radical sign ($\sqrt{\ }$) refers only to the positive root.*	You can find the square root of a number by factoring it and removing any factors that occur more than once. For example, $\sqrt{50} = \sqrt{25 \times 2} = \sqrt{5 \times 5 \times 2} = 5\sqrt{2}$.

Name: _____ **Date:** _____

Think Sheet

Directions: Write your answers to the questions from your teacher. After the mathematics reading assignment or activity, write any thoughts or questions that you have about the topic.

Main Issue: _____

Teacher Questions	My Questions/Thoughts

Free-Association Brainstorming

Background Information

The Free-Association Brainstorming strategy supports students' divergent thinking and helps them generate many ideas on a given subject. It also helps students access their prior knowledge on the subject being studied without requiring them to organize that information. Often, students have some content knowledge but are not prepared to organize it in a systematic fashion. This strategy is best implemented during the prewriting phase of the writing process.

Grade Levels/Standards Addressed

See page 64 for the standards this strategy addresses, or refer to the Digital Resource CD (standards.pdf) to read the correlating standards in their entirety.

Genres

Expository, Narrative, Persuasive

Stage of Writing Process

Prewrite

Activity

Distribute the *Free-Association Brainstorming* activity sheet (page 79, freeassociation.pdf) to help students in planning their written work during the prewriting phase. Write the topic on the board, and have students write it at the center of the map. Do not discuss this topic or explain it. Instruct students to write in the surrounding ovals any words, thoughts, ideas, or examples that come to mind. If there are not enough ovals, students can continue to add more. Next, meet as a class and share all the ideas that students came up with.

Remind them that they may continue to think of new ideas and can add them to their maps. The maps can be used as a springboard to writing or a way to access and/or organize prior knowledge on the subject being studied.

Variation

In primary grade classes, this activity is best completed as a class because it is meant to focus on the prewriting process of generating ideas—both good and bad—as quickly as possible. Write students' contributions on the board so that writing will not hinder them. Use of the *Free-Association Brainstorming* activity sheet can be altered to fit the needs of the lesson and students: it can be used independently (to assess each student's prior knowledge), in pairs or small groups (to generate additional ideas), or as a whole class (to allow for teacher prompting, modeling, or scaffolding).

Differentiation

Encourage English language learners to draw pictures or diagrams if that helps them more easily communicate their ideas. Challenge above-level students with a more complex concept that requires higher-order thinking skills. Have below-level students work with partners to assist in getting their ideas on paper. Remind them that the purpose is simply to get their ideas on paper without worrying about spelling or grammar.

Free-Association Brainstorming *(cont.)*

Grades 1–2 Example

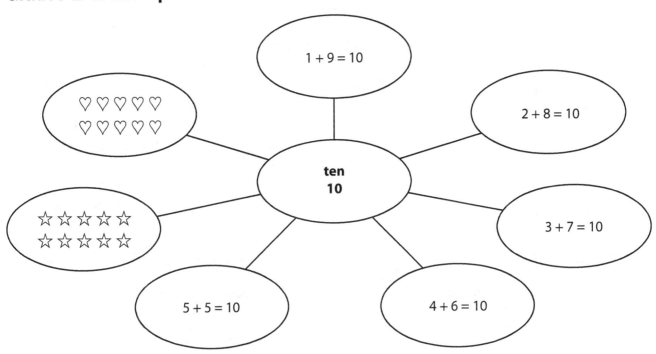

Grades 3–5 Example

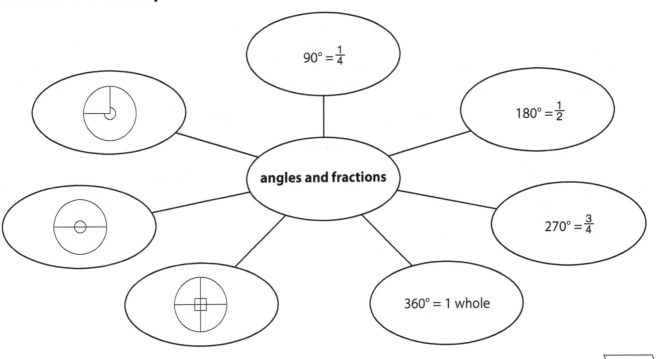

#51153—Writing Strategies for Mathematics Second Edition

Free-Association Brainstorming *(cont.)*

Grades 6–8 Example

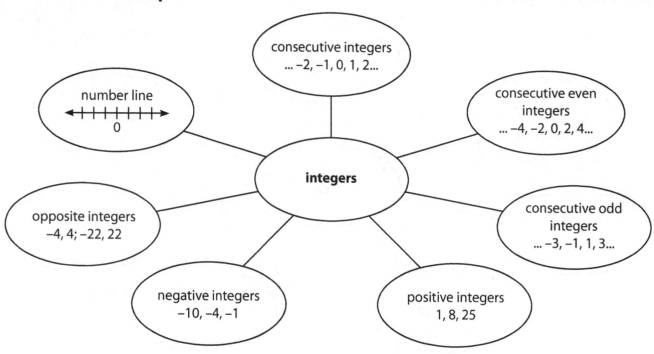

Grades 9–12 Example

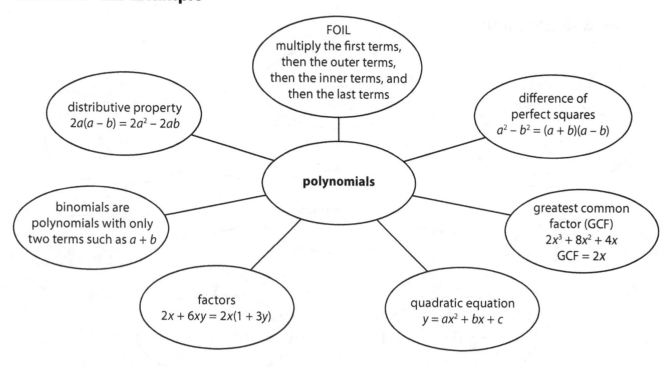

Free-Association Brainstorming

Directions: Write the topic in the center oval. Then, add any words, thoughts, ideas, or examples in the surrounding ovals.

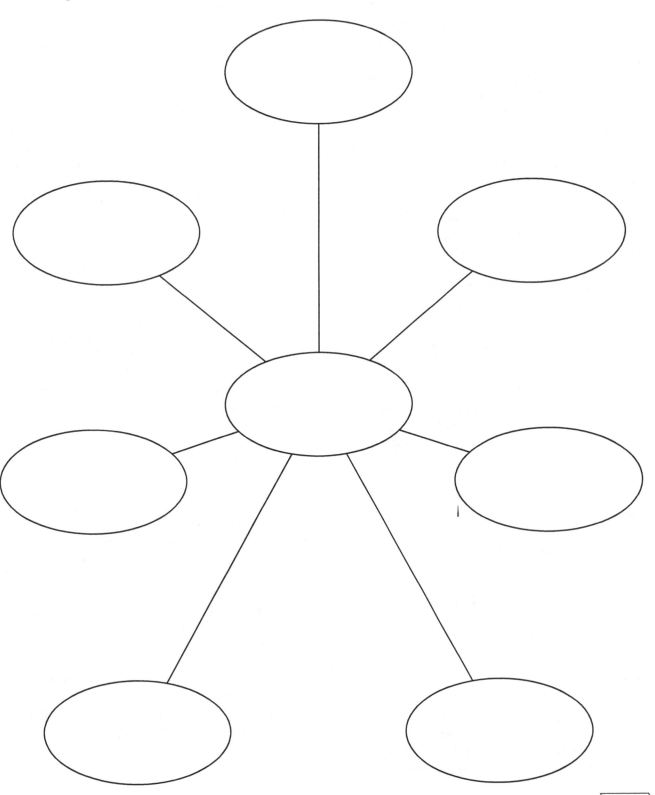

Probable Passages

Background Information

The Probable Passages strategy (Wood 1984) incorporates writing directly into a mathematics lesson. This strategy is primarily used with basal readers, but John Readence, Thomas Bean, and R. Scott Baldwin (1981) suggest that this strategy can be adapted for use with expository text. Its focus is to use key concepts or terms to make predictions about the content of a text. Students use key terms or concepts provided by the teacher to write short passages that could appear in the text. The goal is not necessarily to have their information correct the first time but to examine a topic and convey their ideas through writing. The goal is to write using the types of language and sentence structure common to the genre and use the process of analyzing relevant information against a reliable source.

Grade Levels/Standards Addressed

See page 64 for the standards this strategy addresses, or refer to the Digital Resource CD (standards.pdf) to read the correlating standards in their entirety.

Genres

Expository, Summary, Narrative, Persuasive

Stages of Writing Process

Prewrite, Draft, Revise

Activity

Before reading an informational mathematics text, distribute the *Probable Passages* activity sheet (page 84, probablepassages.pdf) to students. Introduce the topic and write the key vocabulary words on the board or display them using a document camera. Discuss the meanings of these words, and then call on students to define and use the words orally in sentences. Once students are familiar with the words, have them look for relationships among the words in the same way that writers look for related information while composing a rough draft. *Which word might be a main idea? Which words have common meanings or definitions? Which words go together? Which words are examples of another word?* Support students in constructing a simple outline or diagram of how the words might be related as a quick prewriting scaffold in order to help students develop and strengthen their writing. Then, instruct students to write a short passage using the outline. There is no strict format to follow except that the key words must be utilized. Allow time for students to share their passages with their partners or table for feedback and input. After reading the informational mathematics text, have students compare and contrast their Probable Passages with the text. This step is key because students are analyzing their own writing against published writing to verify information and analyze content.

Differentiation

Provide clear, simple definitions and visuals of the key terms for English language learners to refer to as they write their paragraphs because it might be difficult for them to use complex terms they have just learned. Provide sentence frames and examples of how to write a paragraph for English language learners as well. Instruct above-level students to write more than one paragraph or provide additional words for them to incorporate. Also, challenge them to write the passage and leave the key words blank. Then, have students exchange with a partner to see if they can fill in the blanks. For below-level students, spend individual time in a writing conference working through the writing of the paragraph. Also, provide definitions for the key terms.

Probable Passages *(cont.)*

Grades 1–2 Example

Key Concepts:

numbers 1–12, minute hand, hour hand, clock, second hand

Prewrite:

clock
numbers 1–12
hour hand
minute hand
second hand

Probable Passage:

The clock has numbers 1–12. It has a short hand that is the hour hand. It has a longer hand that is called the minute hand. Some clocks also have a skinny red hand called a second hand.

How does your passage compare to the text?

My information is correct. The book gives more descriptions.

Grades 3–5 Example

Key Concepts:

tenths place, hundredths place, thousandths place, decimals, rounding, estimating

Prewrite:

rounding
estimating
decimals
tenths place
hundredths place
thousandths place

Probable Passage:

Sometimes it helps to use estimating and rounding when adding numbers with decimals. The first number after the decimal is in the tenths place. The second number is in the hundredths place. The third number is in the thousandths place. To round a number, you have to decide which place you are rounding to first. Then, you look at the digit that is to the right of that number. If it is 5 or more, you round up, and if it is less than 5, you round down. Then, you can add the numbers together for a good estimate.

How does your passage compare to the text?

My paragraph made sense and was organized. The book did not use the word *you*. It gave examples of each way to round, along with real-life examples of when to round and estimate.

Probable Passages (cont.)

Grades 6–8 Example

Key Concepts:

slope, *x*-intercept, *y*-intercept, *x*-axis, linear function, coordinate plane, *y*-axis, constant, graphing, origin, *x*-coordinate, *y*-coordinate

Prewrite:

graphing
    coordinate plane
        origin
        x-axis
        y-axis
        x-coordinate
        y-coordinate
    linear function
        x-intercept
        y-intercept
        slope
        constant

Probable Passage:

To begin graphing, a person must start with a coordinate plane. This includes an *x*-axis, which is a horizontal line, and a *y*-axis, which is a vertical line. The *x*-coordinate is a number to the right or left on the *x*-axis. The *y*-coordinate is a number up or down on the *y*-axis. Where the lines intersect is called the origin. It has a value of zero. Many times, it is necessary to graph a linear function. This is an equation that is often put in the following form: $y = mx + b$. The *x*-intercept is the place where the line crosses the *x*-axis. The *y*-intercept is where the line crosses the *y*-axis. The letter *m* is the slope and tells you whether the line goes up or down and how steep it is. The letter *b* is the constant because it has no variable and it is also the *y*-intercept.

How does your passage compare to the text?

I did a good job and used all of the words. The book stated that the lines on a coordinate plane are perpendicular. Also, the book explained that the *x*-intercept is where the equation crosses the *x*-axis when $y = 0$, and the *y*-intercept is where the equation crosses the *y*-axis when $x = 0$. The text started most sentences with words other than *the*.

Probable Passages (cont.)

Grades 9–12 Example

Key Concepts:

circle, radius, tangent, chord, central angle, circumference, arc, diameter, concentric circle, sector, semicircle, area

Prewrite:

circle
- **A.** semicircle
- **B.** concentric circle
- **C.** circumference
  - **i.** arc
- **D.** radius
  - **i.** diameter
- **E.** area
  - **i.** sector
  - **ii.** central angle
- **F.** tangent
- **G.** chord

Probable Passage:

A circle has many different parts. A semicircle is half a circle, and a concentric circle is a circle that is a different size but shares the same center point. A circle has a circumference, which is the measurement of the distance around the circle. A circle may also have one or more arcs, or portions of the circumference between certain points on the circle. Inside the circle, there is the radius, or the line from the center to any point on the circle. If you double the radius, you get the diameter, or the length of a straight line between two points on the circle that passes through the center. You use the radius to find the area of the circle. You can also find the area of a sector, or the portion of the circle made up of two radiuses and an arc. The angle formed by the two radiuses at the center of the circle is called the central angle. Circles can also have chords, which are lines that connect two points on the circle and do not pass through the center. Circles also have tangents, which are lines that touch only one point on the circumference of the circle.

How does your passage compare to the text?

I used all the words correctly. The book has a picture with the parts of the circle labeled and it refers to the picture to help define the different words. It is very helpful to refer to the picture. The book uses the plural "radii" when talking about multiple radiuses. The book also doesn't use the word *you*.

Probable Passages

Directions: Write down the key concepts for the lesson. Use a prewriting strategy and then write a probable passage using these words. After reading, compare your passage to the text.

Key Concepts:

_____

_____

Prewrite:

_____

_____

_____

_____

_____

_____

Probable Passage:

_____

_____

_____

_____

How does your passage compare to the text?

_____

_____

_____

_____

Guided Free Write

Background Information

The Guided Free Write strategy, introduced by Peter Elbow (1973), is a slight variation of free writing. The difference is that students are guided in the topics they write about instead of writing about whatever comes to mind. Using this strategy in a mathematics class encourages students to write routinely for a designated amount of time for a range of tasks, including demonstrations or hands-on activities completed in class. It encourages students to record observations about what they are learning and thinking and to generate questions about mathematics concepts. The Guided Free Write strategy allows students to practice writing using mathematics terms and concepts with support from the teacher. This builds confidence in writing, enhances vocabulary development, cements understanding, and leads to further discovery. This "thinking through" helps them clarify exactly what it is they do not understand. The primary focus is not on spelling, grammar, or mechanics. The intent is for students to think and write about their thinking.

Grade Levels/Standards Addressed

See page 65 for the standards this strategy addresses, or refer to the Digital Resource CD (standards.pdf) to read the correlating standards in their entirety.

Genres

Expository, Summary, Narrative, Persuasive

Stage of Writing Process

Draft

Activity

Prepare for the Guided Free Write by thinking of the central mathematics concept or theme that is being taught, and determine a question or questions that will generate thought about the subject. Asking questions as opposed to describing a concept encourages higher-order thinking. These questions may be controversial or may simply encourage students to think further on a given topic. To begin, write the question on the board and instruct students to write on this topic in a notebook or on a sheet of paper. Here are some suggestions for using Guided Free Writes:

- Be sure that all students have access to paper and pencils so they can spend the entire time thinking and writing.

- Tell students not to cross out any information but rather to continually add to their writing. There are no bad ideas. Many of these beginning thoughts will lead to new ideas or trails of thought.

- Keep the classroom free of distractions and noise so that students can focus on their writing.

- Set a timer for 10–20 minutes. This may differ depending on the age of students and the purpose of the Guided Free Write. Remind students that if they are actively thinking on the topic, then it is okay to pause in their writing.

- Remind students not to focus on spelling, grammar, or punctuation. The focus is on getting ideas on paper.

Guided Free Write (cont.)

Variation

Allow students in the primary grades to draw pictures along with writing to explain their thoughts. You may choose to have some students complete the Guided Free Write on the computer. Both typing on the computer and writing on paper provide students with informal writing experience.

Differentiation

Allow English language learners to write words or phrases or draw pictures related to what they are thinking about. Provide sentence frames to model how to begin the answers. Encourage English language learners to put concepts down on paper and not to worry about correct tense or wording. Have them share their free writing with you in order to bring voice to what they have written or drawn. Coach above-level students to write about higher-level concepts or processes. The more complex the concept, the more questions, concerns, and solutions will be generated. For below-level students, provide time for discussion before writing to build their confidence. Also allow these students to use pictures, words, phrases, etc., if necessary, instead of writing complete sentences and paragraphs.

Guided Free Write (cont.)

Grades 1–2 Example

Question:

How do you measure something?

Student Free Write:

There are lots of ways to measure something. If you are measuring the size of a book, you would use a ruler. You could also measure the height of a jar with a ruler. My mom uses a measuring cup to measure flour to bake a cake. Sometimes you have to put in 1 cup of flour or $\frac{1}{2}$ cup of sugar. She also uses measuring spoons. She puts 1 tsp. of vanilla into her cookie dough. Sometimes you have to measure something really big, and you need a tape measure. You can measure the length of a room with a tape measure.

Grades 3–5 Example

Question:

What are the similarities between area and volume?

Student Free Write:

Area and volume both measure the inside of something. With area, you measure the space inside a square or a rectangle. If you were going to tile a floor, you would need to know the area of the space so you know how much tile to buy. With volume, you are measuring the inside of a box or a whole container. Volume is how much something will hold. Maybe you want to make punch and you are going to use many different juices. You would have to know how much your punch bowl would hold before you started adding the juices.

Guided Free Write (cont.)

Grades 6–8 Example

Question:

How do you solve an equation?

Student Free Write:

It depends on what kind of equation it is and how many variables there are. If the equation has only one variable, then the goal is to get that variable all by itself. I first look for parentheses. I use the distributive property to remove all of the parentheses first. Then, I look for denominators. If there are denominators under many of the terms, I have to multiply both sides by the denominator so that there are no more fractions in the problem. Then, I always try and put all the variables on the left side of the equal sign and everything else on the right side. In order to do this, I have to add or subtract them from both sides. Once everything has been moved, I can combine all the like terms. Then, I am only left with the number that is attached to the variable. I usually have to multiply both sides by the reciprocal and then I am done.

Grades 9–12 Example

Question:

What is a function?

Student Free Write:

A function is a mathematical relationship between two different variables or sets of numbers. Functions can be graphed using x- and y-axes. These graphs can have lots of different shapes like straight lines, curved lines, and parabolas. You can also solve functions for certain variables. For every function there can be different answers depending on the input, but for every input, there is only one output. The input is called the independent variable because it can be whatever you want, and the output is called the dependent variable because its value depends on what you put in for the independent variable. You can have a set of numbers that includes all possible values for the input and that is the domain. The range is the set of all possible values for the dependent variable. Functions can have one variable or more.

End-of-Class Reflection

Background Information

With the End-of-Class Reflection, students produce clear and coherent writing on a notecard that includes the two or three most important things learned from a lesson, mathematics activity, or demonstration, as well as two or three questions they want to ask about the central topic. This strategy meets many mathematics classroom needs: students have an opportunity to summarize and glean the main concepts, articulate their learning, and ask questions of the teacher. Teachers are able to quickly assess student understanding and analyze student reflections to direct future lessons. Research shows that writing about learning is a key way to create lifelong learning.

Grade Levels/Standards Addressed

See page 65 for the standards this strategy addresses, or refer to the Digital Resource CD (standards.pdf) to read the correlating standards in their entirety.

Genre

Expository

Stage of Writing Process

Draft

Activity

At the end of a given mathematics lesson, instruct students to write down three key things they learned during the lesson and three questions they still have about the topic. This activity can be completed in a student journal or on a 3" × 5" notecard that can be collected for teacher review.

Variation

For younger students who are still learning to write, consider recording students' dictated responses on the board. With upper grades, ask students to rank their key points in order of priority or emphasis, then lead a brief discussion to review key concepts, analyze rankings, and discuss any questions that were raised.

Differentiation

Allow English language learners to write words, phrases, or draw pictures to explain their key points or questions. Encourage them to get concepts down on paper and not worry about correct verb tense or wording. Expect above-level students to write more than three key points or to write an analysis of the learning they gathered from the lesson. Encourage these students to write questions that are open-ended and encourage higher-level thinking. For below-level students, provide time—perhaps in a Think-Pair-Share—for discussion before writing. If students have an opportunity to discuss what they have learned, it will be easier for them to write. Model a sample response, or simply the beginning of a sample response, to show students how to get started. Then, ask them to use the model to write down their own thoughts.

End-of-Class Reflection *(cont.)*

Grades 1–2 Example

Learning:

I learned that $\frac{1}{2}$ of a pizza is more than $\frac{1}{4}$.

I learned that 2 halves is one whole.

I learned that when you give an equal amount of something to 4 different people, you are giving , you are giving each person $\frac{1}{4}$ of the total.

Questions:

Why is it that 2 is smaller than 4, but $\frac{1}{2}$ is bigger than $\frac{1}{4}$?

Is there a limit to how many pieces you can divide something into?

If you start out with 11 pieces of candy and have 4 people, what fraction would you give each person?

Grades 3–5 Example

Learning:

I learned that a coordinate plane has 4 quadrants.

I learned that the straight line that runs across the middle is the *x*-axis.

I learned that the straight line that runs up and down is the *y*-axis.

I learned how to plot different points on a coordinate plane.

Questions:

What do you do if one of the points includes the number 0?

How do you make a coordinate plane yourself?

Can you ever label the plane starting with 5 and then have the next number be 10, or does it always have to start with 1 and then 2?

End-of-Class Reflection *(cont.)*

Grades 6–8 Example

Learning:

I learned that exponents tell you how many times to multiply a number by itself.

I learned that the number on the bottom is called the base.

I learned that the number that is smaller in size and raised on the top is called the power.

Questions:

What would happen if the number was raised to a negative power?

What do you do if the number is raised to 0 as a power?

Can a number be raised to a power that is a fraction?

Grades 9–12 Example

Learning:

I learned that a quadratic function is a polynomial function and the highest power in the function is 2.

I learned that the graph of a quadratic function is a parabola.

I learned that to graph quadratic functions, it is easier to graph by first putting them into vertex form.

Questions:

How do you determine where the parabola starts on the graph and whether it opens upwards or

downwards?

How can I change a quadratic function into vertex form so I can graph it?

What is the quadratic formula and when is it used?

Reader-Response Writing Chart

Background Information

The Reader-Response Writing Chart strategy, introduced by Allen Carey-Webb (2001), asks students to think about what they bring to a reading passage and what the author of the text brings to the passage. When writing expository mathematics pieces, students need to try to remain neutral and focus on facts, data, or research. In contrast, when writing persuasive pieces in mathematics, students must establish a clear point of view. This strategy helps students become more aware of their biases and in what types of writing it is appropriate to use them and also helps students in producing clear and coherent writing that is appropriate to task, purpose, and audience.

Grade Levels/Standards Addressed

See page 65 for the standards this strategy addresses, or refer to the Digital Resource CD (standards.pdf) to read the correlating standards in their entirety.

Genres

Expository, Narrative, Persuasive

Stage of Writing Process

Draft

Activity

After reading a selected mathematics text, distribute the *Reader-Response Writing Chart* activity sheet (page 95, readerresponse.pdf). On the left side, students write down the author's point of view on the topic as well as any examples of bias or prejudice. For older students, require them to cite examples from the text to support their ideas.

On the right side, students record the bias or prejudice that they had going into the reading. Discuss the following questions with students:

- What do you know about the subject?
- What are your feelings about this topic?
- Have you read anything about this subject before?
- What did you think about this subject?
- What tone does the author use in the text?
- Can you tell what the author is thinking?
- Do you think the author has preconceptions about the topic?

In conclusion, ask students to record whether their views or opinions changed after reading.

Variation

For primary grade classes, re-create the *Reader-Response Writing Chart* on the board or on a large sheet of chart paper. Lead a class discussion about each question, and allow students to help formulate responses to add to the chart.

Differentiation

Encourage English language learners to work with partners when using this strategy to lower anxiety levels and promote collaboration. These students can record answers and share in the discussion. Challenge above-level students to identify examples from the text to support their views of the author's bias and prejudice. Ask them to write about how these influence the author's writing. Then, challenge them to write a synthesis of what they have learned. Take time to define and provide examples of bias and prejudice in a level-appropriate text for below-level students.

Reader-Response Writing Chart *(cont.)*

Grades 3–5 Example

The Author	Me
The graph above shows how temperatures are dramatically increasing across the United States due to global warming, which is a direct result of pollution from things like car exhaust.	This statement makes it seem like humans are the only ones responsible for the increasing temperatures. It also names car exhaust, which makes it seem like that is the main cause. There are lots of other pollutants that could contribute to global warming. I recently saw on the news that if you change all the lightbulbs in your house to the energy-efficient ones, it is like eliminating 30 cars from the road.

Grades 6–8 Example

The Author	Me
The table above shows high school dropout rates for the past 5 years. It is clear that there are more high school dropouts now than ever before. Many students seem uninterested in learning now.	I don't think it is fair to say that students seem uninterested in learning. There are a lot of reasons why students drop out. Maybe some of them have to help take care of the family and work. Also, some areas have so much crime that kids feel they have no choice but to drop out. Finally, the table does not tell us the percentage of dropouts compared to the total number of students. It would make sense that the numbers are higher each year if the population has increased each year.

Reader-Response Writing Chart (cont.)

Grades 9–12 Example

The Author	Me
The graph shows how the population of the United States is increasing exponentially. At this rate, American farmland will no longer be able to provide enough food for future generations and food shortages will occur.	This text assumes that farmland is the only source of food in the United States. The author did not take into account alternative farming methods, like hydroponic farms, that do not depend on vast amounts of land. The author also should consider other methods of obtaining food like importing from other countries before assuming that population growth will lead to food shortages.

Reader-Response Writing Chart

Directions: On the left side, write down the author's point of view on the topic. Also, note any examples of prejudice or bias. On the right side, record your own point of view regarding the subject.

The Author	Me

Journal Writing Overview

Benefits of Journal Writing

The quote, "How do I know what I think until I see what I say?" by novelist E. M. Forster makes journal writing extremely relevant to students in the mathematics class. Even in this crowded, technological world, there is still room for personal writing. Being able to express personal feelings in writing will always be vital to making sense of this world. Journal writing in mathematics allows the writer to use words to express his or her understanding of mathematics concepts and how these concepts relate to the real world.

There are many benefits to using journal-writing strategies in the mathematics classroom. Journal writing provides a means for students to absorb the complex processes, vague concepts, and large amounts of information presented in mathematics. Journal writing is a way for students to sort out all the new information. Writing about what they are learning helps students make sense of it. By writing in a daily journal, students become more confident in their writing and increase the number of words they are writing as well. This is another way for students to see their writing progress.

Journals mean different things to different educators, and they are used for a variety of purposes. However, the support for journal writing seems almost universal. Many different types of journal-writing exercises can be incorporated into the mathematics classroom. Robert Yinger (1985, 31) states that "writing is a powerful tool for learning as well as for communicating."

How to Implement Journal Writing

Incorporating journal writing into the mathematics classroom is easy because it does not take much class time and there is little or no teacher preparation. Journals do not need to be graded; the focus is on content, not on students' writing abilities or spelling, grammar, and punctuation skills. Be sure that students respond positively to writing each day in their journal. Do not make it seem like a punishment; your attitude as a teacher will mean everything.

Create or designate a mathematics journal for each student—and you—to use regularly. Students should date each entry so that it becomes a written record, documenting their growth and progress in learning. Be sure students have notebooks and pencils ready at journal time so that they can spend the entire time writing instead of looking for materials. Model good writing behavior by writing in your own journal.

Set aside a specific time each day during class for journal writing. Be sure to allow enough time for students to write a meaningful entry but not so much that it becomes boring and tedious. Select certain days throughout the week to have students share their journal entries with one another.

Journal Writing Overview *(cont.)*

Standards Addressed

The following chart shows the correlating standards for each strategy in this section. Refer to the Digital Resource CD (standards.pdf) to read the correlating standards in their entirety.

Strategy	McREL Standards	Common Core State Standards
Vocabulary Journal	Grades 1–2 (1.8) Grades 3–5 (1.5, 1.6) Grades 6–8 (1.5) Grades 9–12 (1.5, 1.6)	Grade 1 (CCRA.W.4) Grade 2 (CCRA.W.4) Grade 3 (W.3.4) Grade 4 (W.4.4) Grade 5 (W.5.4) Grade 6 (W.6.4) Grade 7 (W.7.4) Grade 8 (W.8.4) Grades 9–10 (W.9-10.4) Grades 11–12 (W.11-12.4)
Dialogue Journal	Grades 1–2 (1.6) Grades 3–5 (1.5, 1.10) Grades 6–8 (1.5) Grades 9–12 (1.5)	Grade 1 (CCRA.W.4) Grade 2 (CCRA.W.4) Grade 3 (W.3.4) Grade 4 (W.4.4) Grade 5 (W.5.4) Grade 6 (W.6.4) Grade 7 (W.7.4) Grade 8 (W.8.4) Grades 9–10 (W.9-10.4) Grades 11–12 (W.11-12.4)
Highlighted Journal	Grades 1–2 (1.1) Grades 3–5 (1.1, 4.1) Grades 6–8 (1.1, 4.3) Grades 9–12 (1.1)	Grade 1 (CCRA.W.4, CCRA.W.10) Grade 2 (CCRA.W.4, CCRA.W.10) Grade 3 (W.3.4, W.3.10) Grade 4 (W.4.4, W.4.10) Grade 5 (W.5.4, W.5.10) Grade 6 (W.6.4, W.6.10) Grade 7 (W.7.4, W.7.10) Grade 8 (W.8.4, W.8.10) Grades 9–10 (W.9-10.4, W.9-10.10) Grades 11–12 (W.11-12.4, W.11-12.10)

Journal Writing Overview (cont.)

Strategy	McREL Standards	Common Core State Standards
Key Phrase Journal	Grades 1–2 (1.2) Grades 3–5 (1.2) Grades 6–8 (1.2) Grades 9–12 (1.2)	Grade 1 (CCRA.W.10, L.1.6) Grade 2 (CCRA.W.10, L.2.6) Grade 3 (W.3.10, L.3.6) Grade 4 (W.4.10, L.4.6) Grade 5 (W.5.10, L.5.6) Grade 6 (W.6.10, L.6.6) Grade 7 (W.7.10, L.7.6) Grade 8 (W.8.10, L.8.6) Grades 9–10 (W.9-10.10, L.9-10.6) Grades 11–12 (W.11-12.10, L.11-12.6)
Double-Entry Journal	Grades 3–5 (1.10, 1.11) Grades 6–8 (1.12) Grades 9–12 (1.12)	Grade 3 (CCRA.W.9) Grade 4 (W.4.9) Grade 5 (W.5.9) Grade 6 (W.6.9) Grade 7 (W.7.9) Grade 8 (W.8.9) Grades 9–10 (W.9-10.9) Grades 11–12 (W.11-12.9)
Critical Incident Journal	Grades 1–2 (1.6) Grades 3–5 (1.8, 1.10) Grades 6–8 (1.7, 1.8) Grades 9–12 (1.8, 1.11)	Grade 1 (CCRA.W.4, W.1.5) Grade 2 (CCRA.W.4, W.2.5) Grade 3 (W.3.4) Grade 4 (W.4.4) Grade 5 (W.5.4) Grade 6 (W.6.4) Grade 7 (W.7.4) Grade 8 (W.8.4) Grades 9–10 (W.9-10.4) Grades 11–12 (W.11-12.4)
Three-Part Journal	Grades 1–2 (1.6, 1.8) Grades 3–5 (1.5, 1.6, 1.10) Grades 6–8 (1.5, 1.8) Grades 9–12 (1.5, 1.8)	Grade 1 (CCRA.W.4) Grade 2 (CCRA.W.4) Grade 3 (W.3.4) Grade 4 (W.4.4) Grade 5 (W.5.4) Grade 6 (W.6.4) Grade 7 (W.7.4) Grade 8 (W.8.4) Grades 9–10 (W.9-10.4) Grades 11–12 (W.11-12.4)

Vocabulary Journal

Background Information

The Vocabulary Journal provides an opportunity for students to produce clear and coherent writing to communicate their learning, and it can lead to self-reflection and growth. The Vocabulary Journal is an excellent resource for the mathematics classroom because it allows students to write personally about the words they are learning in mathematics. The entries in a Vocabulary Journal vary—each one meets a specific need or skill. Expectations for the writing in the Vocabulary Journal vary according to students' levels, purpose, and intended audience.

Grade Levels/Standards Addressed

See page 97 for the standards this strategy addresses, or refer to the Digital Resource CD (standards.pdf) to read the correlating standards in their entirety.

Genres

Expository, Narrative

Stage of Writing Process

Draft

Activity

Designate or create a notebook for each student to use as a Vocabulary Journal. This journal helps students keep track of and reflect on the many new words that are introduced in the study of mathematics. The following is a variety of strategies to use with the Vocabulary Journal:

- Log mathematics vocabulary words and their definitions as well as synonyms, antonyms, comparisons, etc.

- Write about the words students are learning. Ask students: *What has the experience been like? What have you learned? What do you hope to remember? What strategies can you use to retain these words? How does learning the meanings of words help you better understand concepts and information?*

- Explain the strategies that can be used when students encounter an unfamiliar word.

- Create a piece of fiction, such as a letter or story, using the new mathematics vocabulary words.

- Write sentences using the vocabulary words.

- List the resources that are available for students to use when researching new vocabulary words.

- Design a journal entry to be shared with a partner or small group.

Variation

For primary grade students, create a class Vocabulary Journal. Allow students to dictate entries to be recorded by the teacher. This provides an opportunity for the teacher to model good writing skills. Or provide students with their own journals and allow them to draw and label pictures of vocabulary words. If students are able to use the word in a sentence or explain what it means orally, then challenge them to write their responses in their journals.

Vocabulary Journal *(cont.)*

Differentiation

Select Vocabulary Journal strategies that will encourage growth for English language learners but not overwhelm them, such as recording new vocabulary terms with their definitions, synonyms, examples, etc. Remind them to draw pictures to help create a visual connection. Challenge above-level students to write about complex mathematics terms in their Vocabulary Journal. Allow them to select words and entries that they are personally interested in. Limit the number of vocabulary words that below-level students write about. Provide them with sentence frames to help them meet the expectations of the assigned activity.

Vocabulary Journal *(cont.)*

Grades 1–2 Example

Vocabulary Words

1. **circle**—a round shape with no sides or corners

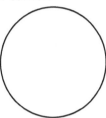

2. **triangle**—a shape with 3 sides and 3 corners

3. **square**—a shape with 4 equal sides and 4 equal corners

Grades 3–5 Example

What strategies can I use when I come across a word I do not know? There are many things that I can do. One thing I can do is look at the other words in the sentence to see if there are clues that can help me. Sometimes I recognize parts of the word, such as a prefix, suffix, or root. I can use those to help me figure out what the word means. If I'm lucky, the author used a context clue, and the definition is right there in the sentence. If none of these strategies work, I can look up the unfamiliar word in a dictionary or in a thesaurus.

Vocabulary Journal *(cont.)*

Grades 6–8 Example

Absolute value is the distance on a number line between a number and the origin. Therefore, it is always positive.

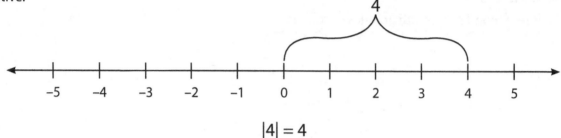

$$|4| = 4$$

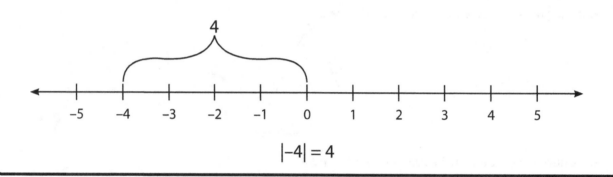

$$|-4| = 4$$

Grades 9–12 Example

1. **sine** $= \frac{a}{c}$, or the ratio of the length of the opposite side over the length of the hypotenuse, sin Θ

2. **cosine** $= \frac{b}{c}$, or the ratio of the length of the adjacent side over the length of the hypotenuse, cos Θ

3. **tangent** $= \frac{a}{b}$, or the ratio of the length of the opposite side over the length of the adjacent side, tan Θ

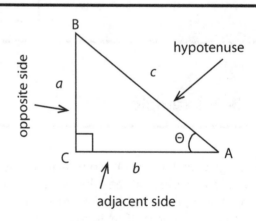

Dialogue Journal

Background Information

A Dialogue Journal (Staton 1980) is just what the name implies—a dialogue between two or more people. Dialogue Journals can be shared between a student and a teacher or between two students. This strategy does entail more work for teachers, but the dialogue exchange and extra effort are rewarding, informative, and provides the teacher with immediate feedback about students' writing skills. Using this strategy, teachers can recognize areas of student concern or misunderstanding with respect to the mathematics content as well as student progress in communicating thoughts and ideas in writing. Students benefit from having an audience for their writing and frequent opportunities for using writing as an authentic form of communication as they produce a dialogue that is appropriate to task, purpose, and audience.

Grade Levels/Standards Addressed

See page 97 for the standards this strategy addresses, or refer to the Digital Resource CD (standards.pdf) to read the correlating standards in their entirety.

Genre

Narrative

Stage of Writing Process

Draft

Activity

Designate a notebook or binder to be used as the mathematics Dialogue Journal. Ask students to respond to a prompt or question, or occasionally allow them to write about a topic of their own. Using a combination of both adds variety to the strategy. Students should exchange Dialogue Journals with the teacher or a peer who then reads the journal entry and responds to questions or adds comments. Then, exchange again and write a new entry to continue the dialogue.

Variation

Create a teacher-class Dialogue Journal for primary grade students, or provide a question or prompt with a frame for the answer to assist these students.

Differentiation

Remind English language learners that this is a personal assignment, so they can respond in a way that is comfortable for them. Allow them to choose how they would like to communicate. Challenge above-level students by giving them specific feedback that will stimulate challenging thoughts and ideas and develop more effective writing skills. Encourage them to research ideas further and write about their findings in the next journal entry. When dialoguing with below-level students, be sure to keep your writing clear, concise, and easy to read, and model correct spelling. Use the journal as an opportunity to challenge students' thinking even if the reading or writing skills are not high. Carefully consider who to pair these students with when they exchange journals with each other.

Dialogue Journal *(cont.)*

Grades 1–2 Example

Student: I like using pictures to help me solve math problems.

Teacher: That is a great strategy. What kinds of problems has that strategy helped you solve?

Student: I think it is really helpful when we do word problems like the one we did today where we had to figure out how many outfit combinations were possible with the different-colored shirts, shorts, and socks.

Teacher: That is a great problem to draw a picture of. Can you think of another way you could have solved that problem?

Student: I did think that I could have used multiplication if I understood it better. Are we going to learn more about multiplication this year?

Teacher: We are going to learn a little more about multiplication this year, but our next topic is going to be measurement. What do you already know about measurement? Maybe you could see if you can find some information about measurement on the Internet.

Grades 3–5 Example

Student: Today we reviewed how to do subtraction with borrowing and carrying. It helped when you called me up to the board, and you and the class helped me do a problem myself. I hope that when I go home to do the homework, I will remember what to do.

Teacher: I was really proud of you for coming up to the board. I know that it helped the other kids to see you do it. I know you have an older brother, too. Don't be afraid to ask him for help. Would you like me to do the first few problems with you right after school?

Student: Thanks for helping me after school yesterday. I was able to do the problems myself after we did the first two together. My brother helped me a little bit, too. That was a good idea. I still get stuck when I go to borrow and the number is a 0. What do I do then?

Teacher: Remember that if you have to borrow and the number is 0, then you have to go to the next place to the left of the 0 and borrow from that number.

Dialogue Journal *(cont.)*

Grades 6–8 Example

Student: I really enjoyed the rate experiment we did today. I was excited to see whether the boys in our class would run as fast or faster than the girls. I really understand how to calculate rate now, too. Do you think we could do the experiment again but over a longer distance?

Teacher: I am really glad that you liked the experiment. That is a really good question. I don't know if it would change our results. What would be some factors that might affect the experiment?

Student: Well, in this experiment, we only sprinted 60 feet and the boys seemed to win hands down. In P.E. class when we run the mile, it seems that the girls finish ahead of the boys. If we timed everyone running the mile and then calculated average rate, I think we might get different results. Also, our class is right after lunch and the kids had just eaten, but PE is at the end of the day. That might affect the outcome.

Teacher: That is a great suggestion. I will talk to your PE teacher and see if I can coordinate things. It depends on which students are in the PE class also. Perhaps your PE class has more girls in it who are in athletics than our regular class. I do think it would be fun to use what we learned about rate and find out if a greater distance makes a difference in our results.

Grades 9–12 Example

Student: I really liked talking about compound interest in class today. It seems like there are a lot of situations in life where it is important to know how to calculate compound interest. I've been thinking about putting the money I received for my birthday into a certificate of deposit (CD) at the bank. Do you think that's a good idea?

Teacher: Yes, I think CDs are a good way to earn some extra money on your savings. Different banks offer different rates of return on your investment so you need to do some research and figure out which bank is offering the best rate. Also, the rates often depend on the length of the CD. You can use what you learned in class to figure out how much interest you'll make depending on the rate and length of investment. That should help you make your decision.

Student: I researched several different banks. I found that the longer the CD, the better the return on your investment. Now I just need to consider whether I will want to access that money in the near future or whether I should put it in a longer CD to make more money.

Teacher: That is exactly right. Banks offer better rates for longer investments. Also, we learned that compound interest grows exponentially so that is more incentive to make a longer investment for you. I'm glad to see that you're applying our classroom learning to help you make decisions in your personal life!

Highlighted Journal

Background Information

The Highlighted Journal is a strategy that assists students in making connections with their learning. Students need to write routinely in their journals for at least a month before trying this strategy. Students read through their journals and highlight key points—significant information or discoveries, points from class discussions, or concepts from a mathematics text. This strategy helps develop research skills by asking students to analyze their written work for trends, commonalities, main ideas, themes, etc., which is crucial to the prewriting stage of the writing process.

Grade Levels/Standards Addressed

See page 97 for the standards this strategy addresses, or refer to the Digital Resource CD (standards.pdf) to read the correlating standards in their entirety.

Genre

Expository

Stage of Writing Process

Prewrite

Activity

Have students routinely write in their journals for at least a month so that they will have enough writing to analyze and highlight. Tell them to read through their journals, looking for key words or concepts, common themes, or interesting points. Provide highlighters or allow students to use pencils to underline key points in their journal entries. Ask them to share their highlighted selections and the reasons why they chose them with each other or with the class.

Variation

For a primary grade class using a single journal between the teacher and the class, read through the journal entries together and ask students to identify the key points to highlight.

Differentiation

Prompt English language learners to look for common words that they see throughout their journals, as these are likely some of the key concepts and important vocabulary words that they need to know. Using this strategy serves as an effective review tool for them. Consider having above-level students explain to the class how they chose their highlighted points. For below-level students, take time to explicitly model how to identify significant information or common ideas in your own journal before asking them to apply the strategy.

Highlighted Journal *(cont.)*

Grades 1–2 Example

November 2

We practiced putting things <u>below</u> each other.

November 3

Putting things <u>below</u> is like putting them <u>underneath</u>.

November 4

We practiced more <u>location words</u> like <u>next to</u> and <u>above</u>.

November 7

We learned how to tell between our <u>right and left</u>. I remember it easily because I write with my <u>right</u> hand.

Grades 3–5 Example

February 10

<u>Fractions</u> are used to <u>divide bigger things into smaller pieces</u>. The <u>numerator</u> goes on top and the <u>denominator</u> goes on the bottom.

February 11

You can add <u>fractions</u> together easily when they have the same <u>denominator</u>. When you add pieces together, you can end up with one whole. If you cut a pie into 8 pieces and everyone got one piece and ate it, you would say that everyone ate $\frac{8}{8}$ total. That is the <u>same as 1 whole</u>.

February 12

You can also <u>convert fractions</u>. With the pie example from yesterday, you can say that 2 pieces of the pie is $\frac{2}{8}$, which is the <u>same as</u> $\frac{1}{4}$. Also, $\frac{4}{8}$ would be the <u>same as</u> $\frac{1}{2}$.

February 15

<u>Fractions</u> are <u>linked to money</u>, too. A <u>quarter</u> is worth 25 cents, and it is $\frac{1}{4}$ <u>of a dollar</u>. <u>Two quarters</u> are worth 50 cents and are $\frac{1}{2}$ <u>of a dollar</u>.

Highlighted Journal *(cont.)*

Grades 6–8 Example

January 8

The least common multiple is also called the LCM. It is the smallest number that is a multiple of the numbers in a set. For example, the LCM of the numbers 12 and 30 is 60. That is 12×5 and 30×2.

January 11

The greatest common factor is also called the GCF. It is the biggest number that can be divided into a set of numbers. For example, the GCF of 12 and 30 is 6.
$12 \div 6 = 2$ and $30 \div 6 = 5$.

January 12

The GCF is very helpful in reducing fractions. For example, if you have the fraction $\frac{12}{30}$ and you knew that the GCF was 6, you could divide both numbers by 6 and the fraction would be $\frac{2}{5}$. That is the simplest form of the fraction.

Grades 9–12 Example

March 2

The probability of a particular event (x) occurring is determined by dividing the number of outcomes resulting in x by the total number of possible outcomes. For example, if you're trying to figure out the chances that you'll roll a 4 on a number cube, you divide 1 (there's only one side with the number 4 on a number cube) by 6 (because there are six different possible outcomes, or numbers, on a number cube). So the probability is $\frac{1}{6}$.

March 3

If you're trying to figure out the probability that either event A or event B will occur, you have to figure out if the events are mutually exclusive. If the events cannot happen at the same time (you cannot roll both a 2 and a 5 at the same time on a number cube), then you can add the probability of each event occurring to find the probability of one or the other happening. If the events are not mutually exclusive, then you take the probability of A plus the probability of B and subtract the probability of A and B occurring together.

March 6

You use multiplication to figure out the probability of multiple events occurring together. If the events are independent of one another, then you multiply the probability of A times the probability of B to figure out the probability of A and B occurring together. If A and B are dependent on one another, then the probability of A and B occurring together equals the probability of A times the probability of B *after A has occurred*.

Key Phrase Journal

Background Information

The Key Phrase Journal (Bringle and Hatcher 1996) is a strategy that assists students in routinely incorporating new mathematics vocabulary and phrases into their writing. During a mathematics lesson, the teacher selects a list of mathematics terms students are to use in a journal entry. By using this strategy on a regular basis, students can develop a more solid understanding of the mathematics terms and become more adept at accurately using them in writing. This strategy is most commonly used with a reading selection, but it can also be used when conducting a mathematics experiment or observation activity.

Grade Levels/Standards Addressed

See page 98 for the standards this strategy addresses, or refer to the Digital Resource CD (standards.pdf) to read the correlating standards in their entirety.

Genres

Expository, Persuasive

Stage of Writing Process

Draft

Activity

Prior to teaching a mathematics lesson, make a list of words or phrases that students should understand thoroughly. Throughout the reading lesson or activity, introduce the words and use them in sentences, or point them out in the text. Discuss the meanings of the words with students. After the lesson or later in the day, write the list of words and phrases on the board and instruct students to write an entry in their journals accurately using those words.

Variation

With primary grade students, create sentences orally as a class. Write the sentences on the board or invite students to write them. To challenge upper grade students, let them select the words to incorporate into the journal entries, and ask them to persuade you to agree with their choices.

Differentiation

For English language learners, select from the list only the terms with which they are somewhat familiar—words that have been discussed as a class and defined on numerous occasions. Have them use only those words in their Key Phrase Journal so that they are not frustrated. Challenge above-level students to use words that are more difficult or less familiar to them by researching the terms and determining ways to incorporate them into the journal entry. For below-level students, allow them to select only one or two words to use in their journal entry and to use resources to look up these words, if needed.

Key Phrase Journal (cont.)

Grades 1–2 Example

Key Words:

one more than, one less than, 10 more than, 10 less than

Journal Entry:

The number 3 is one more than 2. The number 1 is one less than 2. The number 30 is 10 more than 20. The number 10 is 10 less than 20.

Grades 3–5 Example

Key Words:

ones place, tens place, hundreds place, thousands place, ten thousands place, hundred thousands place

Journal Entry:

It is easy to identify the place value of each digit in the number 154,879. The 9 is in the ones place. The 7 is in the tens place. The 8 is in the hundreds place. The 4 is in the thousands place. The 5 is in the ten thousands place, and the 1 is in the hundred thousands place.

Key Phrase Journal *(cont.)*

Grades 6–8 Example

Key Words:

perimeter, width, length, base, height, pi, diameter, area, circumference

Journal Entry:

The perimeter of a rectangle is two times the width of an object plus two times the length of an object. The formula is $P = 2w + 2l$. The area of a triangle is one half the base times the height of the triangle. The formula is $A = \frac{1}{2}bh$. The circumference of a circle is pi (π) times the diameter of the circle itself. The formula is $C = \pi d$.

Grades 9–12 Example

Key Words:

conic sections, circle, ellipse, parabola, vertex, axis of symmetry, focus, major axis, minor axis, center

Journal Entry:

Conic sections are the shapes formed when a plane passes through a cone. When a plane passes through a cone at a centered or flat angle, a circle is formed. When a plane passes through a cone at an off-center angle, an ellipse is formed. An ellipse is oval-shaped and is defined by its major axis (long distance) and minor axis (short distance). Ellipses contain a center point and two foci. All points on an ellipse are the same distance from the sum of the foci. A parabola is formed when a cone is intersected by a plane that is perpendicular to the base of the cone. Parabolas are u-shaped and may open upwards or downwards. They have an axis of symmetry that bisects the figure and a vertex, or point, where the parabola crosses the axis of symmetry.

Double-Entry Journal

Background Information

The Double-Entry Journal (Angelo and Cross 1993) is a strategy to help students summarize what they read and connect the reading with their own words and understanding. A Double-Entry Journal has two columns: one for notes, paraphrasing, summaries, and textual evidence from the mathematics reading; and the other for entries that express students' thoughts in their own words. This strategy allows teachers to immediately gauge student comprehension of the objectives and use that information to inform future instruction. It also focuses on the prewriting skills of note-taking and information analysis. Students analyze, synthesize, question, and write about what they are reading as well as personalize and reflect on what they have learned by drawing on information in the text to support their analyses.

Grade Levels/Standards Addressed

See page 98 for the standards this strategy addresses, or refer to the Digital Resource CD (standards.pdf) to read the correlating standards in their entirety.

Genres

Expository, Narrative, Persuasive

Stage of Writing Process

Prewrite

Activity

Distribute the *Double-Entry Journal* activity sheet (page 115, doubleentry.pdf). On the left side, have students write notes or summaries of the reading, using text evidence to support their summaries, and on the right side, have them record personal reflections, observations, or questions. Select passages to focus on content or clarify misunderstandings, or allow students to select their own passages because of particular interest or questions they have about them.

When students have completed both sides of their journal entries, have them draw arrows to show the connections and relationships between the summary of the content and their personal thoughts and reflections. This reinforces for students what they are learning.

Differentiation

For English language learners, scaffold the activity by providing notes and key concepts for the left column in simple sentences that are easy to understand. Have these students read and discuss the notes before writing about them. Once they have written the personal reflection, suggest that English language learners draw arrows to show connections between the notes and their own words. Challenge above-level students to also write what they are thinking about as they write their notes. Another term for this is "thinking aloud." Once the note-taking, summarizing, and thinking aloud is completed, have them write personal reflections. For below-level students, have them focus on only one or two key points to summarize from the lesson. Instruct them to keep their notes brief and limited so they can focus on their personal reflection without being overwhelmed by too many concepts to discuss.

Double-Entry Journal *(cont.)*

Grades 3–5 Example

Title: <u>Favorite Colors and Bar Graphs</u>

Text Passage	Student Response
"Jill and Tony decided to take a survey of their classmates' favorite colors. There were 19 students in their class. They found that 4 people liked red, 3 people liked blue, 6 people liked purple, and 6 people liked green. It is important to be able to show data in different ways. One way to show data is by creating a bar graph. To make a bar graph of this data, you would start by naming the colors along the bottom of the graph. Along the left side of the graph, with even spacing, you would label the numbers 1–10. That is as high as you would need to go because the biggest number in your data is 6."	This reminds me of when my family was trying to order pizza. I have 3 sisters, 2 brothers, my parents, my grandma and me all living at my house. We had to take a survey of the different pizza toppings everyone wanted so that we could decide what kind of pizza to order. That would have made a good bar graph, too. I could put the toppings along the bottom and the numbers on the left side. I can think of many ways we could gather data for a bar graph. We should survey the students' favorite ice cream flavors and make a bar graph.

Grades 6–8 Example

Title: <u>Mean, Median, and Mode</u>

Text Passage	Student Response
"Ms. Nelson's class of 25 students took a math test with 20 questions. The test was worth 100 points. Understanding mean, median, and mode can help us understand how the students did on the test. By taking all the students' scores and dividing them by 25, it gives us the average test score, or the mean test score. The mean test score for Ms. Nelson's class was 75%. Ms. Nelson asked the students to write down all the problems that they got wrong. She found that 20 of the 25 students got problem number 16 wrong. That problem number was the mode of the list because it occurred most often on the students' lists."	This reminds me of the test we just took. You said that the class average was 85%. This is the same as saying that the mean test score for our class was 85%. I also remember that you paired us up to work in partners, making sure that someone with a higher test score worked with someone who had a lower test score. I also remember that it seemed like everyone got problem number 12 wrong. I bet if everyone listed the problems they got wrong on a single piece of paper, the number 12 would occur the most, and that would be the mode.

Double-Entry Journal *(cont.)*

Grades 9–12 Example

Title: <u>Probability</u>

Text Passage	Student Response
"A child is playing with a bag of marbles. In the bag, there are 3 green marbles, 4 red marbles and 5 blue marbles. The child reaches into the bag and draws out one marble. Then the child reaches into the bag again and draws out a second marble. What is the probability that the child pulls out two red marbles? Each of the two marbles chosen represents separate events. The probability that the first marble is red is $\frac{4}{12}$, or $\frac{1}{3}$, since there are 4 red marbles and twelve marbles altogether. For the second marble, the chances are 3 (number of red marbles left) out of 11 (total number of marbles left). The chances of both events occurring together is the product of the probability of each event occurring: $\frac{4}{12} \times \frac{3}{11} = \frac{12}{132}$ or $\frac{1}{11}$."	This reminds me of the time I went to an arcade with my best friend. We played a game where you put a coin into a machine and the machine randomly grabs a prize from a box for you. My friend and I both wanted to win yo-yos from the prize box, but we didn't think we'd be able to since there were only two yo-yos and 18 other prizes in the box. The chance of one of us getting a yo-yo was $\frac{2}{20}$, or $\frac{1}{10}$, and the chance of the other person getting a yo-yo was $\frac{1}{19}$. Therefore, the probability of us both winning a yo-yo was $\frac{1}{10} \times \frac{1}{19} = \frac{1}{190}$, which is very slim, but we decided to take our chances anyway. Neither of us ended up getting a yo-yo, but we liked our prizes anyway.

Name: _____ **Date:** _____

Double-Entry Journal

Title: _____

Text Passage	Student Response
• Write the passage directly from the text. • Write notes from the text. • Write a summary of a section of text.	• What are your reactions to the text? • What does it remind you of? • What questions do you still have?

Critical Incident Journal

Background Information

The Critical Incident Journal (Bringle and Hatcher 1996) focuses on a specific event that occurred in class. The critical incident will be different for each student. Examples of critical incidents in a mathematics class may include the results of a photo analysis, an "aha!" moment when a student finally understands the material, the confusing part of a lesson, a low test grade, a reaction to a hands-on activity, or another type of personal experience. This quick writing strategy provides a springboard for future writing or research activities and aids students in producing clear and coherent writing that is appropriate to task, purpose, and audience.

Grade Levels/Standards Addressed

See page 98 for the standards this strategy addresses, or refer to the Digital Resource CD (standards.pdf) to read the correlating standards in their entirety.

Genres

Expository, Narrative

Stage of Writing Process

Draft

Activity

Prior to teaching a mathematics lesson, explain that students should look for a critical incident throughout the course of a lesson. Describe a critical incident and give examples. Explain that students should identify the critical incident during the lesson and be prepared to write about it in their journals in a clear and coherent manner. Here are some questions to consider:

- What is the significant event you would like to write about in your journal?
- Why is this event important to you?
- What was your favorite or least favorite part of the lesson today?
- Describe the event. What happened?
- What did you learn from this experience?
- How does this fit in with what you are learning in mathematics class?

Variation

For grades 1–2, invite students to draw and label their critical incidents and display the drawings on the board. Those who are able can then write sentences to explain their choice of critical incidents. This strategy may be especially meaningful following a hands-on activity.

Differentiation

For English language learners, create a shared experience that they can discuss with other students, such as classifying solid figures, making their own clocks, or creating physical representations of fractions. After students have had time to discuss, allow time for students to write in their journals. Ask above-level students to write about their critical incident in a specific genre: use vivid imagery and descriptive language to describe the critical incident, use persuasive language to show why the incident is the most critical, or compare and contrast the critical incident with a previous one. Encourage above-level students to identify critical incidents in newspapers or other resources (e.g., trends in population growth, major political developments). Provide examples of the critical incident journal for below-level students. Allow them to work with partners to discuss events during the mathematics lesson so that they feel more confident about writing about them.

Critical Incident Journal *(cont.)*

Grades 1–2 Example

Today we were learning about patterns with shapes. We came up with the pattern square, circle, circle, triangle. I drew the square on the board for the first part of the pattern. Then Jose drew the two circles, and Jenny drew the triangle to finish the pattern. It was fun.

 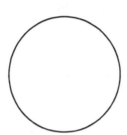 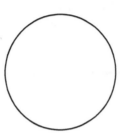 

Grades 3–5 Example

It was fun working with perimeter today in class. I found that the length of our math book is 12 inches and the width was 8 inches. The total perimeter was 40 inches. April used yardsticks to measure the perimeter of the classroom. It was 86 feet! I wonder how many inches that is. It was a lot of fun.

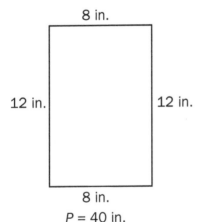 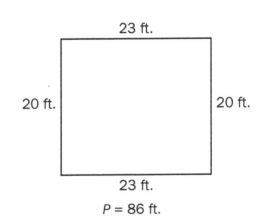

Critical Incident Journal (cont.)

Grades 6–8 Example

It was really exciting in math class today because we were able to "buy" snacks and drinks using math. Each item was given an original price and a discount price. The only way you could buy the item was if you were the first person to correctly calculate the final price. I was able to buy a bottle of water because the original price was $2.38 and it was marked down by 24%. That meant the total cost was $1.81. I wish we could have used calculators.

Grades 9–12 Example

Today we learned about factorials in class and it was lots of fun. Even factorials of small numbers like 5! add up to big numbers because factorials increase exponentially: $5! = 5 \times 4 \times 3 \times 2 \times 1 = 120$. Mr. Larsen told us that if we could figure out 7!, he would give each of us that number of pennies, but I know he was joking because $7! = 5040$. That would be $50.40 for each of us and I don't think Mr. Larsen can afford to give each of us that much money!

Three-Part Journal

Background Information

The Three-Part Journal (Bringle and Hatcher 1996) asks students to divide the journal page into thirds. On a weekly basis, students are asked to write in their Three-Part Journals as they produce clear and coherent journal entries that are appropriate to task, purpose, and audience as it relates to a mathematics concept of study.

Grade Levels/Standards Addressed

See page 98 for the standards this strategy addresses, or refer to the Digital Resource CD (standards.pdf) to read the correlating standards in their entirety.

Genres

Expository, Narrative

Stage of Writing Process

Draft

Activity

Designate or create a notebook for students to use for this strategy. Distribute the *Three-Part Journal* activity sheet (page 122, threepartjournal.pdf) to students. Primary grade teachers may want to use this strategy as a class until students are able to complete it independently. In the first section, students describe insights that they gained from the lesson. Questions to prompt students might include:

- What information did you learn?
- What was your favorite part?
- What do you think about what you have learned?

In the second section, students write about how this new information or experience fits in with what they already know. Ask students to explain what they knew previously about this topic, and then show what new information they have learned. Ask questions such as these to prompt students:

- What did you already know about this topic?
- What new information did you learn?
- How does the new information fit in with the old information, or information you already knew?

In the last section, students write about how the new knowledge relates or can be applied to their personal lives. This will vary, as each student will apply the mathematics material in a different way. Consider writing some prompts on the board:

- How might you relate this new learning to your life?
- How does this information change your views of the topic?
- How might you use this information in your own life?

Finally, allow time for students to share what they have written.

Differentiation

Explain the different sections of the journal page to English language learners to ensure that they understand the purpose of each section. Model how to complete the journal and provide sentence stems for each section to help these students express their thoughts. Remind them to focus on content rather than grammar and mechanics. Challenge above-level students to research the concepts being discussed in class and share further research information in their journals. Allow below-level students to complete the section they are most comfortable with first to build their confidence. Guide a small group to complete the remainder of the sections.

Three-Part Journal (cont.)

Grades 1–2 Example

Part 1: What new information did you learn? What was your favorite part?
I learned that there are many different numbers that can add up to 10.

Part 2: What did you already know? How does the new information fit in with the old?
I knew that 5 + 5 = 10 and 6 + 4 = 10, but now I know all the combinations of numbers that add up to 10.

Part 3: How can you use this information in your own life?
When my mother and I went to the store and she said I could spend 10 dollars, I used to look for two things that were each 5 dollars. Now if I find something for 2 dollars, I can look for something that is 8 dollars. Or if I find something that is 7 dollars, I will look for something that is 3 dollars.

Grades 3–5 Example

Part 1: What new information did you learn? What was your favorite part?
I learned what expanded notation is and how to use it.

Part 2: What did you already know? How does the new information fit in with the old?
I figured that 20 + 5 would be 25, but I did not even think of doing the same thing with bigger numbers. Now I can not only put numbers together but break them apart, too.

Part 3: How can you use this information in your own life?
This can help with estimation. I used to think that estimation was difficult, but if you look at each place value as a separate number, it makes more sense.

Three-Part Journal *(cont.)*

Grades 6–8 Example

Part 1: What new information did you learn? What was your favorite part?
I learned that the speed you travel down a freeway is just a ratio. For example, if you are traveling 60 miles per hour, that means that for every 60 miles traveled, it would take one hour. I never thought of speed as a ratio.
Part 2: What did you already know? How does the new information fit in with the old?
I knew how to read the speedometer of a car. Now that I understand that it is a ratio, I see that ratios apply to all kinds of things besides speed. Batting averages are also ratios.
Part 3: How can you use this information in your own life?
This is really helpful for car trips. I used to ask my mom how long it would take us to get somewhere. Now I can figure it out myself if she gives me the number of miles away that it is and how fast we are traveling.

Grades 9–12 Example

Part 1: What new information did you learn? What was your favorite part?
I learned that you can find the surface area of a sphere by using the equation $SA = 4\pi r^2$. I also learned that a sphere's volume is $\frac{4}{3}\pi r^3$. I liked learning about the properties of spheres because lots of things in our lives are spheres, like balls, globes, oranges, etc.
Part 2: What did you already know? How does the new information fit in with the old?
I already knew that the area of a circle is πr^2. It makes sense that the volume of a sphere is bigger than the area of a circle (πr^2 vs. $\frac{4}{3}\pi r^3$) since a circle is a two-dimensional figure and a sphere is three-dimensional.
Part 3: How can you use this information in your own life?
I love to play basketball, and sometimes I like to take my basketball with us when my family goes on vacation. Whenever we fly somewhere, my mom says I have to leave my basketball at home because it takes up too much space in my suitcase. Now I can use this information to explain to her that all I need to do is deflate the ball and I will be able to fit it in my suitcase. I can tell her that the surface area of a sphere (actually it would only be half the surface area since the ball will be folded in half) is much less than the volume of a full sphere.

Three-Part Journal

Part 1: What new information did you learn? What was your favorite part?

Part 2: What did you already know? How does the new information fit in with the old?

Part 3: How can you use this information in your own life?

Note-Taking Overview

Note-taking is a crucial skill for students in upper elementary grades and beyond. High school and college students do a significant amount of note-taking during classes and while reading, so it makes sense for this skill to be taught to our younger students as well. Teachers often ask students to take notes or copy modeled notes during a lecture. Some ask for notes as evidence of completing assigned independent reading. Additionally, notes can be useful as a review tool before an assessment.

Note-taking is also an important research skill, as it provides a system for organizing information. As students read various research sources, they must extract the larger overarching ideas and the supporting details. If students are to apply this information in a meaningful way, they must arrange the information in such a way that makes sense. Otherwise, the notes are simply a laundry list of random information. By providing instruction on effective note-taking systems, teachers can help their students become more efficient researchers.

It is important to note that this skill needs to be taught with a clear explanation, teacher modeling, guided practice, and explicit feedback. As with any other strategy, students must reach a level of proficiency before they are expected to use the strategy independently. Teachers can employ the same instructional strategies that are effective when teaching other skills: display the selection with a document camera, conduct a think-aloud as the main ideas and details are identified, model how to use the designated note-taking strategy with a document camera or with chart paper, and ask for student assistance to complete the notes. Upper elementary students may need the notes scaffolded for them, with some of the information filled in, in order to develop a useful set of notes.

Teachers can make the connection between reading and writing explicit by discussing how text structures are mirrored between the two. Students who are familiar with various text structures will be better able to learn and use the notes strategies. Informational text that is organized by main ideas will lend themselves well to a strategy such as a T-List (pages 133–136), where main ideas are listed in one column and the corresponding details are listed in the other. Additionally, text that describes a series of concepts may be better suited to the Note-Taking System for Learning (pages 129–132), where each concept has a section within the outline. Teachers may want to introduce one of these strategies immediately following a reading lesson on main ideas and details. In this way, teachers can provide an authentic opportunity for students to apply that reading skill to a writing strategy.

To extend the value of note-taking, teachers can show students how to use their notes to apply new knowledge to a writing activity. Well-organized notes are an excellent foundation for a well-written assignment. Teachers can remind students to make use of their notes to begin a piece of writing, as they serve as an effective prewriting strategy. Again, this can show students the connection between reading and writing.

Note-Taking Overview (cont.)

Standards Addressed

The following chart shows the correlating standards for each strategy in this section. Refer to the Digital Resource CD (standards.pdf) to read the correlating standards in their entirety.

Strategy	McREL Standards	Common Core State Standards
Cornell Note-Taking System	Grades 3–5 (4.7) Grades 6–8 (4.3) Grades 9–12 (4.6)	Grade 3 (W.3.4) Grade 4 (W.4.4) Grade 5 (W.5.4) Grade 6 (W.6.4) Grade 7 (W.7.4) Grade 8 (W.8.4) Grades 9–10 (W.9-10.4) Grades 11–12 (W.11-12.4)
Note-Taking System for Learning	Grades 3–5 (4.7) Grades 6–8 (4.3) Grades 9–12 (4.6)	Grade 3 (W.3.4) Grade 4 (W.4.4) Grade 5 (W.5.4) Grade 6 (W.6.4) Grade 7 (W.7.4) Grade 8 (W.8.4) Grades 9–10 (W.9-10.4) Grades 11–12 (W.11-12.4)
T-List	Grades 3–5 (4.7) Grades 6–8 (4.3) Grades 9–12 (4.6)	Grade 3 (W.3.4) Grade 4 (W.4.4) Grade 5 (W.5.4) Grade 6 (W.6.4) Grade 7 (W.7.4) Grade 8 (W.8.4) Grades 9–10 (W.9-10.4) Grades 11–12 (W.11-12.4)

Cornell Note-Taking System

Background Information

The Cornell Note-Taking System (Pauk 1988) strategy assists in teaching students how to effectively take notes during a mathematics lecture to produce writing that is appropriate for the task of note-taking. This strategy teaches students to take clean notes and to organize the notes for the best study options later. It requires a lot of practice time for students. Teach the Cornell Note-Taking System by modeling or practicing each day and slowly incorporating the different stages of the system.

Grade Levels/Standards Addressed

See page 124 for the standards this strategy addresses, or refer to the Digital Resource CD (standards.pdf) to read the correlating standards in their entirety.

Genre

Expository

Stage of Writing Process

Prewrite

Activity

Create or designate a notebook for the *Cornell Note-Taking System* activity sheet (page 128, cornellsystem.pdf) so that sheets can be added or removed. Instruct students to write on only one side of the paper. The right side is the Notes column for notes taken during the lecture. The left column of the page is the Recall column where key words or phrases that summarize the notes are recorded. Before beginning a mathematics lecture, explain that students should first focus on the Notes column. With your guidance and support, encourage students to use abbreviations or phrases and to write down the big ideas when taking notes. Students may need to skip lines to leave room for adding information later. Discuss the notes that could be gleaned from the lecture, and discuss the different ways that students can record this information. Remind students to focus on the main ideas and key terms of the content and to not get bogged down with too many details. After the lecture, instruct students to read through their Notes and write down key points or terms in the Recall column. These key words or phrases will help them recall the main idea of each section of notes without having to read through the whole Notes section. Remind students to review their notes each day to place the information into long-term memory.

Variation

When students are finished, have them use their Notes to write questions about the material that might be asked on future tests. Or instruct students to cover up the Notes side and use the cue words on the Recall side to describe the details of each concept. Students can verify what they have recited by uncovering the Notes column and checking their work.

Differentiation

When working with English language learners, scaffold the Notes column by supplying some of the main ideas; this will give a preview of the information and shape their focus for the lecture. Challenge above-level students to add diagrams, maps, and charts in the Notes column to visually portray processes or important concepts. For below-level students, preview the main ideas of the lecture and explain how to identify important as well as extraneous information. This discussion will help these students organize and understand their notes, and it will help cement information taught during the lecture.

Cornell Note-Taking System *(cont.)*

Grades 3–5 Example

Topic: <u>Negative Numbers</u>

Recall	Notes
Negative numbers can be written on a number line. Seen often in temperature Also useful with money Can be added	• Negative numbers are written to the left of the 0, and positive numbers are written to the right of the 0. • In really cold weather, you may see that a temperature becomes negative. For example, –4°C is for degrees below 0, or freezing. • If money is owed, it will be shown with a negative. For example, –$10 means that the person owes 10 dollars or has to pay 10 dollars. • If you add two numbers that are negative, you get a bigger negative number (with less value). For example, –3 + –4 = –7.

Grades 6–8 Example

Topic: <u>Fractions</u>

Recall	Notes
Numerator goes on top Denominator goes on bottom Find LCM to add fractions Find GCF to reduce fractions	• The numerator tells you how many parts of the whole are included. • The denominator tells you how many parts there are total. • To add fractions with different denominators, you need to find the least common multiple (LCM) and convert both fractions to the same denominator. • To reduce a fraction, you divide both the numerator and the denominator by the greatest common factor (GCF).

Cornell Note-Taking System *(cont.)*

. . . .

Grades 9–12 Example

Topic: Quadratic Functions

Recall	Notes
Highest power is 2 and the function can have one or more terms Two forms: vertex and standard Graph is a parabola	• The highest power in a quadratic function is 2 and quadratic functions can have one term or more (i.e., $2xy^2$ or $x^2 + 4$) • Quadratic equations can be written in either standard form ($f(x) = ax^2 + bx + c$) or vertex form ($y = a(x - h)^2 + k$) • When graphed, quadratic functions have u-shaped graphs, called parabolas, that can open upward or downward.

Name: _____ **Date:** _____

Cornell Note-Taking System

Directions: During a lecture, take notes in the Notes column, using short phrases and abbreviations. After the lecture, review your notes and write the key points in the Recall column.

Topic: _____

Recall	Notes

Note-Taking System for Learning

Background Information

Students in the upper elementary, middle, and high school grades are required to take notes on lectures and presentations, demonstrating writing in the form of note-taking that is appropriate to the lecture or discussion taking place. Often, students do not have experience with or the understanding of how to take notes, and the Note-Taking System for Learning strategy (Palmatier 1973) helps students learn this valuable skill.

Grade Levels/Standards Addressed

See page 124 for the standards this strategy addresses, or refer to the Digital Resource CD (standards.pdf) to read the correlating standards in their entirety.

Genre

Expository

Stage of Writing Process

Prewrite

Activity

Before introducing this strategy, distribute the *Note-Taking System for Learning* activity sheet (page 132, notesystemlearning.pdf). The strategy has three main components:

1. **Recording**—During a lecture, have students develop their writing for the task by writing down the main ideas and supporting details in outline form. Instruct them to leave space between main ideas as needed for future notes and additions. Robert Palmatier suggests writing only on the front of the pages to avoid confusion later. Model for students how to take notes; after reading a passage from a mathematics text, take notes on a chart and display the notes using a document camera to show how to choose the key points. Give students plenty of practice taking notes before expecting them to do it independently.

2. **Organizing**—When students have completed their notes, have them number the pages and staple them in order. Next, have students read through their notes and add labels in the left margin that describe the gist of the notes. This allows time for students to review what they have written and helps them identify any confusion they may have about the content. Students may also add to their notes, incorporating information from the text, lecture, or additional research that clarifies existing information. Students may use the blank side of the paper for this information.

3. **Studying**—Once students have organized all the information in one place, instruct them to use their notes to study. The labels and information in the left margin provide a summary and overview of their notes.

Differentiation

Scaffold notes for English language learners by providing them with the main points. Then, have them focus on adding details during the note-taking process. They will still have the opportunity to summarize and label their notes in the left margin. Challenge above-level students to add to their notes by reading another mathematics text. Be sure the new materials are at a challenging reading level. For below-level students, clearly define main ideas and details and provide examples of completed notes pages. Prior to the lecture, provide them with the main ideas so that they can listen for and record the details.

Note-Taking System for Learning *(cont.)*

Grades 3–5 Example

Subject: Rounding

I. Rounding to the Nearest Hundreds

    a. Look at the number in the tens place.

    b. If it is under 5, then make the tens and ones place a 0 and leave the hundreds alone.

        1. 127 = 100

        2. 831 = 800

    c. If it is 5 or more, make the tens and ones place a 0 and increase the hundreds place by one.

        1. 157 = 200

        2. 381 = 400

Grades 6–8 Example

Subject: Opposites and Absolute Value

I. Opposites

    a. opposites—any two points on a number line that are equal in distance from 0

    b. (−3, 3)—both numbers are 3 points away from the origin.

    c. "−" is often used to mean "the opposite of."

    d. −(4) = −4 is read as "the opposite of 4 is negative 4."

        1. If the number is positive, then its opposite is negative.

    e. −(−4) = 4 is read as "the opposite of negative 4 is 4."

        1. If the number is negative, then its opposite is positive.

II. Absolute Value

    a. always the positive of the given number

    b. $|4| = 4$ is "the absolute value of 4 is 4."

    c. $|-4| = 4$ is "the absolute value of negative 4 is 4."

III. Put it Together

    a. How would you read this, and what is the answer? $-|-(-8)|$

        1. The opposite of the absolute value of the opposite of negative 8 is negative 8.

Note-Taking System for Learning *(cont.)*

Grades 9–12 Example

Subject: Factoring Polynomials

I. Greatest Common Factor (GCF)
   a. look at the coefficients and determine their GCF
   b. look at the variables and determine their GCF
   c. combine the coefficient and variable GCFs
      1. in the equation $4x^3 + 8x^2 + 32x$, all of the coefficients are divisible by 4 and the variable GCF is x, so the GCF for the expression is $4x$
   d. the GCF can also be a binomial
      1. example: $x(y - 2) + 2(y - 2)$ has the GCF $(y - 2)$

II. Special Polynomials
   a. these polynomials can be factored in special ways
      1. it is helpful to memorize these relationships to make factoring polynomials easier
   b. perfect-square trinomials—some trinomials can be factored into squared binomials
      1. equations in the form $a^2 + 2ab + b^2$ can be factored to equal $(a + b)^2$
   c. difference of squares
      1. $(a^2 - b^2) = (a + b)(a - b)$

Note-Taking System for Learning

Directions: During a lecture, write down the main ideas and supporting details in outline form.

Subject: _____

I. _____

    a. _____

    b. _____

    c. _____

    d. _____

II. _____

    a. _____

    b. _____

    c. _____

    d. _____

III. _____

    a. _____

    b. _____

    c. _____

    d. _____

T-List

Background Information

The T-List strategy (Chamot and O'Malley 1994; Hamp-Lyons 1983) organizes information into main ideas and details to assist students in developing their writing for this particular writing task. It is also an effective alternative to quizzes and short-answer tests for assessing student comprehension. This strategy can facilitate question-and-answer discussions and oral summaries. The T-List is a visual representation of information that students can use to write about a given topic.

Grade Levels/Standards Addressed

See page 124 for the standards this strategy addresses, or refer to the Digital Resource CD (standards.pdf) to read the correlating standards in their entirety.

Genre

Expository

Stage of Writing Process

Prewrite

Activity

Distribute the *T-List* activity sheet (page 136, tlist. pdf) or have students create their own by drawing a large *T* on a blank sheet of paper. On the left side of the T-List, students list main ideas or key concepts from the reading passage or lecture. On the right side of the T-List, students record the corresponding details that support the main ideas. With your guidance and support, explain to students that they will organize the main ideas and details of a mathematics text or lecture on the chart. As the lesson proceeds, guide students in identifying the main ideas (in only two or three words) and writing them in the left-hand column. Students should then write the corresponding details in their own words rather than copying them from the text.

Differentiation

Fill in portions of the *T-List* activity sheet prior to giving it to English language learners, and have them identify supporting details as they read. Also, be sure to preteach any challenging vocabulary words they might encounter. Challenge above-level students with the T-List by assigning a chapter and have students create and fill in a T-List independently. Organize them in a small group to compare their T-Lists and justify their decisions. For below-level students, provide the main ideas for the left-hand column as a scaffold.

T-List *(cont.)*

Grades 3–5 Example

Topic: Division

Main Ideas	Details
long division	• For each step, you find a number that will go into the first or first two numbers of your dividend. • Multiply that number by the divisor and write the answer under the dividend. • Subtract to find the remaining value, and pull down the next number of the dividend. • Repeat the process until you reach the end of the dividend and have either no remainder, a remainder, or a decimal value.
short division	• For each step, mentally perform the multiplication of the divisor and the start of the quotient. • Mentally subtract the values. • Write the remaining value in front of the next number in the dividend. • Repeat the process until you reach the end of the dividend and have either no remainder, a remainder, or a decimal value.

Grades 6–8 Example

Topic: Rational and Irrational Numbers

Main Ideas	Details
rational numbers	• whole numbers, fractions, mixed numbers, decimals, and their negative values as well • can be written as a fraction, terminating decimal, or repeating decimal
irrational numbers	• number that cannot be written as a fraction, terminating decimal, or repeating decimal • examples: the square root of 2 ($\sqrt{2}$), pi (π)

T-List *(cont.)*

· ·

Grades 9–12 Example

Topic: <u>Symmetry in Function Graphs</u>

Main Ideas	Details
even functions	<ul><li>even functions have even-numbered exponents</li><li>an even function is symmetrical across the y-axis</li><li>$f(x) = x^4$ is an example of an even function</li><li>for even functions, $f(x) = f(-x)$, so the y-value will always be the same regardless of whether you plug in a positive or negative number for x</li></ul>
odd functions	<ul><li>odd functions have odd-numbered exponents</li><li>odd functions are symmetrical with the origin</li><li>$f(x) = x^5$ is an example of an odd function</li><li>$f(x) = -f(x)$ for odd functions so for any x-value put into the function, the result will be the opposite y-value</li></ul>

T-List

Directions: Write the main ideas gained from the reading in the left-hand column. Then, add details that support each main idea in the column on the right.

Topic: _____

Main Ideas	Details

Using Diagrams and Maps Overview

The Reading/Writing Connection

Just as using diagrams and maps can help students identify the text structure to improve their reading comprehension, these tools can also improve students' writing abilities. Students must be able to recognize the patterns in a variety of writing genres in order to apply those same patterns to their own writing. Diagrams and maps are not only used for reading comprehension; they are also the key to effectively beginning a writing piece to plan and organize information. Therefore, mathematics teachers who are working toward developing the writing skills of their students can emphasize this with their students.

Text Structure

There are different elements to text structure worthy of examination. Instructional approaches range from highlighting external text features (e.g., illustrations, chapter headings, indexes) to identifying sentence and paragraph organizational patterns (e.g., compare and contrast, description) to visually representing the organization of the ideas in the text through graphic organizers (e.g., Venn diagrams, concept maps).

The direct instruction of text structure is intended to help students anticipate, monitor, and comprehend what they are reading in order to organize and communicate the information in writing. Using text structures helps students study model texts for their own writing pieces. If students know what the features are of each particular genre, they spend less time reworking a writing piece and more time effectively planning it in the early stages of writing. In addition, students who are familiar and comfortable with a wide variety of text structures can write with greater ease and can choose to write in the structure that best suits their needs.

Internal Text Structure

The internal text structure refers to how the words and paragraphs are put together. The purpose of informational text is to tell, show, describe, or explain (Vacca and Vacca 2005). For the writer to communicate information easily, the information must be presented through the logical connections that exist between ideas. Text patterns have emerged in informational texts to aid in the expression of these logical connections. According to Richard Vacca and Jo Anne Vacca (2005), there are five patterns of text that dominate informational writing: description, sequence, compare and contrast, cause and effect, and problem and solution. Each structure is represented in this section by a diagram or map that students can use to plan their writing.

See the *Internal Text Structure Reference Sheet* in Appendix A: Additional Resources (page 246, internaltextstructure.pdf) for a list of internal text features frequently found in informational texts.

Using Diagrams and Maps Overview *(cont.)*

Standards Addressed

The following chart shows the correlating standards for each strategy in this section. Refer to the Digital Resource CD (standards.pdf) to read the correlating standards in their entirety.

Strategy	McREL Standards	Common Core State Standards
Frame	Grades 3–5 (1.1, 4.7) Grades 6–8 (1.1, 4.3) Grades 9–12 (1.1, 4.6)	Grade 3 (W.3.5) Grade 4 (W.4.5) Grade 5 (W.5.5) Grade 6 (W.6.5) Grade 7 (W.7.5) Grade 8 (W.8.5) Grades 9–10 (W.9-10.5) Grades 11–12 (W.11-12.5)
Venn Diagram	Grades 1–2 (1.1, 4.2) Grades 3–5 (1.1, 4.7) Grades 6–8 (1.1, 4.3) Grades 9–12 (1.1, 4.6)	Grade 1 (CCRA.W.4) Grade 2 (CCRA.W.4) Grade 3 (W.3.4) Grade 4 (W.4.4) Grade 5 (W.5.4) Grade 6 (W.6.4) Grade 7 (W.7.4) Grade 8 (W.8.4) Grades 9–10 (W.9-10.4) Grades 11–12 (W.11-12.4)
Triangular Venn Diagram	Grades 3–5 (1.1, 4.7) Grades 6–8 (1.1, 4.3) Grades 9–12 (1.1, 4.6)	Grade 3 (W.3.4) Grade 4 (W.4.4) Grade 5 (W.5.4) Grade 6 (W.6.4) Grade 7 (W.7.4) Grade 8 (W.8.4) Grades 9–10 (W.9-10.4) Grades 11–12 (W.11-12.4)
Cause-and-Effect Map	Grades 1–2 (1.1, 4.2) Grades 3–5 (1.1, 4.7) Grades 6–8 (1.1, 4.3) Grades 9–12 (1.1, 4.6)	Grade 1 (CCRA.W.4) Grade 2 (CCRA.W.4) Grade 3 (W.3.4) Grade 4 (W.4.4) Grade 5 (W.5.4) Grade 6 (W.6.4) Grade 7 (W.7.4) Grade 8 (W.8.4) Grades 9–10 (W.9-10.4) Grades 11–12 (W.11-12.4)

Using Diagrams and Maps Overview (cont.)

Strategy	McREL Standards	Common Core State Standards
Semantic Word Map	Grades 1–2 (1.1, 4.2) Grades 3–5 (1.1, 4.7) Grades 6–8 (1.1, 4.3) Grades 9–12 (1.1, 4.6)	Grade 1 (CCRA.W.4) Grade 2 (CCRA.W.4) Grade 3 (W.3.4) Grade 4 (W.4.4) Grade 5 (W.5.4) Grade 6 (W.6.4) Grade 7 (W.7.4) Grade 8 (W.8.4) Grades 9–10 (W.9-10.4) Grades 11–12 (W.11-12.4)
Concept Map	Grades 3–5 (1.1, 4.7) Grades 6–8 (1.1, 4.3) Grades 9–12 (1.1, 4.6)	Grade 3 (W.3.4) Grade 4 (W.4.4) Grade 5 (W.5.4) Grade 6 (W.6.4) Grade 7 (W.7.4) Grade 8 (W.8.4) Grades 9–10 (W.9-10.4) Grades 11–12 (W.11-12.4)
Problem-Solution Map	Grades 1–2 (1.1, 4.2) Grades 3–5 (1.1, 4.7) Grades 6–8 (1.1, 4.3) Grades 9–12 (1.1, 4.6)	Grade 1 (CCRA.W.4) Grade 2 (CCRA.W.4) Grade 3 (W.3.4) Grade 4 (W.4.4) Grade 5 (W.5.4) Grade 6 (W.6.4) Grade 7 (W.7.4) Grade 8 (W.8.4) Grades 9–10 (W.9-10.4) Grades 11–12 (W.11-12.4)
Time Order Map	Grades 1–2 (1.1, 4.2) Grades 3–5 (1.1, 4.7) Grades 6–8 (1.1, 4.3) Grades 9–12 (1.1, 4.6)	Grade 1 (CCRA.W.4) Grade 2 (CCRA.W.4) Grade 3 (W.3.4) Grade 4 (W.4.4) Grade 5 (W.5.4) Grade 6 (W.6.4) Grade 7 (W.7.4) Grade 8 (W.8.4) Grades 9–10 (W.9-10.4) Grades 11–12 (W.11-12.4)

Frame

Background Information

Frames (Ryder and Graves 2003) are charts that organize important information in rows and columns to illustrate relationships between the main ideas and details. Frames assist students in distinguishing important concepts from less important details and help them to compare and contrast information, which supports students in strengthening and developing their writing as they use this strategy to help plan written work. Different types of Frames can be used for different purposes (Ryder and Graves 2003). Matrix Frames are best used in mathematics classes to compare and contrast information, examine cause-and-effect relationships, and analyze forms and functions. Frames help students write about nonfiction mathematics topics by organizing and structuring information. When students write summaries based on the information in the Frame, it allows them to reflect on the content, elaborate on the application, and note relationships or draw distinctions between broader concepts and related information (Ryder and Graves 2003).

Grade Levels/Standards Addressed

See page 138 for the standards this strategy addresses, or refer to the Digital Resource CD (standards.pdf) to read the correlating standards in their entirety.

Genre

Expository

Stage of Writing Process

Prewrite

Preparation

Consider how the main ideas from the selected text can be compared, what features they share, and what specific features or characteristics they possess (Ryder and Graves 2003). Draw the *Frame* activity sheet (page 142, frame.pdf) on the board by creating and labeling the columns and rows or display the activity sheet using a document camera. Write the main topics, ideas, and concepts in the rows and list the categories for the characteristics and/or relationships in the columns.

Activity

Tell students they will use a graphic organizer called a Frame to organize the key information in a selection of text to help them plan written work, which will help develop their writing. Remind them that good writers need to gather information before writing, and it helps to keep this information as organized as possible. Distribute the prepared *Frame* activity sheet with the rows and columns labeled. Allow time for students to review the Frame and predict what information might fit within it. After reading the selected text, discuss the content and have students fill in the cells in each row and column as a class or in small groups. Encourage students to add their prior knowledge to the Frame as well. Students can use the information to assist them in writing a summary or a report on the assigned topic.

Differentiation

Discuss any unfamiliar words and information with English language learners before beginning the lesson to assist them in completing the *Frame* activity sheet. Challenge above-level students to complete the Frame independently, including determining the column and row titles. In addition, have them create a new Frame with a different text passage and compare the two. Give below-level students a Frame that is partially completed to assist them.

Frame (cont.)

· ·

Grades 3–5 Example

Topic: Expanded Notation

Thousands	Hundreds	Tens	Ones	Total Value
3,000	+ 200	+ 50	+ 2	= 3,252
6,000	+ 500	+ 40	+ 8	= 6,548
1,000	+ 700	+ 80	+ 4	= 1,784

Grades 6–8 Example

Topic: Rate

Distance	Time	Rate
126 miles	÷ 3 hours	= 42 miles per hour
72 meters	÷ 8 seconds	= 9 meters per second
840 yards	÷ 10 minutes	= 84 yards per minute

Grades 9–12 Example

Topic: Difference of Two Squares

Polynomial	First Term	Second Term	Factored Product
$16x^2 - 1$	$16x^2 = (4x)^2$	$1 = 1^2$	$(4x + 1)(4x - 1)$
$x^2 - 9$	$x^2 = (x)^2$	$9 = 3^2$	$(x + 3)(x - 3)$
$25x^2 - 16$	$25x^2 = (5x)^2$	$16 = 4^2$	$(5x + 4)(5x - 4)$

Name: _____ **Date:** _____

Frame

Directions: Write in the topic for the Frame and the titles for each column. Then, fill in each box with information from the text.

Topic: _____

#51153—*Writing Strategies for Mathematics Second Edition*

Venn Diagram

Background Information

The Venn Diagram (Venn 1880) compares and contrasts two items, terms, or concepts to help students strengthen and develop writing that is appropriate for a particular writing task. In the mathematics classroom, the Venn Diagram is especially useful in helping students articulate and write about what they are learning in a manner that visually illustrates similarities and differences. Using the Venn Diagram also requires students to write descriptions in their own words and to condense and summarize their statements. It is also a useful prewriting strategy because it organizes the information so that students can begin writing an effective draft.

Grade Levels/Standards Addressed

See page 138 for the standards this strategy addresses, or refer to the Digital Resource CD (standards.pdf) to read the correlating standards in their entirety.

Genre

Expository

Stage of Writing Process

Prewrite

Activity

Select two mathematics concepts to have students compare and contrast. Begin by telling students that they will organize information using a graphic organizer called a Venn Diagram to compare and contrast two topics or concepts. Distribute the *Venn Diagram* activity sheet (page 146, venndiagram.pdf) and emphasize that similarities are listed in the center and differences are listed in the outer sections of the circles. With your guidance and support, have students write the concepts at the top of each circle and discuss these two concepts to activate prior knowledge about their similarities and differences. As students read the selected text, instruct them to look for information to include on their diagrams. List the unique characteristics and attributes of each concept in the appropriate outer sections and the commonalities in the center section.

Differentiation

Scaffold the Venn Diagram for English language learners by listing some of the characteristics. Provide a few examples to get them started and to clarify what you are looking for in this assignment. Instruct above-level students to complete the Venn Diagram without any discussion or support from the text. Have those students verify their characteristics and attributes with reading after they have completed the Venn Diagram. When finished, above-level students can then write a compare/contrast essay using the notes they recorded on the Venn Diagram. Allow below-level students to work with a partner or small group.

Venn Diagram *(cont.)*

Grades 1–2 Example

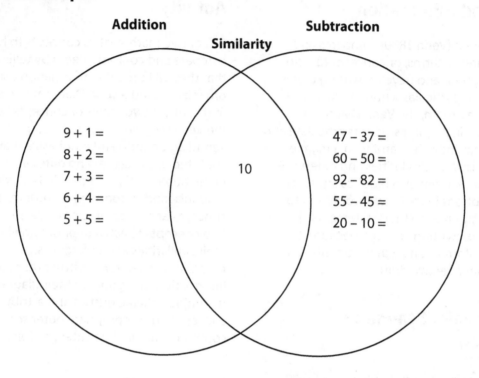

Addition **Similarity** **Subtraction**

$9 + 1 =$
$8 + 2 =$
$7 + 3 =$
$6 + 4 =$
$5 + 5 =$

10

$47 - 37 =$
$60 - 50 =$
$92 - 82 =$
$55 - 45 =$
$20 - 10 =$

Grades 3–5 Example

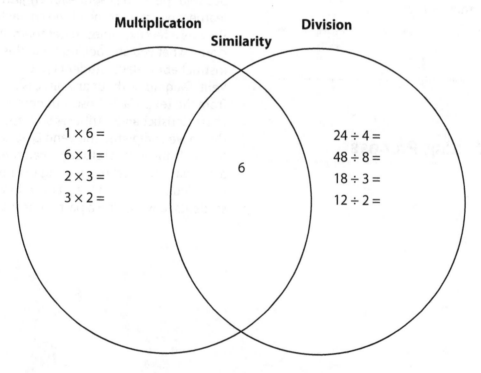

Multiplication **Similarity** **Division**

$1 \times 6 =$
$6 \times 1 =$
$2 \times 3 =$
$3 \times 2 =$

6

$24 \div 4 =$
$48 \div 8 =$
$18 \div 3 =$
$12 \div 2 =$

Venn Diagram *(cont.)*

Grades 6–8 Example

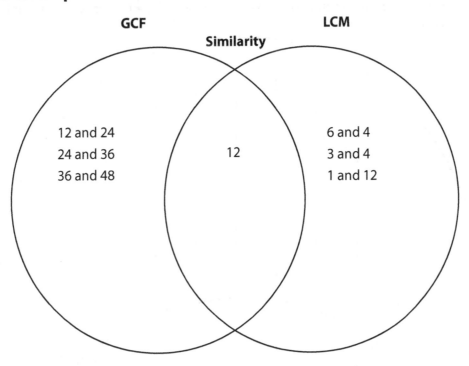

GCF   **Similarity**   **LCM**

12 and 24

24 and 36

36 and 48

12

6 and 4

3 and 4

1 and 12

Grades 9–12 Example

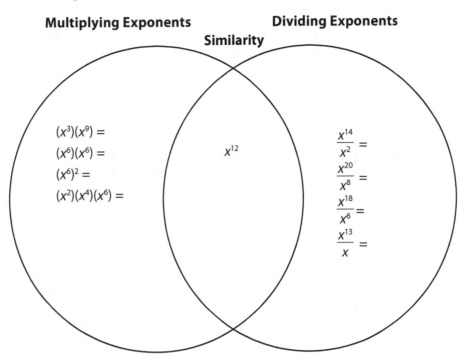

Multiplying Exponents   **Similarity**   **Dividing Exponents**

$(x^3)(x^9) =$

$(x^6)(x^6) =$

$(x^6)^2 =$

$(x^2)(x^4)(x^6) =$

x^{12}

$\dfrac{x^{14}}{x^2} =$

$\dfrac{x^{20}}{x^8} =$

$\dfrac{x^{18}}{x^6} =$

$\dfrac{x^{13}}{x} =$

#51153—Writing Strategies for Mathematics Second Edition

Venn Diagram

Directions: Write on the top two lines the concepts you are comparing and contrasting. List the ways in which they are similar in the center section of the Venn Diagram. Write the ways they are unique in the outer sections of the circles.

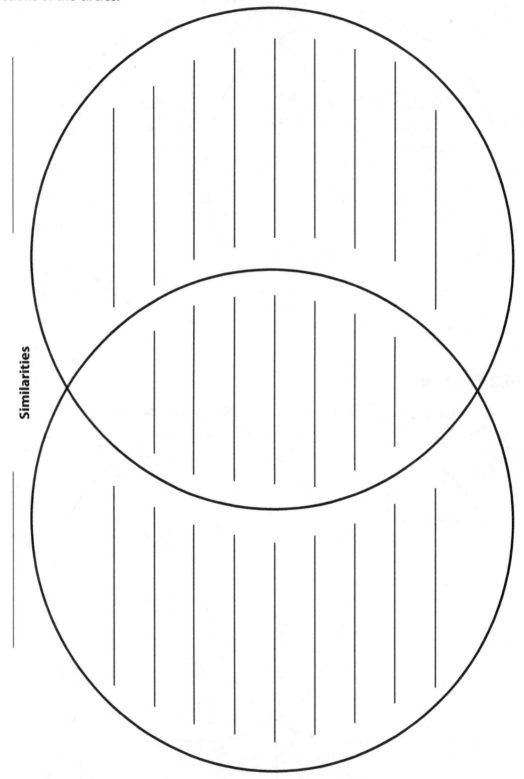

Triangular Venn Diagram

Background Information

Use the Triangular Venn Diagram to compare three topics or concepts. It not only compares the items but also shows the interconnectedness among all three topics or concepts to help students strengthen and develop their writing for a particular writing task. When introducing this strategy, use basic concepts that are easy to understand so that students can learn the procedure. Remind students that the purpose of using a graphic organizer is to arrange the information in a way that makes sense so it can be used later to plan writing activities or projects.

Grade Levels/Standards Addressed

See page 138 for the standards this strategy addresses, or refer to the Digital Resource CD (standards.pdf) to read the correlating standards in their entirety.

Genre

Expository

Stage of Writing Process

Prewrite

Activity

Determine the three concepts to discuss and compare. Distribute the *Triangular Venn Diagram* activity sheet (page 150, triangularvenn.pdf) and label each of the large shaded triangles with the three concepts to compare. With your guidance and support, discuss as a class the attributes of each concept:

- **How are these three concepts unique?** Write characteristics under each heading. These notes should give a brief summary or overview of each concept, stating how each concept is unique and different from the others.

- **How is each pair of concepts similar to one another?** Compare each concept individually with another concept and discuss the characteristics that they share. Record this information inside the small white triangles in between the shaded triangles.

- **How are these three concepts interconnected?** Record information that all three concepts share in the center shaded triangle. This information must be valid for all three concepts.

On the back of the *Triangular Venn Diagram* activity sheet, have students record information that they learned from this process in writing. What insights did they gain? How will this new information change the way they think about these concepts? Discuss student findings as a class.

Differentiation

English language learners will need scaffolding on the Triangular Venn Diagram. Fill in portions of the characteristics for each concept. Encourage above-level students to complete this activity independently, and then model for other students how to complete the diagram and how to determine which characteristics are important and which are extraneous information. Provide small-group instruction and preteaching of the diagram for below-level students.

Triangular Venn Diagram *(cont.)*

Grades 3–8 Example

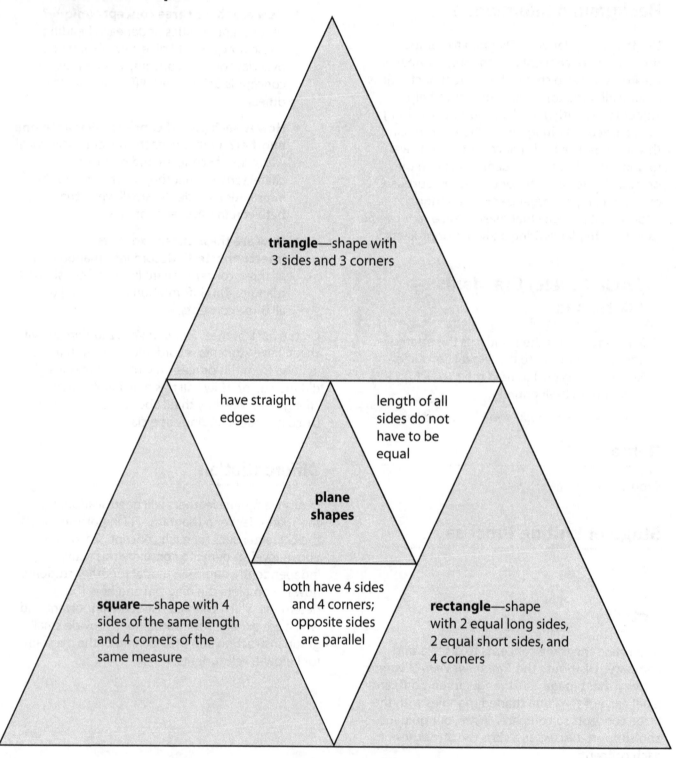

triangle—shape with 3 sides and 3 corners

have straight edges

length of all sides do not have to be equal

plane shapes

square—shape with 4 sides of the same length and 4 corners of the same measure

both have 4 sides and 4 corners; opposite sides are parallel

rectangle—shape with 2 equal long sides, 2 equal short sides, and 4 corners

Triangular Venn Diagram *(cont.)*

Grades 9–12 Example

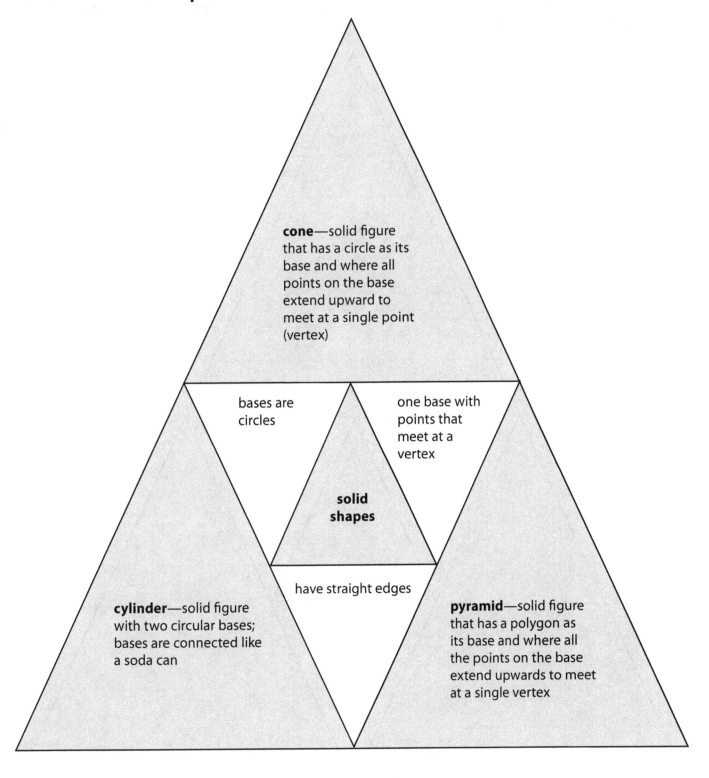

cone—solid figure that has a circle as its base and where all points on the base extend upward to meet at a single point (vertex)

bases are circles

one base with points that meet at a vertex

solid shapes

have straight edges

cylinder—solid figure with two circular bases; bases are connected like a soda can

pyramid—solid figure that has a polygon as its base and where all the points on the base extend upwards to meet at a single vertex

Triangular Venn Diagram

Directions: Use this diagram to compare and contrast three topics or concepts. In the outer triangles, write the unique features of each topic or concept. In the three interior triangles, record how each pair of concepts are similar. In the center triangle, write what all three topics have in common.

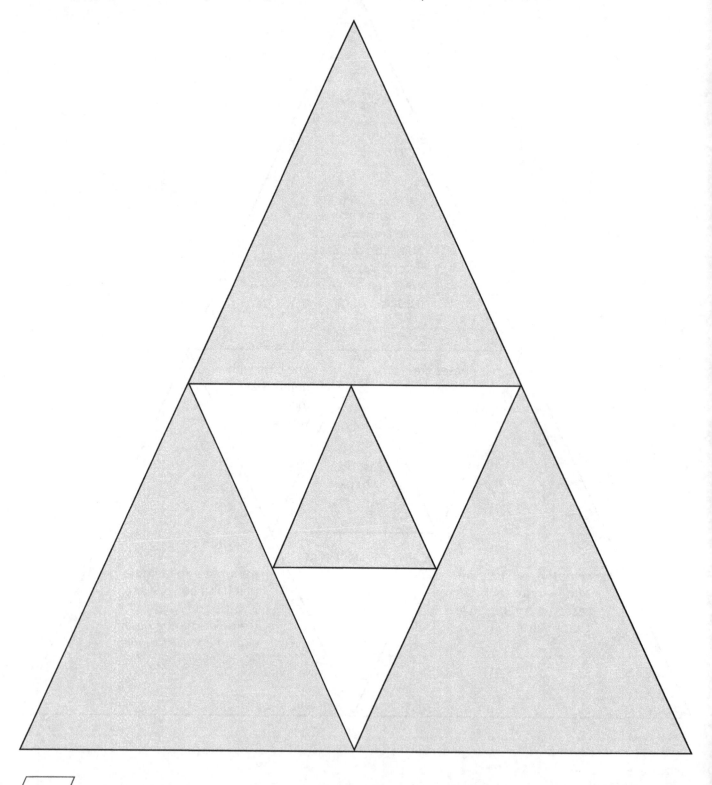

Cause-and-Effect Map

Background Information

A Cause-and-Effect Map is a graphic organizer that helps organize information about the causes or effects of an event, a crucial skill needed for studying mathematics, in order to produce writing in which the development and organization are appropriate to the writing task at hand. The Cause-and-Effect Map encourages students to use higher-order thinking skills, which are key to understanding mathematics concepts. Students can then use the Cause-and-Effect Map to organize information for different mathematics writing projects.

Grade Levels/Standards Addressed

See page 138 for the standards this strategy addresses, or refer to the Digital Resource CD (standards.pdf) to read the correlating standards in their entirety.

Genre

Expository

Stage of Writing Process

Prewrite

Activity

Prior to reading about a specific mathematics topic or completing a mathematics activity, explain that students will analyze causes and effects throughout the course of this activity. If needed, share several examples of cause-and-effect relationships, especially in the primary grades. Distribute the *Cause-and-Effect Map* activity sheet (page 154, causeeffect.pdf) for students to complete and make sure they understand

how to use it. Depending on the nature of the mathematics text or the activity, focus on either the cause(s) or effect(s) first with your guidance and support.

- Ask questions that can help identify the cause(s): *What happens or changes the situation? Where does everything begin? What produces the effect?* Once students have identified the cause, they write a description of it. The more descriptive they are, the better they will be able to identify the effects.

- Ask questions that can help students identify the effect(s): *What is the result of the cause? What happened after the cause or the change? What happened next?* Make sure that students identify all the effects if there are more than one. Encourage them to think about any effects that may not be obvious.

Differentiation

Model how to complete the *Cause-and-Effect Map* activity sheet and provide examples for English language learners. Encourage discussion first, then allow them to work in pairs to complete the activity sheet. They can also use pictures. Encourage above-level students to use higher-level thinking skills. Have them alter the causes and predict how the effects would be different based on those causes. Use prompting and questioning with below-level students to help them identify the more complex effects or results. Or provide the information for one side of the map and ask them to complete the other side.

Cause-and-Effect Map *(cont.)*

Grades 1–2 Example

Cause(s):

You have 4 pizzas and 20 people in your class.

You have 6 pizzas and 36 people in your class.

Effect(s):

You must divide each pizza into 5 equal pieces in order for everyone to get a piece.

You must divide each pizza into 6 equal pieces in order for everyone to get a piece.

Grades 3–5 Example

Cause(s):

You multiply a number by 3.

You divide a number by 4.

Effect(s):

You can divide the result by 3 in order to check the answer.

You can multiply the result by 4 in order to check the answer.

Cause-and-Effect Map *(cont.)*

Grades 6–8 Example

Cause(s):

The cost to bowl is $6 per person plus a $2 lane fee, and each lane holds 5 bowlers.

Effect(s):

- The cost of 1 bowler would be $8.
- The cost of 2 bowlers would be $14.
- The cost of 3 bowlers would be $20.

Grades 9–12 Example

Cause(s):

You raise a negative number to an even power.

$(-2)^4$

You raise a negative number to an odd power.

$(-2)^3$

Effect(s):

A negative number multiplied an even number of times will always equal a positive number.

$(-2)(-2)(-2)(-2) = 16$

A negative number multiplied an odd number of times will always equal a negative number.

$(-2)(-2)(-2) = -8$

Cause-and-Effect Map

Directions: Complete the graphic organizer by writing the causes and effects.

Cause(s):

What event creates change?

Where does everything begin?

Effect(s):

What are the results of the cause?

What happened after the change?

Semantic Word Map

Background Information

Semantic Word Maps (Heimlich and Pittelman 1986, as cited by Ryder and Graves 2003) allow students to clarify the meaning of concepts and identify connections to other related words by creating a map. This strategy is appropriate for studying a specific concept that has multiple vocabulary words and helps students strengthen and develop writing about the mathematics concept of focus. According to William Nagy and Judith Scott (2000), mapping the interconnectedness of mathematics vocabulary words is a way for students to organize and store information in the brain. Because this strategy builds a bridge between new information and previous knowledge and prior experiences, it also can be used as a pre-assessment to see what students already know about a given topic. Students can add to their Semantic Word Maps after they have completed the reading in order to plan for written work. Students also can use the maps to help them review information at the end of a unit of study or to write a paragraph or essay.

Grade Levels/Standards Addressed

See page 139 for the standards this strategy addresses, or refer to the Digital Resource CD (standards.pdf) to read the correlating standards in their entirety.

Genre

Expository

Stage of Writing Process

Prewrite

Activity

Determine the central concept of the assigned reading passage. After introducing the concept, lead a brainstorming session to create a list of words about it. Record all student ideas on the board or use a document camera to record and display students' ideas. Distribute the *Semantic Word Map* activity sheet (page 158, semanticwordmap.pdf) to students. Encourage students to explain how these words relate to bigger ideas, events, characteristics, and examples, and help them move from the words to the concepts. Once the bigger categories have been determined, have students organize the words into categories with your guidance and support on the activity sheet. Students' maps will show big ideas, small ideas, and how all the ideas interconnect. Instruct students to share and explain their maps in small groups, making sure to justify and explain their reasons for choosing each word for each category.

Differentiation

Allow English language learners to work in small groups on this activity so they can hear how other students determine categories and fit words into these categories. Encourage above-level students to incorporate additional or more complex words and categories, using resources to help them determine appropriate placement. Below-level students should work independently to generate a list of words and then work with a partner to determine the categories and the placement of the words. Working with partners provides students with support. Do not place these students in groups for this activity, as they will "fall through the cracks."

Semantic Word Map *(cont.)*

Grades 1–2 Example

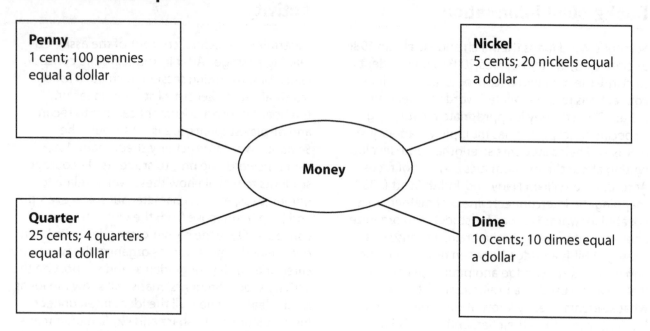

Grades 3–5 Example

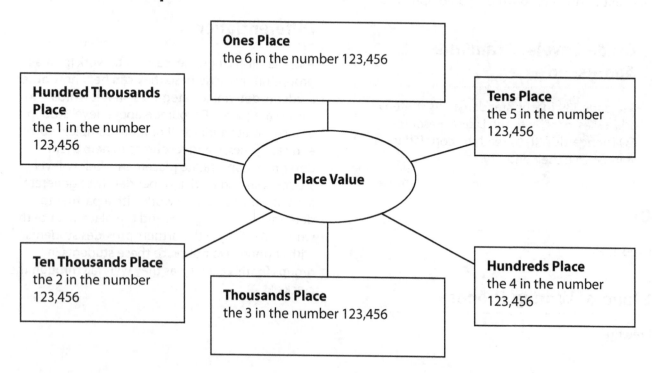

Semantic Word Map (cont.)

Grades 6–8 Example

y
the value of *y* in an ordered pair of (*x*,*y*)

m
the slope of the line; indicates the direction and steepness of the line

Parts of a Linear Function
(*y* = *mx* + *b*)

b
the constant, or the *y*-intercept

x
the value of *x* in an ordered pair of (*x*,*y*)

Grades 9–12 Example

Sphere
a three-dimensional circle where all points are equal distance from the center point
$V = \frac{4}{3}\pi r^3$

Cube
a special type of rectangular prism where all sides are of equal length
$V = l^3$ (*l* = edge length)

Cylinder
a solid figure with two circular bases on parallel planes
$V = \pi r^2 h$

Volume of Solid Figures

Rectangular Solid
two congruent rectangular bases on parallel planes connected by corresponding points (at 90° angles)
$V = lwh$
(*l* = length, *w* = width, *h* = height)

Pyramid
a solid figure with a polygon as a base; the base extends upwards to meet at a single point, or vertex
$V = \frac{1}{3}Bh$ (*B* = area of base)

Cone
a solid figure with a circular base; the base extends upwards to meet at a vertex
$V = \frac{1}{3}\pi r^2 h$

Semantic Word Map

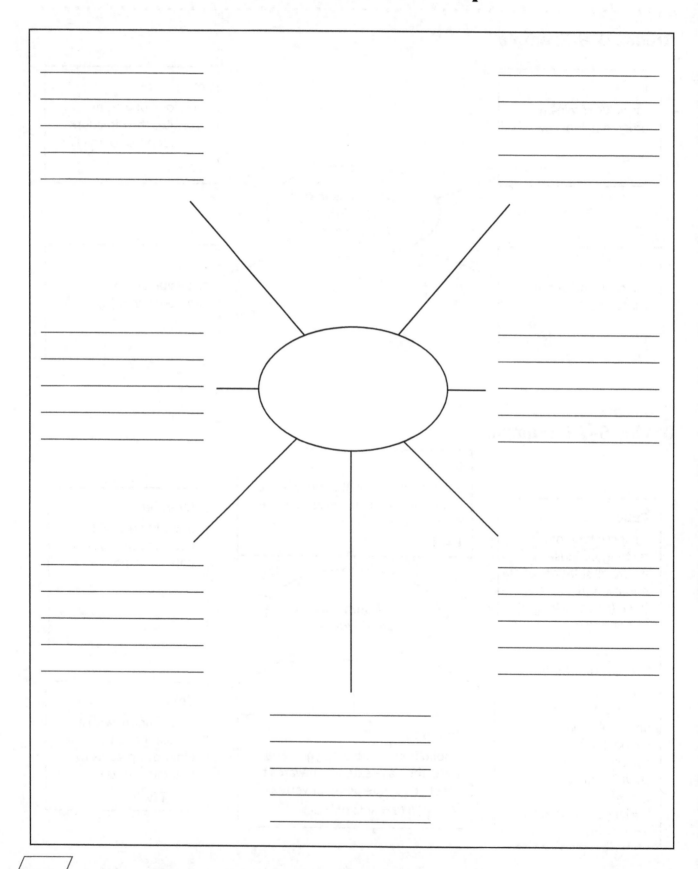

#51153—Writing Strategies for Mathematics Second Edition

Concept Map

Background Information

The Concept Map graphic organizer displays a visual representation of concepts and their relationships discussed in mathematics texts (West, Farmer, and Wolff 1991). A Concept Map is generally organized in a hierarchical manner, moving from broad categories to specific categories. It resembles a flow chart in that the concepts are linked together with lines and arrows. This is an effective strategy to use prior to a mathematics reading assignment; it prepares students for the material they will be reading and assists them in making connections between concepts. Following the reading, students can use their research skills to add or revise information. Concept Maps also help students organize information as they plan for a writing assignment, which helps them produce writing in which the development and organization are appropriate to the purpose of the writing task. Each concept and its supporting details can then be logically and easily developed into a paragraph.

Grade Levels/Standards Addressed

See page 139 for the standards this strategy addresses, or refer to the Digital Resource CD (standards.pdf) to read the correlating standards in their entirety.

Genre

Expository

Stage of Writing Process

Prewrite

Preparation

Read the assigned material and identify the most important concepts, as well as words and phrases related to these concepts. Then, organize the concepts and identify the relationships and connections among them. Create an outline of the concept map (without the concepts filled in).

Activity

Display the prepared Concept Map—outline only—on a chart or use a document camera to display. Create and distribute the blank Concept Map so that students can write down their own information and learn to create the map independently. Write the title on the class map and have students predict what they think the reading passage will be about. Allow plenty of time for students to share, either in pairs or as a whole class, their background knowledge. Have students read the text, and then meet again as a class to determine the most important concepts presented in the text. Write these on the Concept Map. With your guidance and support, instruct students to identify and record on their maps details relating to each major concept. When finished, allow students to share their findings with a small group. Reassemble as a class and invite students to present the information they gathered. Incorporate their information into the class map. Use the presentation time to clarify misunderstandings and determine the level of knowledge students have developed about the topic.

Variation

Reverse the activity by making a list of all of the terms and categories that belong in a Concept Map. Distribute a blank Concept Map and have students place all the information in the correct spaces on the Concept Map. When finished, have students compare their maps with each other.

Concept Map *(cont.)*

Differentiation

Scaffold the map for English language learners and below-level students by providing some of the concepts to help guide them as they fill out the map. Use specific shapes and colors on the map to create a more visual connection for these students. If desired, pair these students with partners to complete the Concept Maps. Challenge above-level students to read an additional piece of text and add to their maps.

Extension

Use the Concept Map as a guide for further reading on the topics presented or as an outline for writing mathematics assignments. Encourage students to continue to add information, highlight key points, and use the map for review.

Concept Map *(cont.)*

· ·

Grades 3–5 Example

multiplication property of 0
any number multiplied by 0
is 0

Multiplication Properties

multiplication property of 1
any number multiplied by 1 is
the original number

Grades 6–8 Example

rate = distance ÷ time

Rate

time = distance ÷ rate

distance = rate × time

Grades 9–12 Example

Negative Exponents
A negative exponent
is the reciprocal of the
fraction with a positive
exponent.

$4^{-2} = \frac{1}{4^2}$

Zero Exponents
Any number except zero,
raised to the zero power,
equals 1.

$-4^0 = 1$

Special Exponents

Power of a power
When you raise a power
to a power, you multiply
the powers and keep the
base number the same.

$(5^3)^2 = 5^6$

Fractions as Exponents
A fraction as an
exponent is the same
as finding the root of
the base number; the
denominator of the
exponent indicates the
root ($x^{\frac{1}{2}} = \sqrt{x}$).

Problem-Solution Map

Background Information

The Problem-Solution Map is a graphic organizer that assists students in analyzing and solving mathematics problems encountered in the real world as they prepare to write about a mathematics concept. Scott Willis (1992) notes the advantages of teaching in units organized around a problem. Clearly identifying a problem in the real world is the first step in understanding the problem. Writing about a problem in one's own words is an effective way for students to understand the problem.

A Problem-Solution Map can be used prior to, during, or after reading in order to help students produce writing in which the development and organization are appropriate to the purpose of the assignment. At each point, this strategy can help reinforce valuable skills. Set up students for success by explaining that no specific answers are expected. A Problem-Solution Map teaches problem-solving skills, so the more ideas that students generate, the better! There are no specific answers and no right or wrong answers because a failed suggestion may turn out to provide ideas and more successful solutions.

Grade Levels/Standards Addressed

See page 139 for the standards this strategy addresses, or refer to the Digital Resource CD (standards.pdf) to read the correlating standards in their entirety.

Genres

Expository, Narrative

Stage of Writing Process

Prewrite

Activity

Determine the mathematics-related problem for the focus of this lesson. Write the problem on the board or display it using a document camera. Discuss it as a class. *How can it be defined as a problem?* Distribute the *Problem-Solution Map* activity sheet (page 167, problemsolution.pdf) to students. With your guidance and support, instruct students to write as much as they know about this problem, using their own words. Ask the following questions to prompt students:

- What is the problem?
- Why is it a problem?
- Who or what is affected by this problem?
- When did this become a problem?
- When does this problem present itself? Daily? Weekly? Seasonally?
- Are there any obvious solutions?
- Have any steps already been tried to solve the problem and failed?
- Is there anything that can be learned from these attempts?

Have students outline their solutions on the *Problem-Solution Map* activity sheet. Allow them to share their ideas in small groups and discuss the expected results of their proposed solutions. If possible, students should apply their solutions, record the results in writing, and share their findings with the class.

Problem-Solution Map *(cont.)*

· ·

Variation

Have students research mathematics resources to see if the solutions they suggest have been tested or tried before. Students can share their information in a report explaining and predicting the success of their solution.

Differentiation

Pair English language learners with partners who can help them discuss and articulate their thoughts and ideas prior to filling out the *Problem-Solution Map* activity sheet. Encourage above-level students to suggest more than one solution and to document their suggestions with research. If time allows, have above-level students present their research findings to enhance the lesson topic. Have below-level students determine possible solutions and work with partners to write out their plans to build confidence.

Problem-Solution Map (cont.)

Grades 1–2 Example

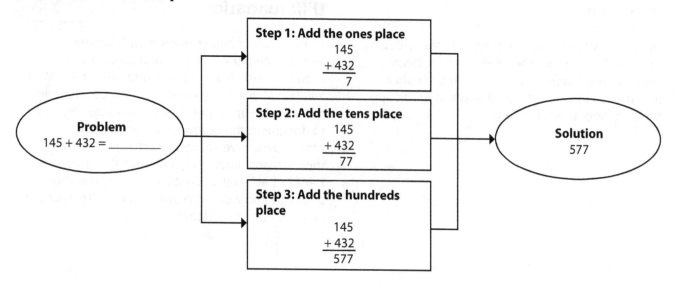

Grades 3–5 Example

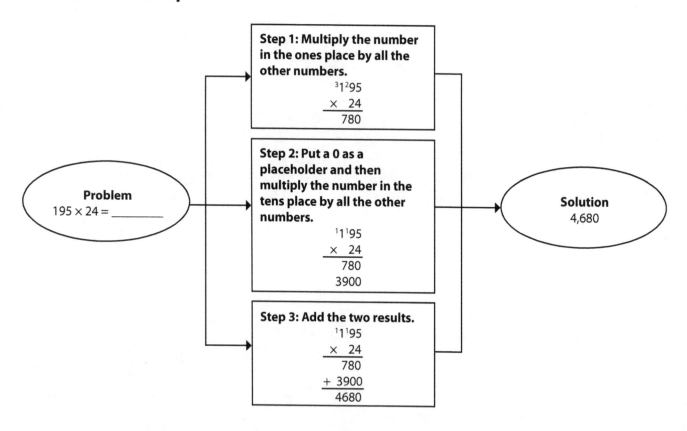

Problem-Solution Map *(cont.)*

Grades 6–8 Example

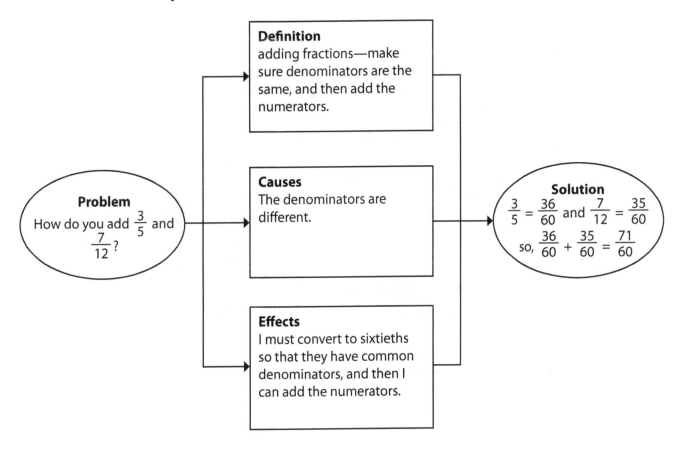

Definition
adding fractions—make sure denominators are the same, and then add the numerators.

Causes
The denominators are different.

Problem
How do you add $\frac{3}{5}$ and $\frac{7}{12}$?

Effects
I must convert to sixtieths so that they have common denominators, and then I can add the numerators.

Solution
$\frac{3}{5} = \frac{36}{60}$ and $\frac{7}{12} = \frac{35}{60}$

so, $\frac{36}{60} + \frac{35}{60} = \frac{71}{60}$

Problem-Solution Map *(cont.)*

Grades 9–12 Example

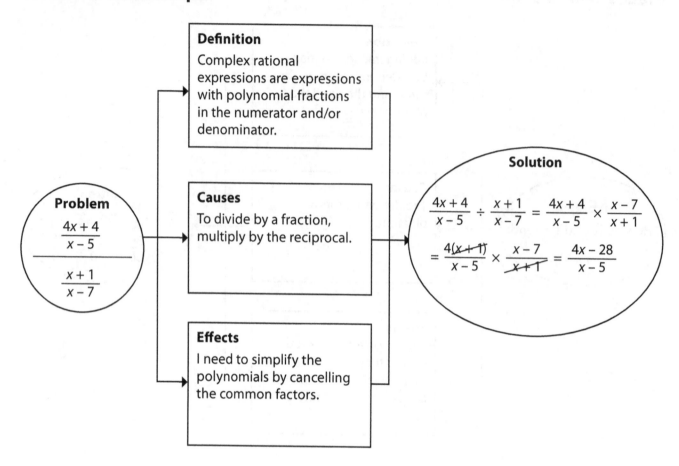

Problem-Solution Map

Directions: Write the problem in the left-hand oval. Read, research, and/or discuss with others the definition, causes, effects, and solutions.

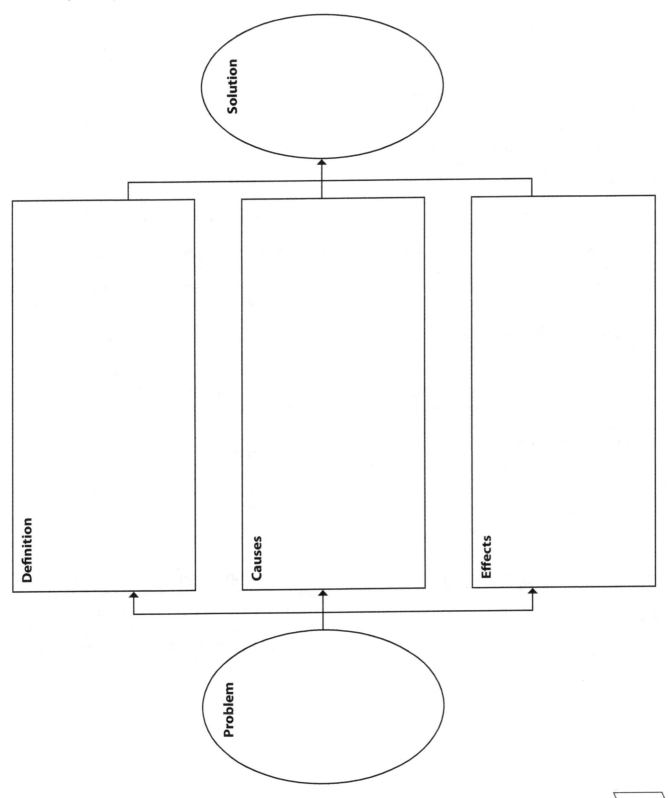

Time Order Map

Background Information

David Perkins and Gavriel Salomon (1988) recommend organizing instruction so that students are better able to apply knowledge and skills from one context to another. This transfer of understanding and knowledge encourages students to broaden their thinking and apply the new information to a variety of situations. The Time Order Map helps organize information to show the passage of time so the writing that students produce is appropriate to the development and organization of the assignment. Sequence is a critical element of mathematics. Capturing sequence in a graphic organizer helps students visualize the process, identify and describe each step of a sequence over time, and write more analytically about the process.

Grade Levels/Standards Addressed

See page 139 for the standards this strategy addresses, or refer to the Digital Resource CD (standards.pdf) to read the correlating standards in their entirety.

Genre

Expository

Stage of Writing Process

Prewrite

Activity

Identify a mathematics topic in a text or lecture that demonstrates a sequence of events or the passage of time: classroom schedules, travel schedules, steps for converting fractions to decimals, etc. Tell students that they will study the time sequence of a concept and organize the information on a graphic organizer called a Time Order Map with your guidance and suport.

Distribute the appropriate *Time Order Map* activity sheet (pages 171–172, timeorder.pdf), and conduct a short brainstorming session to activate prior knowledge about the selected concept. Assign a passage of text on this subject for students to read that portrays the steps or events over time. As students read, instruct them to add to their *Time Order Map* activity sheet. Primary students may draw and label pictures in the Time Order Map. Encourage upper-grade students to locate and access outside information on the topic using television, radio, magazines, or newspapers, as well as typical sources such as mathematics books and other informational texts.

Differentiation

Preteach any new vocabulary words to English language learners to improve their comprehension. Also, pair them with partners to provide plenty of discussion time. Challenge above-level students to explain the causes and effects that occur at each phase of the process and to analyze the process deeper than on a surface level. Model how to complete the map for below-level students so that they understand the organization of the map. Then, provide frequent feedback and prompting to keep them organized as they work. Remind these students to use the text as a tool to help them complete their maps.

Time Order Map *(cont.)*

Grades 1–2 Example

Subject: Patterns

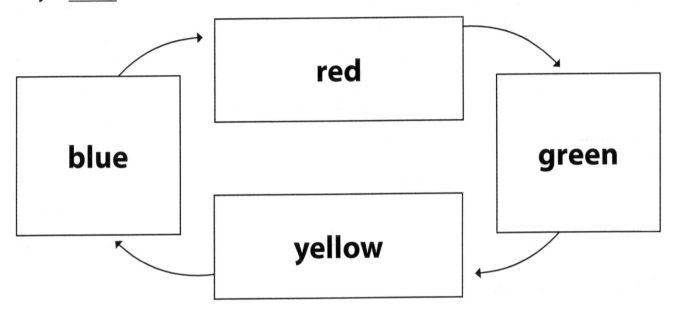

Grades 3–5 Example

Subject: Probability

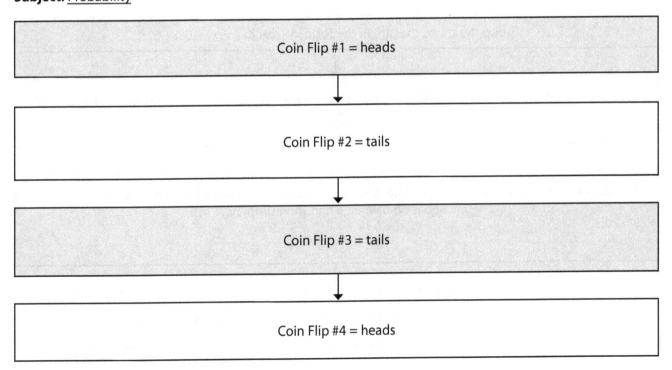

Time Order Map (cont.)

Grades 6–8 Example

Subject: <u>FOIL: $(2x + 7)(3x - 12)$</u>

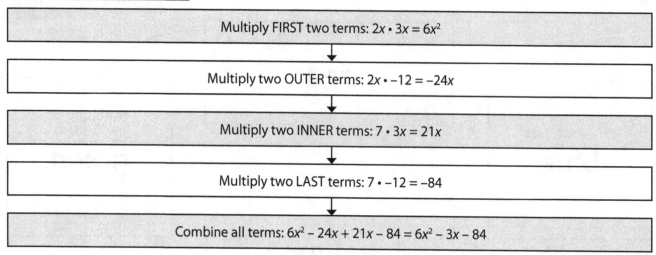

Multiply FIRST two terms: $2x \cdot 3x = 6x^2$

Multiply two OUTER terms: $2x \cdot -12 = -24x$

Multiply two INNER terms: $7 \cdot 3x = 21x$

Multiply two LAST terms: $7 \cdot -12 = -84$

Combine all terms: $6x^2 - 24x + 21x - 84 = 6x^2 - 3x - 84$

Grades 9–12 Example

Subject: <u>Standard form to vertex form using the completing the square method</u>

Write the quadratic equation: $f(x) = x^2 + 6x + 5$

Group the terms that are in the form $x^2 + bx$: $f(x) = (x^2 + 6x) + 5$

Divide the coefficient of x by 2 and then square it to find the number needed to complete the perfect trinomial: $\frac{6}{2} = 3, 3^2 = 9$

Add the number you found inside the parentheses and subtract it outside the parentheses to keep the equation balanced and then simplify:
$f(x) = (x^2 + 6x + 9) + 5 - 9 =$
$f(x) = (x + 3)^2 - 4$

Write the equation in vertex form: $y = (x + 3)^2 - 4$

Time Order Map

Directions: Use this map to show the sequence of events. Write the first event in the top box and the second event in the second box. Continue until you have described the entire chain of events.

Subject: _____

Time Order Map

Directions: Use this map to show how a sequence of events happens in a circular manner. Write the events in order in the boxes.

Topic: _____

Authoring Overview

This book has previously established the strong connection between reading and writing. The quote from Gay Su Pinnell in the article "Success of Children at Risk in a Program That Combines Writing and Reading" bears repeating: "As children read and write they make the connections that form their basic understandings about both. Learning in one area enhances learning in the other. There is ample evidence to suggest that the processes are inseparable and that we should examine pedagogy in the light of these relationships. Hence, the two activities should be integrated in instructional settings. Teachers need to create supportive situations in which children have opportunities to explore the whole range of literacy learning, and they need to design instruction that helps children make connections between reading and writing" (1988).

Reading and writing are critical to all learning. Writing to apply new knowledge can be more challenging for students because they need to not only understand the content and be able to process it at a higher level, but also communicate it using the strategies of the writing process, the features of the chosen genre, and the conventions of the grade level. Through authoring, students can make personal connections with the new content information they are learning.

Carol Santa, Lynn Havens, and Shirley Harrison (1996) make several key points with regard to this connection.

1. **Writing helps students become more active learners of the mathematics content.** Creating writing pieces that utilize mathematics content knowledge requires students to think more deeply about the content, analyze it, and reconstruct it into a piece of writing.

2. **Writing assists students in understanding the complexities of mathematics.** Writing can provide opportunities for students to analyze new concepts, internalize new vocabulary, and explore patterns and relationships between concepts.

3. **Writing forces learners to organize their thinking and to evaluate whether they have understood a concept.** In order to communicate in writing, students must carefully consider how to approach the writing activity. For example, students who are asked to write a newspaper article about a current event must not only organize the content information that they intend to include but also meld it with the style appropriate for the genre. Within the framework of the genre, students must decide how best to communicate their information.

4. **One cannot write about something one does not understand.** The process of creating a clear explanation of a concept will challenge students to think carefully about the best way to explain it. In working through this challenge, students can develop a deeper understanding of the concept.

Authoring Overview (cont.)

Standards Addressed

The following chart shows the correlating standards for each strategy in this section. Refer to the Digital Resource CD (standards.pdf) to read the correlating standards in their entirety.

Strategy	McREL Standards	Common Core State Standards
Guided Writing Procedure	Grades 3–5 (1.1, 1.2) Grades 6–8 (1.1, 1.2) Grades 9–12 (1.1, 1.2)	Grade 3 (W.3.5) Grade 4 (W.4.5) Grade 5 (W.5.5) Grade 6 (W.6.5) Grade 7 (W.7.5) Grade 8 (W.8.5) Grades 9–10 (W.9-10.5) Grades 11–12 (W.11-12.5)
Reading-Writing Workbench	Grades 3–5 (1.1, 1.2) Grades 6–8 (1.1, 1.2) Grades 9–12 (1.1, 1.2)	Grade 3 (W.3.5, W.3.8) Grade 4 (W.4.5, W.4.8) Grade 5 (W.5.5, W.5.8) Grade 6 (W.6.5, W.6.8) Grade 7 (W.7.5, W.7.8) Grade 8 (W.8.5, W.8.8) Grades 9–10 (W.9-10.5, W.9-10.8) Grades 11–12 (W.11-12.5, W.11-12.8)
Author's Chair	Grades 1–2 (1.4) Grades 3–5 (1.4) Grades 6–8 (1.4) Grades 9–12 (1.4)	Grade 1 (CCRA.W.4, SL.1.1) Grade 2 (CCRA.W.4, SL.2.1) Grade 3 (W.3.4, SL.3.1) Grade 4 (W.4.4, SL.4.1) Grade 5 (W.5.4, SL.5.1) Grade 6 (W.6.4, SL.6.1) Grade 7 (W.7.4, SL.7.1) Grade 8 (W.8.4, SL.8.1) Grades 9–10 (W.9-10.4, SL.9-10.1) Grades 11–12 (W.11-12.4, SL.11-12.1)
Read, Encode, Annotate, Ponder	Grades 3–5 (1.4, 1.11) Grades 6–8 (1.4, 1.12) Grades 9–12 (1.4, 1.12)	Grade 3 (W.3.4, SL.3.1) Grade 4 (W.4.4, SL.4.1) Grade 5 (W.5.4, SL.5.1) Grade 6 (W.6.4, SL.6.1) Grade 7 (W.7.4, SL.7.1) Grade 8 (W.8.4, SL.8.1) Grades 9–10 (W.9-10.4, SL.9-10.1) Grades 11–12 (W.11-12.4, SL.11-12.1)

Guided Writing Procedure

Background Information

The Guided Writing Procedure (Smith and Bean 1980) uses writing as a vehicle for activating students' prior knowledge and synthesizing existing and new information in mathematics. Students brainstorm about a topic to lay a foundation for building new mathematics content knowledge, then analyze the information for patterns and relationships to create an outline, just as good writers do during the prewriting phase. After writing a paragraph, students compare their work with that of the mathematics informational text, article, or trade book to look for similarities and differences, as well as opportunities to add or change information. This strategy aids students in developing and strengthening their writing as they plan to write on mathematics topics and concepts.

Grade Levels/Standards Addressed

See page 174 for the standards this strategy addresses, or refer to the Digital Resource CD (standards.pdf) to read the correlating standards in their entirety.

Genres

Expository, Summary, Narrative, Persuasive

Stages of Writing Process

Prewrite, Draft, Revise

Activity

Write the key concept for the reading lesson on the board or display the concept using a document camera. Ask students to brainstorm everything they know about that concept, and write their responses on the board. Remind them that there are no "wrong" ideas in brainstorming. Then, review the brainstormed ideas as a class, decide which of them are major points and which are supporting details, and create a simple outline as a prewriting strategy. Provide time for students to draft a paragraph or two using the class outline. Next, have students read the assigned text and analyze their work against the mathematics text. They should see how well the class outline matches the mathematics text, look for similarities and differences between their own paragraph(s) and the text, and identify information that could be added or deleted from their writing based on the mathematics text. With your guidance and support, have students return to their drafts and revise their writing based on what they observed when comparing and contrasting their drafts against informational mathematics texts.

Differentiation

Scaffold notes or create an outline for English language learners to use as they write their paragraphs. Model the strategy and provide examples of completed paragraphs for these students to refer to. Have above-level students write more than a paragraph, perhaps a report, on the topic. Conduct writing conferences with below-level students to explicitly instruct how to use notes from the prewriting stage to create a draft. Also, provide models of good paragraphs and spend time in the conferences analyzing the good writing traits shown in the examples. Use students' work to guide them through analyzing their writing and the text for similarities and differences. Understanding and being able to recognize good writing helps these students become better writers themselves.

Guided Writing Procedure *(cont.)*

Grades 3–5 Example

Concept: three-dimensional shapes

Brainstorming:

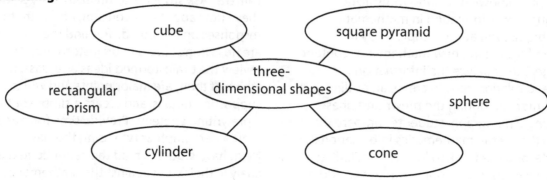

Sample Paragraph:

There are many kinds of three-dimensional shapes. A cube is very similar to a box that has equal sides. A square pyramid has four sides shaped like triangles and a bottom that is a square. There are very big pyramids in Egypt. A sphere is just a ball, like a basketball or tennis ball. A cone has a flat, circular bottom and a point at the top, like an ice cream cone. A cylinder is like a can of soup. Its side is round with a flat bottom and a flat top.

Grades 6–8 Example

Concept: parts of a linear function

Brainstorming:

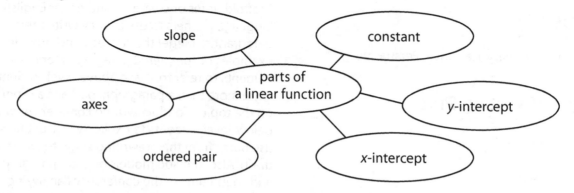

Sample Paragraph:

A linear function has several parts. The slope is the number or fraction that represents how steep the line is and whether it goes up or down. The constant is the b-value and is also the y-intercept. The y-intercept is the value of y when the value of $x = 0$. The x-intercept is the value of x when the value of $y = 0$. An ordered pair is a pair of points that will accurately make the equation true for a value of x.

Guided Writing Procedure (cont.)

Grades 9–12 Example

Concept: <u>shapes of coordinate geometry</u>

Brainstorming:

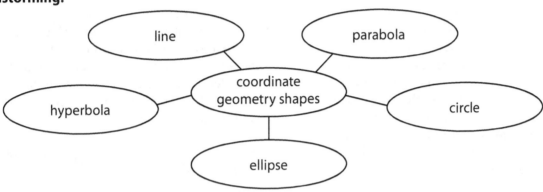

Sample Paragraph:

There are many different types of shapes that can be created by graphing functions on a coordinate plane, five of which are shown in the diagram. A line refers to a straight line, while a parabola is a curved, u-shaped graph of a quadratic function. A circle is created when all points are the same distance from the center point. An ellipse is like a circle but is oval-shaped. All points in an ellipse are equal distance from the sum of two fixed points called foci. A hyperbola looks like two parabolas extending away from each other on a graph. A hyperbola has two asymptotes, or lines that run along the two branches of the hyperbola. A hyperbola is like the opposite of an ellipse because it is defined by the difference of the distance between two fixed points.

Reading-Writing Workbench

Background Information

The Reading-Writing Workbench strategy (Tierney et al. 1989) incorporates writing as a pre-reading activity and teaches students how to use resources as they read and plan to write about mathematics concepts. After students explore and recall information from their own experiences relating to a theme introduced in the mathematics text, they read, discuss, and compare their ideas with their peers and those of professional authors. The "workbench" refers to the way the teacher coordinates the use of and interaction with mathematical, as well as other, resources.

Grade Levels/Standards Addressed

See page 174 for the standards this strategy addresses, or refer to the Digital Resource CD (standards.pdf) to read the correlating standards in their entirety.

Genres

Expository, Summary

Stages of Writing Process

Prewrite, Draft, Revise

Activity

Lead a class discussion about the key concept of the lesson. With your guidance and support, have students recall information from personal experiences or any background knowledge they have relating to this concept in preparation for the writing activity. Next, have students independently write about their experiences. Allow a few minutes for students to share their writing, as well as the techniques they used as the author. Identify the

resources available on this topic: mathematics books, television programs, newspaper articles, etc. Encourage students to bring in the resources they find to share with the class and, if possible, make these resources available to them to read. Ask students in small groups to read their writing and compare it to that of the resources your class has obtained. Here are some questions for students to consider, which are also included on the *Reading-Writing Workbench* activity sheet (page 181, readwriteworkbench.pdf):

- How does your writing compare with other published texts on the same topic?

- How can you incorporate these ideas into your own writing?

- How did you begin and end the piece of writing while maintaining the interest of the audience?

- How did you incorporate mathematics facts and still make it interesting and authentic?

In conclusion, allow time for students to use group comments to reflect on what they have learned through this process.

Differentiation

When working as a whole class, make sure the ideas and background knowledge shared by students are easy to understand for English language learners. This is important when students begin to write about the topic. Repeat and rephrase what students say to make it easier for English language learners to comprehend. Above-level students will benefit from an assignment to incorporate several sources into their writing. Show above-level students how to cite sources in their writing. Provide plenty of discussion time for below-level students. Hold independent writing conferences as necessary to provide support for these students.

Reading-Writing Workbench (cont.)

Grades 3–5 Example

Mathematics Topic: <u>Equivalent Fractions</u>

Background Knowledge/Ideas:

A fraction has a numerator and a denominator.
If denominators are the same, you can add or subtract fractions.
If denominators are different, you must convert fractions to add or subtract.
The word *equivalent* reminds me of the word *equal*.

Student Writing:

Fractions represent part of a whole. For example, if you eat $\frac{3}{5}$ of a pizza, then you have eaten part of the whole pizza. The part of the pizza you ate is shown with the number 3 and is the numerator of the fraction. The total number of pieces of pizza is shown by the number 5 and is the denominator of the fraction. Equivalent fractions are those of which equal parts are shaded or eaten, even though there may be a different number of pieces. For example, if a pizza was cut into 4 pieces and you ate 2 of them, then you ate $\frac{2}{4}$ of the pizza, but that is the same as eating half the pizza, so $\frac{2}{4}$ and $\frac{1}{2}$ are equivalent fractions.

Grades 6–8 Example

Mathematics Topic: <u>Angles</u>

Background Knowledge/Ideas:

A right angle is 90°.
A straight line is 180°.
A circle is 360°.

Student Writing:

There are many ways of classifying angles. A right angle is exactly 90°. An acute angle is less than 90°, so it is smaller than a right angle. An obtuse angle is greater than 90° and less than 180°. It is possible to compare angles as well. If two angles added together make 90°, they are called complementary angles. If two angles added together make 180°, they are called supplementary angles.

Reading-Writing Workbench (cont.)

Grades 9–12 Example

Mathematics Topic: <u>Trigonometry: Sine, Cosine, and Tangent</u>

Background Knowledge/Ideas:

Trigonometry refers to the study of triangles.

Triangles have three sides and three angles.

The sum of the interior angles of a triangle is 180°.

The hypotenuse is the side across from the right angle in a right triangle. It is also the longest leg of a right triangle.

Student Writing:

Trigonometry is the study of triangles and their measurements. Triangles have three sides, also called legs, and three interior angles which total 180°. There are different relationships between a triangle's side lengths and angles. For right triangles (triangles with one 90° angle), you can find the measurement of one acute angle by determining the ratio of various side lengths. The sine of an angle is the ratio of the triangle's opposite side (leg across from the angle) over the length of the hypotenuse. The cosine is the ratio of the adjacent side (leg that forms the angle, but not the hypotenuse) over the hypotenuse. The tangent is the ratio of the opposite side over the adjacent side.

Name: _____ **Date:** _____

Reading-Writing Workbench

Mathematics Topic: _____

Background Knowledge/Ideas:

_____

_____

Student Writing:

_____

_____

_____

_____

_____

How does your writing compare with other published texts on the same topic?

_____

_____

How can you incorporate these ideas into your own writing?

_____

_____

How did you begin and end the piece of writing while maintaining the interest of the audience?

_____

_____

How did you incorporate mathematics facts and still make it interesting and authentic?

_____

_____

Author's Chair

Background Information

The Author's Chair strategy (Karelitz 1982; Boutwell 1983; Calkins 1983; Graves 1983; Graves and Hansen 1983) provides student writers with feedback on their writing as students engage effectively in collaborative discussions and presentations. It has also been called peer conferencing. Researchers and educators continue to confirm the strong connections between reading and writing and between authors and readers. The focus of the Author's Chair strategy is to provide feedback to students on their writing: acknowledging its good qualities, making specific suggestions for improvement, and asking thought-provoking questions of student authors so that students produce writing in which the development and organization are appropriate for the assignment.

Grade Levels/Standards Addressed

See page 174 for the standards this strategy addresses, or refer to the Digital Resource CD (standards.pdf) to read the correlating standards in their entirety.

Genres

Expository, Summary, Narrative, Persuasive

Stage of Writing Process

Revise

Activity

Ask students to select a mathematics writing piece to workshop, and then place them in groups of no more than four to collaborate and discuss the writing. Give each group the following tasks:

- Students take turns reading their pieces of writing aloud.

- Group members listen intently and share their feedback.

- Once all members of the group have shared their writing and received feedback, instruct students to read about their writing topics in mathematics texts and other mathematics resources. *How does their writing compare with professional writers? What can be learned about writing from professional writers? What can be learned about how the authors structure and organize their writing?*

- Allow time for students to edit and revise their writing. Students can use this time to incorporate suggestions from peers into their writing, as well as ideas from professional writers. If time permits, allow small groups to meet again and repeat the strategy.

Variation

With primary grade students, conduct the strategy as a whole class. Choose one or two students to read their writing pieces to the class, and then ask the class to provide feedback. Remind students to offer specific comments.

Differentiation

Hold individual writing conferences with English language learners and below-level students to provide direct instruction and specific feedback. Consider using a lower-level text as a model so that the reading level does not hinder their abilities to analyze writing qualities. These students can join groups when it is time to peruse mathematics materials and texts. Group above-level students with others who will challenge their writing skills. Ask them to share the techniques they learned from a professional writer and how they plan to incorporate these techniques into their own writing.

Author's Chair *(cont.)*

Grades 1–2 Example

Student Writing Sample:

You can make a dollar from any type of coin. A dollar equals 100 pennies. A dollar equals 20 nickels. A dollar equals 10 dimes. A dollar equals 4 quarters. It is also possible to mix coins together to make a dollar.

Class Comments:

Student 1: I liked your topic sentence.

Student 2: Maybe you could add a sentence that gives an example of how a mix of coins can make a dollar.

Student 3: You could also describe what each kind of coin looks like.

Student 4: I liked your last sentence because you could start a whole new paragraph after it.

Grades 3–5 Example

Student Writing Sample:

I love pizza and so do my friends. Jack, Jose, Luis, Vicki, and I all went to the pizza place. We each ordered a mini pizza with only two toppings. I gave the man at the counter exactly $40, and there was no change left. How much was each mini pizza?

Class Comments:

Student 1: I like that you used pizza because I like pizza, too.

Student 2: You could add descriptions of each pizza to have more detail.

Student 3: I like that you picked students from our class because it made the problem more interesting.

Author's Chair (cont.)

Grades 6–8 Example

Student Writing Sample:

At my house, we all love to eat salad. Instead of buying dressing at the grocery store, my mother makes a homemade Italian dressing. Well, salad dressing is basically a mixture of ingredients. My mother uses 2 tablespoons of sugar, which is about $\frac{1}{8}$ cup, $\frac{1}{2}$ cup cider vinegar, $\frac{3}{4}$ cup water, and $\frac{3}{4}$ cup vegetable oil as a base to start the dressing. Using what we have learned about percentages, I looked at what percent of each ingredient is in our homemade salad dressing. The total amount of the ingredients is $2\frac{1}{8}$ cups. Based on that number, our dressing is about 6% sugar, 24% vinegar, 35% water, and 35% vegetable oil, excluding the seasonings that my mother adds later.

Class Comments:

Student 1: I never thought of applying percent values to salad dressing. Cool idea. I am going to try to think of a recipe that I know of to do the same thing with.

Student 2: Your paragraph is well organized, with a good topic sentence. It relates to what we learned about mixtures in science, too.

Student 3: I really liked the topic of your paragraph. I think you should add a strong concluding sentence.

Author's Chair *(cont.)*

Grades 9–12 Example

Student Writing Sample:

My sister and I always combine our Halloween candy into one big bag and share it after we go trick-or-treating. The only problem is that we both have the same favorite candy, bubblegum, so we made a rule that you have to close your eyes and just pick a candy from the bag without looking so that it is fair. This year we got a total of 64 pieces of candy, 18 of which were bubblegum. My sister blindly chose a piece of bubblegum on her very first pick. Then I reached my hand into the bag without looking and I chose a piece of bubblegum, too! I was really surprised that we both picked bubblegum on our first draw, so I decided to figure out the probability of that happening again on the next draw. Now there are only 62 pieces of candy, 16 of which are bubblegum. Since we are trying to find the probability of two dependent events occurring together, we need to multiply the probabilities of each event occurring. The chance that my sister will pick another piece of bubblegum is $\frac{16}{62}$, or $\frac{8}{31}$. The probability that I will pick another piece of gum after her is $\frac{15}{61}$. Therefore, the chance that we will both pick bubblegum on our second draw from the candy bag is $(\frac{8}{31})(\frac{15}{61}) = \frac{120}{1891}$, or approximately a 6% chance that we will both pick bubblegum on our second draw from the candy bag.

Class Comments:

Student 1: That is a neat application of probability. I will have to consider probability the next time I make a deal with my older brother to make sure he is being fair!

Student 2: I like the way you explained probability in a detailed way. Probability always confuses me, but this example makes it seem easy.

Student 3: I liked your paragraph. My only suggestion is that at the end you should explain how you got from the fraction $\frac{120}{1891}$ to 6% in case someone does not understand that.

Read, Encode, Annotate, Ponder

Background Information

The purpose of the Read, Encode, Annotate, Ponder (REAP) strategy (Eanet and Manzo 1976) is to develop in students a greater understanding of the author's role in writing and to improve their reading comprehension as they engage in collaborative discussions with their peers. REAP helps students build a bridge between the mathematics text and their own words to enable them to communicate their understanding of the text in writing in which the development and organization are appropriate for the writing task at hand.

Grade Levels/Standards Addressed

See page 174 for the standards this strategy addresses, or refer to the Digital Resource CD (standards.pdf) to read the correlating standards in their entirety.

Genres

Expository, Persuasive

Stage of Writing Process

Draft

Activity

Distribute the *Read, Encode, Annotate, Ponder* activity sheet (page 190, reap.pdf) prior to reading a selected mathematics text. The steps students follow for this activity come from the acronym REAP:

R—Read and understand the author's ideas. After students read the assigned text, have them discuss the contents of the text with partners, in small groups, or in a whole-class discussion.

E—Encode the author's words into their own words. Have students put in their own words what the text passage says. They should be able to do this without having to reread the material as they talk about it. They should become familiar enough with the text to discuss it comfortably. *What is the main idea? What is the concept being presented? Can I explain what the author is saying?*

A—Annotate what they are reading. Annotation is not just a summary of what students have read. Instead, it is an extension of or elaboration on the text. Prompt students with these questions:

- What is the author's opinion on the subject? How can you tell?

- What is the problem being presented in the text? What are some possible solutions?

- Analyze the writing in the text. Is it clear? Could it be improved? Is it creative in how it is presented? Does it need any clarification or additions?

- What is the author's purpose or intention for writing?

- What can you learn from the author's writing that will help your own writing?

P—Ponder means that students must think about what they have written. Does it make sense? Does it complement or differ from what was said in the text?

Differentiation

Scaffold notes or create an outline for English language learners as they do their writing. Provide examples of writing samples for them. Have above-level students write more than a paragraph, such as a report, on the topic. Explicitly model for below-level students how to respond in each of the sections. Also, spend individual time in writing conferences analyzing each student's writing.

Read, Encode, Annotate, Ponder (cont.)

Grades 3–5 Example

Study Topic/Reading Assignment: Unit and Total Cost

R—Read and understand the author's ideas. Do you understand what you are reading? Do you understand all the words? Do you need help with understanding anything?
I am learning how to calculate the individual cost of things, the total cost of several things together, and the tax on either a single unit or a group of items.
E—Encode the author's words into your own words. What is the author saying? What is the main idea or concept being presented? What did you learn by reading this passage? Explain it in your own words.
First, if I am given a total amount and then told the number of items that were purchased, I simply divide the total dollar amount by the number of items bought and that will give me the unit cost. If I am given the unit cost of an item, I can find out how much any number of them will cost by multiplying the unit cost by the amount that is being purchased. That will allow me to buy multiples of the item and figure out a total cost. Where I live, tax is 7.75%. If I multiply a unit cost or total cost by .0775, that will give me the amount of tax that I must pay. By simply adding that amount to the unit or total cost, I can figure out how much things are.
A—Annotate what you read. What is the author's opinion on the subject? How can you tell? What is the problem being presented in the text? What are some possible solutions? What can you learn from the author's writing that will help your own?
The author thinks that this is important information because in order to buy food or clothing or any of the things a person needs, it is necessary to know how much things will cost. If you do not know how much you will have to pay for something, you do not know if you have enough money. That is very important if you go grocery shopping, like the author wrote about. The author also thinks that it is really important to understand how sales tax works because if you cannot afford the sales tax, then you cannot afford the item.
P—Ponder what you have written. Does it make sense? Would someone else understand what you have written? Is it accurate? Do you need to change anything? Did you use your own words?
I was able to use my own words and I do think that another person would be able to understand it. I wonder if sales tax is different in other states, countries, or cities. I should look on the Internet to see if I can find the sales tax of other areas. Maybe it would be fun to work with another school to see if the cost of grocery items, including tax, is the same where I live, or if it is more or less.

Read, Encode, Annotate, Ponder (cont.)

Grades 6–8 Example

Study Topic/Reading Assignment: <u>Metric System</u>

R—Read and understand the author's ideas. Do you understand what you are reading? Do you understand all the words? Do you need help with understanding anything?

The article that I was reading was about the metric system and how it compares to our system of measurement. The article describes how Europe uses a different system of measurement than we do in the United States.

E—Encode the author's words into your own words. What is the author saying? What is the main idea or concept being presented? What did you learn by reading this passage? Explain it in your own words.

There are metric conversions for length, area, volume, and weight. Common measures of length in the United States are inches and feet. One inch is equal to 2.54 centimeters. One foot is equal to 30.48 centimeters (the length of a typical ruler in the United States). For distances greater than a few feet, Americans measure in yards. In most other parts of the world, meters are used. There are 3.2808 feet and 1.0936 yards in a meter. One of the most common units of measurement in the United States is a mile. Other countries measure distance traveled in kilometers. The process is the same, but the units of measurement are different.

A—Annotate what you read. What is the author's opinion on the subject? How can you tell? What is the problem being presented in the text? What are some possible solutions? What can you learn from the author's writing that will help your own?

The author seems to feel that it is important for Americans to understand how to convert our system of measurement into the metric system. This is because our system is so different from that of the rest of the world. If an American travels to a foreign country that uses the metric system, and he or she does not have at least a basic understanding of the conversions, it would be very difficult to get around.

P—Ponder what you have written. Does it make sense? Would someone else understand what you have written? Is it accurate? Do you need to change anything? Did you use your own words?

I was able to use my own words to help explain the information. I am surprised at how different our system of measurement is, compared to the metric system. I think it would be interesting to research why America uses the system that we do, and perhaps add some of that information to what I have already done.

Read, Encode, Annotate, Ponder (cont.)

Grades 9–12 Example

Study Topic/Reading Assignment: <u>Exponential Functions</u>

R—Read and understand the author's ideas. Do you understand what you are reading? Do you understand all the words? Do you need help with understanding anything?

The assignment I read talked about how exponential functions can be used to illustrate certain things like bacterial growth and compound interest in a bank account. These things do not grow in a straight line, but rather a line that curves upwards.

E—Encode the author's words into your own words. What is the author saying? What is the main idea or concept being presented? What did you learn by reading this passage? Explain it in your own words.

The formula used to determine exponential growth is $A = P(1 + r)^t$ where A = total amount, P = principal amount, or the amount you start with, r = rate of growth and t = time. To find the final amount, first you need to convert the rate of growth to a decimal and add the number one. The reason you add the rate of growth to one is because you are taking the principal amount and adding to it. Next you take that amount to the power of t, or time. This is the exponential part of the function because the growth does not occur linearly. For example, one bacterium divides into two bacteria and then these two bacteria *both* divide to give you a total of 4 bacteria or 2^2. You multiply this amount by the original amount to get the final amount.

A—Annotate what you read. What is the author's opinion on the subject? How can you tell? What is the problem being presented in the text? What are some of the possible solutions? What you can you learn from the author's writing that will help your own?

The author thinks it is important to understand exponential growth because it affects many aspects of our daily lives. When you invest money in a bank account that gives compound interest, you need to be able to figure out how much money you will be making on your initial investment. Exponential growth is also important for calculating things like population growth or carbon dating. Understanding bacterial growth is important for treating infections and studying diseases.

P—Ponder what you have written. Does it make sense? Would someone else understand what you have written? Is it accurate? Do you need to change anything? Did you use your own words?

I used my own words to describe how to use an exponential growth formula. I think that someone else could read my explanation and be able to use it to figure out other cases of exponential growth. I think adding a detailed example would help clarify my explanation even more.

Read, Encode, Annotate, Ponder

Study Topic/Reading Assignment: _____

R—Read and understand the author's ideas. Do you understand what you are reading? Do you understand all the words? Do you need help with understanding anything?

E—Encode the author's words into your own words. What is the author saying? What is the main idea or concept being presented? What did you learn by reading this passage? Explain it in your own words.

A—Annotate what you read. What is the author's opinion on the subject? How can you tell? What is the problem presented in the text? What are some possible solutions? What can you learn from the author's writing that will help your own?

P—Ponder what you have written. Does it make sense? Would someone else understand what you have written? Is it accurate? Do you need to change anything? Did you use your own words?

Summarizing Overview

The Challenge of Summarizing

Summarizing improves readers' ability to locate the main ideas and supporting details, identify and omit unnecessary details and redundant materials, remember what is read, analyze text structure and see how ideas are related, generalize details, clarify meaning, take notes, and rethink what they have read so that they can process it more deeply.

Summarizing is, to a certain extent, like a mathematical process. When students summarize their reading, they distill large sections of text, extract the most essential information, and then create a coherent, more concise text that relates the same information as the original text. In order to effectively summarize, writers must be able to identify the main ideas and differentiate important information from less important information in order to stress the most vital parts and minimize less relevant details.

Condensing text so that the substance of a reading selection is in brief form is no easy task and often leads to artificial, awkward language and organization. Summaries should be revised, as with any finished writing product, so they sound more natural when read. When students translate the ideas they have read into their own words, they can more easily retrieve that information to accomplish a learning task. Students must use their own words to form connections across the concepts and relate the concepts to their own prior knowledge and experiences.

The Steps in Summarizing

Students need to remember three elements to summarize effectively: keep the information in their summaries brief, identify the most important ideas, and mention some supporting details.

The Main Idea

One of the skills involved in summarizing is expressing the main idea. In order to summarize, students must be able to identify the key concepts or chief topic of a passage, a paragraph, and a sentence. The main idea is the central thought, but it can be overlooked when teaching students how to summarize. Therefore, students need instruction and practice in communicating the main idea, as it is the one idea to which all other sentences in a passage relate.

Quick and Easy Main Idea Activities

The following activities are fast, easy ways to highlight how to locate the main idea in reading passages (Dechant 1991):

- Have students categorize words from a passage. This helps them recognize the main ideas.

- Have students locate the topic sentence that best identifies the main idea of a paragraph. Remind them to use these as models.

- Instruct students to identify the main idea of a group of sentences by underlining key words.

- Have students read a newspaper story on a topic and remove the title. Ask them to give the story a title and compare it to the actual title.

Summarizing Overview (cont.)

Standards Addressed

The following chart shows the correlating standards for each strategy in this section. Refer to the Digital Resource CD (standards.pdf) to read the correlating standards in their entirety.

Strategy	McREL Standards	Common Core State Standards
GIST	Grades 3–5 (1.1, 1.2, 1.11) Grades 6–8 (1.1, 1.2, 1.12) Grades 9–12 (1.1, 1.2, 1.12)	Grade 3 (W.3.2, W.3.4) Grade 4 (W.4.2, W.4.4) Grade 5 (W.5.2, W.5.4) Grade 6 (W.6.2, W.6.4) Grade 7 (W.7.2, W.7.4) Grade 8 (W.8.2, W.8.4) Grades 9–10 (W.9-10.2, W.9-10.4) Grades 11–12 (W.11-12.2, W.11-12.4)
Key Words	Grades 1–2 (1.1, 1.2) Grades 3–5 (1.1, 1.2, 1.11)	Grade 1 (W.1.5) Grade 2 (W.2.5) Grade 3 (W.3.5) Grade 4 (W.4.5) Grade 5 (W.5.5)
Guided Reading and Summarizing Procedure	Grades 3–5 (1.1, 1.2, 1.11) Grades 6–8 (1.1, 1.2. 1.12) Grades 9–12 (1.1, 1.2, 1.12)	Grade 3 (W.3.4, W.3.5, W.3.8) Grade 4 (W.4.4, W.4.5, W.4.8) Grade 5 (W.5.4, W.5.5, W.5.8) Grade 6 (W.6.4, W.6.5, W.6.8) Grade 7 (W.7.4, W.7.5, W.7.8) Grade 8 (W.8.4, W.8.5, W.8.8) Grades 9–10 (W.9-10.4, W.9-10.5) Grades 11–12 (W.11-12.4, W.11-12.5)

GIST

Background Information

The GIST strategy (Generating Interactions between Schemata and Text) (Moore et al. 1994) helps students get the "gist" of the mathematics text in order to write a clear, concise summary in 20 words or fewer in which students examine a topic and clearly convey their ideas and mathematics information. As students progress in school, teachers begin to limit the number of words or pages for writing assignments. This strategy strengthens students' writing skills by teaching them to eliminate unnecessary information and determine the key points of the text so students produce more focused writing in which the development and organization are appropriate for the writing task. Therefore, each word used in a GIST must have great importance. Using GIST is valuable not only when summarizing a reading passage but also when writing the summary of a multiparagraph essay. To prepare students, review the features of a high-quality summary.

Grade Levels/Standards Addressed

See page 192 for the standards this strategy addresses, or refer to the Digital Resource CD (standards.pdf) to read the correlating standards in their entirety.

Genres

Expository, Summary

Stages of Writing Process

Prewrite, Draft, Revise

Activity

Assign a mathematics passage for students that is fairly short—no more than three paragraphs—and easy to read, then distribute the *GIST* activity sheet (page 196, gist.pdf). Ask students to identify the main points of the passage and write these on the board or use a document camera to display their ideas. Ask them to list the supporting details or statements to complete a prewriting outline. Next, instruct students to use the class outline to write a summary of no more than 20 words, and then edit and revise it, as good writers do, making sure to convey their ideas clearly and concisely. Put students in groups of no more than four to share their paragraphs and receive feedback, which they can use to revise and edit the summaries. As students become more proficient in using this strategy, gradually eliminate the group and/or whole-class work so that they eventually write and edit their summaries independently.

Differentiation

While working as a class during the modeling phase, use simple vocabulary and discuss the meaning of this vocabulary so that English language learners can understand. Use opportunities to rephrase and repeat these terms. Check for understanding before moving on to the writing phase. For above-level students, assign longer passages to read and challenge them to write shorter summaries. Allow below-level students to work with partners to identify the important ideas and words. If necessary, lengthen the word limit on their summaries.

GIST *(cont.)*

Grades 3–5 Example

Text Passage

Numbers like 546,837 have six digits. Each digit in the number has a different place value. The first digit is in the hundred thousands place. The number 546,837 has 5 hundred thousands. The second digit is in the ten thousands place. In the example, there are 4 groups of ten thousands. The third digit is in the thousands place, so the example has 6 thousands. The next digit is in the hundreds place, so the example has 8 hundreds. The next digit is in the tens place, so the example has 3 tens. Finally, the last digit in the example is in the ones place. This number has 7 ones.

Key Points

Place Value

six digits	hundreds place
hundred thousands place	tens place
ten thousands place	ones place
thousands place	

Summary (No more than 20 words)

The number 546,837 has 5 hundred thousands, 4 ten thousands, 6 thousands, 8 hundreds, 3 tens, and 7 ones.

Grades 6–8 Example

Text Passage

Ratios tell how one number is related to another. It may be written as $a{:}b$ or $\frac{a}{b}$ or by the phrase "*a* to *b*." For example, the ratio of 1:5 is read as "1 to 5," and means that the second number is five times as large as the first. Given the ratio of $a{:}b = 2{:}5$ and asked to find b if $a = 10$, follow these steps:

First, determine how many times the number a is divisible by the corresponding portion of the ratio: $10 \div 2 = 5$.

Then, multiply the answer by the portion of the ratio representing b: $5 \times 5 = 25$.

Therefore, if the ratio of a to b is 2:5 and $a = 10$, then $b = 25$.

Key Points

ratios

tell how numbers relate

$a{:}b$ is 2:5 and $a = 10$

$10 \div 2 = 5$ and $5 \times 5 = 25$

$b = 25$

Summary (No more than 20 words)

Ratios, which tell how numbers relate, are written as $a{:}b$ and read "*a* to *b*." If a ratio is 2:5 and $a = 10$, then $b = 25$.

GIST *(cont.)*

Grades 9–12 Example

Text Passage

In a set of real numbers, negative numbers do not have square roots. Imaginary numbers were created so that negative numbers would have square roots. These numbers start with i, which equals the square root of -1, or $i^2 = -1$. For example, $\sqrt{-18} = \sqrt{-9 \cdot 2} = \sqrt{-9}\sqrt{2} = 3i\sqrt{2}$.

Key Points

imaginary numbers

  are square roots of negative numbers

  are represented by the mathematical number i

  $i = \sqrt{-1}$

  $i^2 = -1$

Summary (No more than 20 words)

Imaginary numbers are the square roots of negative numbers. The number i represents imaginary numbers and $i = \sqrt{-1}$, or $i^2 = -1$.

GIST

Directions: After reading the text, write down the important ideas. Then, write a summary of the reading.

Key Points

_____   _____   _____

_____   _____   _____

_____   _____   _____

_____   _____   _____

_____   _____   _____

Summary (No more than 20 words)

_____

_____

_____

_____

_____

_____

_____

_____

_____

_____

Key Words

Background Information

Key Words (Hoyt 1999) is a summary strategy that is better suited to younger students because it does not limit the number of words used in a summary. It provides greater scaffolding to support students in creating a clear, concise summary where students produce writing in which the development and organization are appropriate for the assignment. Before summarizing, students are asked to simply identify the key words from the text. Those words are then used to compose the summary. Key Words can also be effective for older students who are learning to write summaries in multiparagraph compositions.

Grade Levels/Standards Addressed

See page 192 for the standards this strategy addresses, or refer to the Digital Resource CD (standards.pdf) to read the correlating standards in their entirety.

Genres

Expository, Summary, Persuasive

Stages of Writing Process

Prewrite, Draft, Revise

Activity

Explain that students are to look for the main ideas, or key words, as they read a selected mathematics text. Distribute scrap paper, sticky notes, or notebook paper to students on which to write the key words. After the reading, call on students to share their words, discuss the significance of each one, and justify their choices to develop a class list of the key words from the text. Model and discuss how to organize, rearrange, and delete duplicate key words as needed. Then, write a summary using the key words, either by modeling the entire process or using the Guided Writing Procedure strategy (see pages 175–177). Model for students how to edit and revise the summary so that it flows naturally. Provide adequate guided practice time before allowing students to write a summary independently, providing support for students as needed.

Differentiation

Preview the text and preteach any new vocabulary words for English language learners to improve their comprehension. Guide these students in a small group to develop their summaries. Give above-level students reading materials that are appropriate for their reading levels, and challenge them by limiting the number of words used in their summaries. Scaffold for below-level students by modeling how to identify key words as they read.

Key Words (cont.)

Grades 1–2 Example

Text Passage

When you add two numbers together, you are finding how many you have altogether. When you add one, it is just like counting by ones. When you add two, it is just like counting by twos.

Key Words

add, altogether, counting, ones, twos

Summary

To add means putting things together, and with 1 and 2 it is like counting by ones and twos.

Grades 3–5 Example

Text Passage

A decimal is simply a fractional number. Decimals can be converted to equivalent fractions. For example, the number 0.7 represents $\frac{7}{10}$ and 0.07 represents $\frac{7}{100}$. Since $\frac{70}{100}$ is larger than $\frac{7}{100}$, it is easy to understand that 0.7 is bigger than 0.07.

Key Words

decimal, fractional, represents, equivalent

Summary

Converting decimals to equivalent fractions helps to compare decimals.

Guided Reading and Summarizing Procedure

Background Information

The Guided Reading and Summarizing Procedure (Hayes 1989, as cited by Ryder and Graves 2003; Lenski, Wham, and Johns 1999) teaches students to summarize independently as they gather mathematical information from print and digital sources. Students learn to recall, organize, and self-correct information before composing a summary through teacher modeling in order to strengthen the development and organization of their writing. Ryder and Graves (2003) suggest that students and teacher write summaries individually, and then compare and contrast students' summaries to that of the teacher. According to Ryder and Graves (2003), research suggests that the teacher revise his or her summary based on students' suggestions and make a visible record of these changes to make the revision process more concrete for students.

Grade Levels/Standards Addressed

See page 192 for the standards this strategy addresses, or refer to the Digital Resource CD (standards.pdf) to read the correlating standards in their entirety.

Genres

Expository, Summary, Persuasive

Stages of Writing Process

Prewrite, Draft, Revise

Activity

Explain to students that they will use the Guided Reading and Summarizing Procedure to help them summarize the information they gathered from print and digital sources. Emphasize the importance of learning how to summarize text and knowing when summarizing is needed. When students have finished reading the selected mathematics text, have them share what they remember. Write their comments on the board or display them using a document camera. Then, have students read the text again, this time looking for any information that they missed, that can be elaborated on, or that is inaccurate. Make changes as needed, and then organize the ideas into main ideas and details. Using this class outline, model writing a summary passage for students. Read through the summary as a class to edit and revise it so that it flows naturally and contains all the important points from the text passage. After learning how to use the strategy, students can use the *Guided Reading and Summarizing Procedure* activity sheet (page 203, grasp.pdf) to write their summaries independently.

Differentiation

Remind English language learners and below-level students to use the text as a reference. English language learners might also benefit from having a sheet with the key points that they can use in their summary statements. Above-level students can complete this activity independently from the beginning.

Guided Reading and
Summarizing Procedure *(cont.)*

Grades 3–5 Example

Details Remembered from Reading	Additions/Corrections
• When two numbers are multiplied together, the answer is called the product. • It is the same as repeated addition. • The product of any number and 1 is the original number. • The product of doubles is called a square. • The two numbers being multiplied are factors.	• The product of any number and 0 is 0. • Multiplying by 10 means you just add a 0 to the end of the original number. • All of the products of a particular factor are multiples of that factor.

Main Ideas in Reading

• Two factors multiplied together make a product.

• Numbers multiplied by 0 equal 0, and numbers multiplied by 1 equal the original number.

• Multiplying by tens lets you multiply single digits and just add a 0.

Guided Reading and
Summarizing Procedure *(cont.)*

. . . .

Grades 6–8 Example

Details Remembered from Reading	Additions/Corrections
• The meter is the basic metric unit of length. • A millimeter is $\frac{1}{1,000}$ of a meter. • A centimeter is $\frac{1}{100}$ of a meter. • A kilometer is 1000 meters. • The metric system is based on multiples of 10. • The foot is the U.S. basic unit of length. • One inch is $\frac{1}{12}$ of a foot.	• The metric system is common in European countries. • A decimeter is $\frac{1}{10}$ of a meter. • One yard is equal to 3 feet. • There are 5,280 feet in a mile.

Main Ideas in Reading

• There are two common units for measurement of length: the meter and the foot.

• The metric forms of measurement are based on the number 10.

• The metric system is more commonly used around the world.

Guided Reading and
Summarizing Procedure *(cont.)*

Grades 9–12 Example

Details Remembered from Reading	Additions/Corrections
• The graph of a quadratic function is called a parabola.	• The vertex form of a quadratic function is $y = a(x - h)^2 + k$.
• A parabola is a u-shaped graph that can open upward or downward.	• Point *(h, k)* is the vertex of the parabola.
• A parabola has a vertex which is the point where the parabola crosses the axis of symmetry.	• Line $x = h$ is the axis of symmetry of the parabola.
• The axis of symmetry of a parabola is the vertical line that goes through the vertex and divides the parabola in half.	• If *a* is positive, the parabola opens upward; if *a* is negative, it opens downward.

Main Ideas in Reading
• Quadratic functions have u-shaped graphs called parabolas.
• The vertex form of a quadratic equation specifies the vertex, axis of symmetry and direction of the parabola.

Name: _____ **Date:** _____

Guided Reading and Summarizing Procedure

Directions: Use this chart to help you summarize the main ideas of a reading passage. After the first reading, write the details you remember in the upper left-hand box. After the second reading, write any additions or corrections to your original information. Finally, synthesize the information into a few main ideas, and write them in the bottom box.

Details Remembered from Reading	Additions/Corrections

Main Ideas in Reading

Applying Knowledge Overview

What Does the Research Say?

Research is showing that writing-to-learn activities or expressive writing activities have a place in the mathematics curriculum. This is not to say that the formal types of writing originally found in the mathematics classroom should be excluded. Transactional writing, as Britton et al. (1975) call it, is the kind of writing that has a specific purpose. There is the intent to produce something. There is a specific audience and the writer is responsible for what he or she says. Most transactional writing ends up as a finished product and is often called *product writing*. There is emphasis on what the final product will look like. This type of writing is more formal and is the most common form of writing in the mathematics classroom. Examples of product writing include mathematics fiction pieces, biographies, essays, and research reports, as well as responses to test questions.

Students should be taught how to complete product writing. Students should have models and examples to follow. Teachers should be expected to teach students how to write formal mathematics pieces (Sorenson 1989; Winchester School District 1987; Hamilton-Wieler 1988). With this form of writing, the student is accountable for spelling, grammar, and punctuation decisions. Writing mechanics and organization are as much a part of the grade as the content will be. Strategies on how to incorporate examples of mathematics product writing into the classroom are explained in this section of the book.

Much nonfiction reading and writing readily lends itself to the application of knowledge. It is something we do quite naturally in many situations. Writing-to-apply activities provide students with the opportunity to write about mathematics concepts using established formats such as research reports, essays, and data reports. Writing for an audience requires understanding of subject, organization, and complex cognitive thought. Writing-to-apply activities encourage critical thinking skills in formal settings. These same skills can transfer to writing that will be done throughout life in the workplace and elsewhere.

The more students write, the more familiar and the more comfortable they will become. Students need instruction, direction, experience, and motivation to write. Incorporating transactional or product writing in the mathematics class allows students to develop a knowledge of the writing process and each stage. It also allows students to weave together the language of mathematics into everyday language and conversation. Finally, product writing exposes students to writing for an audience and writing for a variety of purposes.

Applying Knowledge Overview *(cont.)*

Standards Addressed

The following chart shows the correlating standards for each strategy in this section. Refer to the Digital Resource CD (standards.pdf) to read the correlating standards in their entirety.

Strategy	McREL Standards	Common Core State Standards
Summary-Writing Microtheme	Grades 3–5 (1.11) Grades 6–8 (1.12) Grades 9–12 (1.12)	Grade 3 (CCRA.W.9, W.3.2, W.3.5) Grade 4 (W.4.2, W.4.5, W.4.9) Grade 5 (W.5.2, W.5.5, W.5.9) Grade 6 (W.6.2, W.6.5, W.6.9) Grade 7 (W.7.2, W.7.5, W.7.9) Grade 8 (W.8.2, W.8.5, W.8.9) Grades 9–10 (W.9-10.2, W.9-10.5, W.9-10.9) Grades 11–12 (W.11-12.2, W.11-12.5, W.11-12.9)
Thesis-Support Microtheme	Grades 3–5 (1.7) Grades 6–8 (1.6) Grades 9–12 (1.7)	Grade 3 (CCRA.W.9, W.3.2, W.3.5) Grade 4 (W.4.2, W.4.5, W.4.9) Grade 5 (W.5.2, W.5.5, W.5.9) Grade 6 (W.6.2, W.6.5, W.6.9) Grade 7 (W.7.2, W.7.5, W.7.9) Grade 8 (W.8.2, W.8.5, W.8.9) Grades 9–10 (W.9-10.2, W.9-10.5, W.9-10.9) Grades 11–12 (W.11-12.2, W.11-12.5, W.11-12.9)
Data-Provided Microtheme	Grades 3–5 (4.8) Grades 6–8 (4.3) Grades 9–12 (4.6)	Grade 3 (W.3.5) Grade 4 (W.4.5) Grade 5 (W.5.5) Grade 6 (W.6.5) Grade 7 (W.7.5) Grade 8 (W.8.5) Grades 9–10 (W.9-10.5) Grades 11–12 (W.11-12.5)

Applying Knowledge Overview *(cont.)*

Strategy	McREL Standards	Common Core State Standards
Quandary-Posing Microtheme	Grades 3–5 (1.7) Grades 6–8 (1.6, 1.11) Grades 9–12 (1.7)	Grade 3 (W.3.2, W.3.5) Grade 4 (W.4.2, W.4.5) Grade 5 (W.5.2, W.5.5) Grade 6 (W.6.2, W.6.5) Grade 7 (W.7.2, W.7.5) Grade 8 (W.8.2, W.8.5) Grades 9–10 (W.9-10.2, W.9-10.5) Grades 11–12 (W.11-12.2, W.11-12.5)
RAFT Assignment	Grades 1–2 (1.7, 1.8) Grades 3–5 (1.5, 1.6) Grades 6–8 (1.5) Grades 9–12 (1.5, 1.6)	Grade 1 (W.1.2, W.1.5) Grade 2 (W.2.2, W.2.5) Grade 3 (W.3.2, W.3.5) Grade 4 (W.4.2, W.4.5) Grade 5 (W.5.2, W.5.5) Grade 6 (W.6.2, W.6.5) Grade 7 (W.7.2, W.7.5) Grade 8 (W.8.2, W.8.5) Grades 9–10 (W.9-10.2, W.9-10.5) Grades 11–12 (W.11-12.2, W.11-12.5)
Business Letter	Grades 1–2 (1.7) Grades 3–5 (1.12) Grades 6–8 (1.13) Grades 9–12 (1.13)	Grade 1 (CCRA.W.4, W.1.5) Grade 2 (CCRA.W.4, W.2.5) Grade 3 (W.3.4) Grade 4 (W.4.4) Grade 5 (W.5.4) Grade 6 (W.6.4) Grade 7 (W.7.4) Grade 8 (W.8.4) Grades 9–10 (W.9-10.4) Grades 11–12 (W.11-12.4)
Friendly Letter	Grades 1–2 (1.7) Grades 3–5 (1.12) Grades 6–8 (1.13) Grades 9–12 (1.13)	Grade 1 (CCRA.W.4, W.1.5) Grade 2 (CCRA.W.4, W.2.5) Grade 3 (W.3.4) Grade 4 (W.4.4) Grade 5 (W.5.4) Grade 6 (W.6.4) Grade 7 (W.7.4) Grade 8 (W.8.4) Grades 9–10 (W.9-10.4) Grades 11–12 (W.11-12.4)

Applying Knowledge Overview (cont.)

Strategy	McREL Standards	Common Core State Standards
Data Report	Grades 1–2 (1.7) Grades 3–5 (1.7) Grades 6–8 (1.6) Grades 9–12 (1.7)	Grade 1 (CCRA.W.4, W.1.5) Grade 2 (CCRA.W.4, W.2.5) Grade 3 (W.3.4) Grade 4 (W.4.4) Grade 5 (W.5.4) Grade 6 (W.6.4) Grade 7 (W.7.4) Grade 8 (W.8.4) Grades 9–10 (W.9-10.4) Grades 11–12 (W.11-12.4)
Newspaper Article	Grades 1–2 (1.7) Grades 3–5 (1.7) Grades 6–8 (1.6) Grades 9–12 (1.7)	Grade 1 (W.1.2, W.1.5) Grade 2 (W.2.2, W.2.5) Grade 3 (W.3.2, W.3.5) Grade 4 (W.4.2, W.4.5) Grade 5 (W.5.2, W.5.5) Grade 6 (W.6.2, W.6.5) Grade 7 (W.7.2, W.7.5) Grade 8 (W.8.2, W.8.5) Grades 9–10 (W.9-10.2, W.9-10.5) Grades 11–12 (W.11-12.2, W.11-12.5)
Mathematics Fiction Story	Grades 1–2 (1.7) Grades 3–5 (1.8) Grades 6–8 (1.7) Grades 9–12 (1.8)	Grade 1 (W.1.3, W.1.5) Grade 2 (W.2.3, W.2.5) Grade 3 (W.3.3, W.3.5) Grade 4 (W.4.3, W.4.5) Grade 5 (W.5.3, W.5.5) Grade 6 (W.6.3, W.6.5) Grade 7 (W.7.3, W.7.5) Grade 8 (W.8.3, W.8.5) Grades 9–10 (W.9-10.3, W.9-10.5) Grades 11–12 (W.11-12.3, W.11-12.5)
Research Report	Grades 3–5 (4.8) Grades 6–8 (4.3) Grades 9–12 (4.8)	Grade 3 (W.3.5, W.3.8) Grade 4 (W.4.5, W.4.8) Grade 5 (W.5.5, W.5.8) Grade 6 (W.6.5, W.6.8) Grade 7 (W.7.5, W.7.8) Grade 8 (W.8.5, W.8.8) Grades 9–10 (W.9-10.5, W.9-10.8) Grades 11–12 (W.11-12.5, W.11-12.8)

Summary-Writing Microtheme

Background Information

The Microthemes strategy, introduced by John C. Bean (1996), enables students to write what they know about a specific theme. In essence, the microtheme is a condensed version of a research report or essay, written on one side of a 5" × 8" index card. This strategy reveals what students do or do not know about a specific mathematics subject. It provides an opportunity for students to write informally using clear and accurate information for an intended audience, drawing on textual evidence from informational texts to support their summaries. With this microtheme, students determine which details to eliminate and which to condense. Ideally, this application activity would follow practice with GIST, Key Words, or Guided Reading and Summarizing Procedure so that students are well prepared to create their own summaries independently. The focus of the Summary-Writing Microtheme is to improve students' comprehension and summarizing abilities.

Grade Levels/Standards Addressed

See page 205 for the standards this strategy addresses, or refer to the Digital Resource CD (standards.pdf) to read the correlating standards in their entirety.

Genre

Summary

Stages of Writing Process

Prewrite, Draft, Revise, Edit, Publish

Activity

Select a piece of text that is well suited for summary writing. Tell students that they will write a short summary about the text, conveying mathematical information and their ideas in a condensed, concise manner. Display a sample Summary-Writing Microtheme on the board or with a document camera, and discuss the organization (main ideas and details), tone (direct), language (content vocabulary), and other features (transition words). Set clear expectations for students so that they will be successful. Next, model writing a Summary-Writing Microtheme using a prewriting strategy, drafting, revising, editing, and publishing. This is probably best done over several days or class periods. Distribute the *Summary-Writing Microtheme* activity sheet (page 209, summarywriting.pdf) to get students started on the writing process.

Differentiation

If appropriate, allow English language learners to use pictures or other visual representations in their microthemes. Remind these students to focus on summarizing the text in an organized manner. Consider providing them with summary frames or sentence stems if these will help English language learners better communicate the information. Do not hold English language learners accountable for spelling and writing conventions as much as for content. Encourage above-level students to write a report after completing the microtheme. Or have them write a Summary-Writing Microtheme on two different texts about the same topic, and then compare and contrast the information. Provide small-group instruction for below-level students at each stage of the writing process. These students may need support to organize their information in a systematic manner and to use the prewriting work to create drafts. Allow additional time for these students to accomplish the assignment.

Summary-Writing Microtheme

Directions: Use this prewriting planner to organize your Summary-Writing Microtheme.

Main Idea

_____

_____

Detail

_____

_____

Detail

_____

_____

Detail

_____

_____

Closing Statement

_____

_____

Reminders:

- Refer back to the text to identify the main idea.

- Make sure the details support or relate to the main idea.

- Use this outline to write your draft.

- Add transition words (*most importantly*, *for example*, etc.).

Thesis-Support Microtheme

Background Information

With this microtheme, students take a stand on an assigned mathematical issue. After conducting some research on the issue or reviewing notes from class, students are ready to write the Thesis-Support Microtheme by drawing on evidence from informational mathematics texts they read while conducting research or reviewing notes. The main stance or thesis statement by students should include three main supportive statements.

Grade Levels/Standards Addressed

See page 205 for the standards this strategy addresses, or refer to the Digital Resource CD (standards.pdf) to read the correlating standards in their entirety.

Genre

Expository

Stages of Writing Process

Prewrite, Draft, Revise, Edit, Publish

Activity

Identify an issue in mathematics that is well suited for thesis writing. Tell students that they will write a thesis with supporting statements to communicate their position on the issue. Display a sample Thesis-Support Microtheme on the board or with a document camera to discuss the organization (main ideas and details), tone (direct and persuasive), language (content-specific vocabulary and persuasive language), and other features (transition words). Set clear expectations so that students will understand how to be successful.

Next, model writing your own Thesis-Support Microtheme: use a prewriting strategy, draft, revise, edit, and publish. Distribute the *Thesis-Support Microtheme* activity sheet (page 211, thesissupport. pdf) to get students started on the writing process. Have students work in pairs to develop and strengthen their writing based on peer feedback. Although this is a short writing application activity, consider modeling over several days or class periods so students are clear on how to create an effective microtheme.

Differentiation

If appropriate, allow English language learners to use pictures or other visual representations in their microthemes. Remind these students to focus on the organization of the microtheme—a clear stance and three supporting statements. Consider providing them with a list of persuasive words and phrases to incorporate into their writing. Do not hold English language learners accountable for spelling and writing conventions as much as for content. Challenge above-level students to include more supporting statements in their Thesis-Support Microtheme. Or encourage them to develop two Thesis-Support Microthemes— one to support their original thesis and one to support an opposing viewpoint. Provide small-group instruction for below-level students at each stage of the writing process. These students may need support to organize their information in a systematic manner and to use the prewriting work to create drafts. Allow additional time for these students to accomplish the assignment.

Thesis-Support Microtheme

Directions: Use this prewriting planner to organize your Thesis-Support Microtheme.

Thesis Statement/Main Stance

_____

_____

Supporting Information

_____

_____

Supporting Information

_____

_____

Supporting Information

_____

_____

Closing Statement

_____

_____

Reminders:
- Take a clear stance in your first statement.
- Make sure the details support or relate to your thesis.
- Use this outline to write your draft.
- Add transition words (*most importantly, for example,* etc.).

Data-Provided Microtheme

Background Information

The Data-Provided Microtheme is a diagram, table, or chart drawn by students to explain a mathematical process. This graphic should include details and descriptions using color, if necessary. Brief descriptions and details should be thorough and condensed.

Grade Levels/Standards Addressed

See page 205 for the standards this strategy addresses, or refer to the Digital Resource CD (standards.pdf) to read the correlating standards in their entirety.

Genre

Expository

Stages of Writing Process

Prewrite, Draft, Revise, Edit, Publish

Activity

Select a piece of text that is well suited to visual representations. Tell students that they will create a diagram, table, or chart to communicate the important information in the text. Display a sample Data-Provided Microtheme on the board or with a document camera and discuss its features: title, visual representation (diagram, table, or chart), labels (for rows, columns, or diagrams), illustrations (when appropriate), and use of color. Set clear expectations for students so that they will be successful in planning this writing assignment. Next, model creating a Data-Provided Microtheme using a prewriting strategy, drafting, revising, editing, and publishing. Then, distribute the *Data-Provided Microtheme* activity sheet (page 213, dataprovided.pdf) to help students begin the writing process. Although this is a short writing application activity, consider modeling over several days or class periods so students are clear on how to create an effective microtheme. Have students work in pairs, in groups, or as a whole class to fully develop and strengthen their writing for the task at hand.

Differentiation

With adequate teacher modeling, English language learners should be very successful with this microtheme. Challenge above-level students to include more details in their diagrams and more complex categories in the charts and tables. Or encourage them to present their microthemes to the class and explain how they determined the appropriate titles, representation, and labels. Meet with below-level students during the prewriting phase to make sure they are choosing appropriate visual representations and organizing the information correctly. Allow additional time for these students to complete the assignment.

Name: _____ **Date:** _____

Data-Provided Microtheme

Directions: Use this prewriting planner to organize your Data-Provided Microtheme.

Reminders:
- Draw on evidence from the text to gather information, words, or data.
- Choose a visual presentation—chart, graph, diagram, table, graphic organizer, etc.—that will best represent the information.
- Give your Data-Provided Microtheme a title.
- Label rows, columns, headings, etc.
- Use color where appropriate.

Quandary-Posing Microtheme

Background Information

The Quandary-Posing Microtheme poses a mathematics-related problem as presented by students. They must incorporate principles that can be applied in solving the problem as they convey their ideas and mathematics information in writing. The focus is to be creative and accurate in solving the problem while strengthening and developing their written work based on teacher and peer feedback.

Grade Levels/Standards Addressed

See page 206 for the standards this strategy addresses, or refer to the Digital Resource CD (standards.pdf) to read the correlating standards in their entirety.

Genre

Expository

Stages of Writing Process

Prewrite, Draft, Revise, Edit, Publish

Activity

Select a mathematics topic that is well suited to identifying problems and creating solutions. Tell students that they will identify a problem, develop a solution, and clearly convey the solution in writing. Display a sample Quandary-Posing Microtheme on the board or with a document camera and discuss its features: a question about the mathematics topic, a proposed solution, and the reasons why that solution is appropriate. Set clear expectations for students so that they will be successful. Next, model creating a Quandary-Posing Microtheme using a prewriting strategy, drafting, revising, editing, and publishing. Then, distribute the *Quandary-Posing Microtheme* activity sheet (page 215, quandaryposing.pdf) to help students begin the writing process. Although this is a short writing application activity, be sure to model over several days or class periods so students are clear on how to create an effective microtheme. Have students work in pairs, in small groups, or as a whole class to fully develop and strengthen their writing for the task at hand.

Differentiation

Make sure English language learners clearly understand the terms *problem* and *solution*. Explicitly model for English language learners how to organize this microtheme, and provide them with sentence frames to use in their writing. Challenge above-level students to present and describe multiple solutions to their problems. Meet with below-level students during the prewriting phase to make sure their solutions address the problem. This is a good opportunity for discussing possible solutions and their outcomes. Allow additional time for these students to complete the assignment.

Quandary-Posing Microtheme

Directions: Use this prewriting planner to organize your Quandary-Posing Microtheme.

Problem

_____

_____

_____

Possible Solution

_____

_____

_____

Why It Will Work

_____

_____

_____

Closing Statement

_____

_____

_____

Reminders:
- Clearly identify and describe the problem.
- Make sure the solution will solve the problem.
- Explain why your solution will be effective.
- Add cause-and-effect words (*as a result, because, due to*, etc.)

RAFT Assignment

Background Information

RAFT stands for Role, Audience, Format, and Topic, the key ingredients of writing assignments (Santa, Havens, and Harrison 1996). This particular writing assignment alters the usual assignment in which students write a formal essay or report. With this activity, teachers can encourage creative application of mathematics content knowledge. Writers may be asked to write from the point of view of an equal sign (role) speaking to a group of students (audience) in a speech (format) explaining the meaning of an equal sign (topic), all the while being mindful to clearly convey their ideas and mathematical information through writing.

Grade Levels/Standards Addressed

See page 206 for the standards this strategy addresses, or refer to the Digital Resource CD (standards.pdf) to read the correlating standards in their entirety.

Genres

Expository, Summary, Narrative, Persuasive

Stages of Writing Process

Prewrite, Draft, Edit, Revise, Publish

Activity

Prepare the *RAFT Assignment* activity sheet (page 217, raft.pdf) by filling in the RAFT components. Distribute the *RAFT Assignment* activity sheet to students, then hold a brainstorming session to share ideas on how to address each area in the writing. Provide plenty of time for students to collaborate and get excited about the assignment. To support and guide students in developing and strengthening their writing during this process, model writing your own RAFT Assignment, showing each step of the writing process before asking students to work on their own. If needed, provide students with copies of a genre-specific graphic organizer (see pages 137–172) during the prewriting phase. Consider incorporating other authoring strategies throughout the writing process, such as Author's Chair (pages 182–185).

Variation

Primary grade teachers may want to create a RAFT Assignment as a whole class, using the shared writing process on a large sheet of chart paper. Provide a beginning for the writing piece, then ask students to contribute ideas to continue the story. Invite various students to come up and write each sentence on the chart until the story is complete. If grade-level teams are working on the RAFT Assignment, teachers may rotate the complete stories so that students can see the creative ideas of the other classes.

Differentiation

Allow English language learners to draw pictures in a story map to get them started. Modify the writing expectations to meet their individual levels. Above-level students may be thrilled with the freedom of the assignment. They should be able to work independently, but challenge them appropriately to develop their writing skills further. Below-level students may need more explicit instruction in the chosen genre, so consider meeting with these students in small groups to preteach the features of the genre before writing. Also, provide graphic organizers to help them stay organized.

Name: _____ Date: _____

RAFT Assignment

Directions: Use this prewriting planner to organize your RAFT Assignment.

Role: _____

Audience: _____

Format: _____

Topic: _____

Reminders:
- Think carefully about your role and your point of view.
- Consider how to best communicate to your audience.
- Use the traits of the writing format. You may wish to use the box above to create a graphic organizer specific to that genre: for example, a letter, poem, explanation, or story.
- Stay focused on your topic.

Business Letter

Background Information

Writing a business letter is another expressive writing strategy that provides students with the opportunity to persuade others on a mathematics topic while paying particular attention to the task and purpose of the writing assignment. Send the business letters out, and read and post replies as they come into the classroom.

Grade Levels/Standards Addressed

See page 206 for the standards this strategy addresses, or refer to the Digital Resource CD (standards.pdf) to read the correlating standards in their entirety.

Genres

Narrative, Persuasive

Stages of Writing Process

Prewrite, Draft, Revise, Edit, Publish

Activity

Review the following questions with students:

- What is the purpose of a business letter?

- Can you think of an example of a business letter that contains a mathematics topic?

- What key features of a business letter should be included?

- What are some tips for writing a business letter relating to a mathematics topic?

Divide the class into groups of three or four. Have each group make a list of ideas for business letters with a mathematics theme. Examples may include the following:

- Write a letter to the editor about a school funding issue.

- Write a letter to a government worker or public official asking about how tax money is spent.

- Write a letter to an architect or engineer to ask about how he or she uses geometry.

- Write a letter to your city's public information office asking about your city's demographics.

Allow time for students to share their responses with the class. Call on students to share examples of business letters with a mathematics theme. Distribute the *Business Letter* activity sheet (page 219, businessletter.pdf), and allow students to write a business letter on a mathematics topic. Have students continue working in their small groups to strengthen and develop their business letters before sending the letters to the intended real-life recipient(s).

Differentiation

Encourage English language learners to write the letter independently, and pair them with a partner for editing and revising. Pair them with students who are comfortable with writing formally. Encourage above-level students to write letters on controversial mathematics topics to a member of Congress or a local politician. This will require students to present an argument and think through the problem to suggest solutions. Below-level students will benefit from working with a partner to write the letter.

Business Letter

_____
_____
_____
_____

_____
_____
_____

To Whom It May Concern: (or) Dear _____:

_____
_____
_____
_____

_____
_____
_____
_____

_____
_____
_____

_____

_____,

_____

Friendly Letter

Background Information

Writing a friendly letter is another expressive writing strategy that provides students with the opportunity to persuade others on a mathematics topic, while paying particular attention to the task and purpose of the writing assignment. Send friendly letters out, and then read and post replies as they arrive.

Grade Levels/Standards Addressed

See page 206 for the standards this strategy addresses, or refer to the Digital Resource CD (standards.pdf) to read the correlating standards in their entirety.

Genres

Narrative, Persuasive

Stages of Writing Process

Prewrite, Draft, Revise, Edit, Publish

Activity

Review the following questions with students:

- What is the purpose of a friendly letter?
- Can you think of an example of a friendly letter that contains a mathematics topic?
- What key features of a friendly letter should be included?
- What are some tips for writing a friendly letter relating to a mathematics topic?

Divide the class into groups of three or four. Have each group make a list of examples of a friendly letter with a mathematics theme. Examples may include the following:

- Write a letter to a friend explaining a mathematics activity that you enjoyed.
- Write a letter to a family member explaining what has been learned in mathematics.
- Write a letter to a friend encouraging him or her to support a bill on a mathematics-related topic.

Allow time for students to share their responses with the class. Call on students to share examples of friendly letters with a mathematics theme. Distribute the *Friendly Letter* activity sheet (page 221, friendlyletter.pdf), and allow students to write a friendly letter of their own on a mathematics topic. Have students continue working in their small groups to strengthen and develop their friendly letters before sending the letters to the intended real-life recipient(s).

Differentiation

Encourage English language learners to write letters independently and pair them with partners for editing and revising. Pair them with students who are comfortable with writing formally. Encourage above-level students to write about a more complex topic, or challenge them to include more advanced vocabulary and complex sentence structures. Below-level students will benefit from working with a partner to write the letter.

Friendly Letter

_____

Dear _____ ,

_____

_____

_____

_____

_____

_____

_____

_____

_____

_____

_____ ,

_____

Data Report

. . . .

Background Information

The Data Report is an opportunity for students to take on the role of mathematicians and present the findings of the data analysis as appropriate for the task and purpose of the assignment. It is important for students to understand the value of collecting and comparing data as a tool for making comparisons and drawing conclusions. The data report offers students a way to organize their information so that they can communicate it with others effectively, clearly, and concisely.

Grade Levels/Standards Addressed

See page 207 for the standards this strategy addresses, or refer to the Digital Resource CD (standards.pdf) to read the correlating standards in their entirety.

Genres

Expository, Summary

Stages of Writing Process

Prewrite, Draft, Edit, Revise, Publish

Activity

Distribute the *Data Report* activity sheet (page 223, datareport.pdf) to students. Discuss data reports with students and explain the purpose and the process they are to follow.

1. **Purpose**—What is the objective? The data report should begin with a clear introduction explaining the purpose and intent of the information that was gathered and is being summarized and reported.

2. **Materials and Methods**—This is a clear, concise description of how data was obtained. It explains the structure and parameters of the data gathering and tells how and with what materials the work was done. Remind students that this part of the report should not be too detailed but should provide an overall view of the procedures.

3. **Data Results**—This explains what outcomes were received as a result of the gathering of the data. What are the results? This is a simple explanation of the facts that were obtained. The data itself can be presented here in the form of a table, chart, or graph.

4. **Analysis and Conclusions**—The conclusion is where the data is fully discussed and interpreted and where the author speculates about the findings. The author can explain the results and make assumptions based on the information that was gathered or compare and contrast his or her work with that done by others.

5. **References**—Some data reports have many references, while others have none. For example, a data report on the favorite breakfast foods for students of a particular class will not have a reference other than perhaps surveys. However, a comparison of precipitation levels for various parts of the world would likely have several reference sources. In this section, the author lists the sources he or she consulted in an effort to obtain the data that is being published.

Differentiation

Preteach English language learners the names and definitions of each data report section so they will be better prepared to participate in the whole-class explanation. English language learners and below-level students will benefit from frequent writing conferences for feedback and additional scaffolding. Require above-level students to cite and refer to at least three sources and compare and contrast their work and the work done by others.

Name: _____ **Date:** _____

Data Report

Purpose: Begin your report by stating the ultimate goal in gathering and evaluating the data.

_____

_____

Materials: List the materials that were used to obtain the data.

_____

_____

Methods: Explain how the data was obtained. Was it through research or practical application?

_____

_____

_____

Data Results: Provide the data that was obtained. It may be necessary to attach a separate graph or table to fully supply the data.

_____

_____

_____

_____

References: Write down the reference information for the sources you gathered information from.

_____

_____

_____

Analysis and Conclusions: What can be learned from analyzing the data? Make comparisons and inferences based on the findings.

_____

_____

_____

_____

Newspaper Article

Background Information

Writing a newspaper article on a mathematics-related theme is another way for students to use mathematics in everyday life as they clearly convey mathematical information and their ideas in a concise manner. The article usually answers the *who, what, where, when, why,* and *how* questions.

Grade Levels/Standards Addressed

See page 207 for the standards this strategy addresses, or refer to the Digital Resource CD (standards.pdf) to read the correlating standards in their entirety.

Genre

Expository

Stages of Writing Process

Prewrite, Draft, Revise, Edit, Publish

Activity

Divide the class into groups of three or four and give each group a newspaper or age-appropriate periodical to read as a model. Ask groups to locate and cut out an article about a mathematics topic. Write the following list on the board, and discuss the elements of a newspaper article.

A newspaper article has:

- **headline**—This is a short, concise phrase that explains the main point of the article.

- **byline**—This is the name of the person who wrote the newspaper article.

- **dateline**—This lists the month, day, and year the article was written.

- **illustration**—An illustration is optional in a newspaper article. It can help bring the point of the story home to the reader.

- **paragraph 1**—This should answer the *who, what, when,* and *where* questions.

- **paragraph 2**—This should answer the *how* and *why* questions. Answering *how* and *why* takes the reader to the next step.

- **last paragraph**—This is usually a conclusion, summary, or list of future prospects.

Have students mark these features in the article. Explain that a newspaper article typically addresses the five Ws—*who, what, where, when,* and *why*—and anticipates and answers readers' questions. A newspaper article can address difficult issues and questions related to mathematics, or it can document a new trend in mathematics. Have students select a mathematics topic about which they would like to write a newspaper article. Distribute the *Newspaper Article* activity sheet (page 225, newspaperarticle.pdf) to students to help them plan their articles. Then, have them write their articles on separate sheets of paper, being mindful to include some of the text features they observed from reading the original newspaper article. Students should work with their groups to provide feedback to one another in order to develop and strengthen the newspaper article.

Differentiation

Make sure English language learners understand the topic through review and discussion before beginning to write. Then, provide resource books for them during the writing process so they can look up words. Make sure all of the words on the board are defined and understood by below-level students. Use visuals whenever possible. Both English language learners and below-level students will benefit from working in mixed-ability groups. Have above-level students work in teams to design a mathematics newspaper dedicated to the mathematics topics being studied in class.

Name: _____ **Date:** _____

Newspaper Article

Directions: Answer the questions below as they relate to your mathematics topic. Then, write your newspaper article on a separate sheet of paper, making sure to include some of the text features you marked in the original newspaper article.

Topic: _____

Headline: _____

Who?

Who is the article about? _____

Who would be interested in reading it? _____

Who is the audience? _____

What?

What is the purpose of the article? _____

What is the main idea of the article? How does it relate to mathematics? _____

_____

What is the author's desired result? _____

When?

When does the event in the story take place? _____

When was the story written? _____

Where?

Where does the news story take place? _____

Where is the newspaper circulated? _____

Why?

Why was this printed in the newspaper instead of a book or other reference? _____

_____

Why did the events in the news story happen? _____

Why did the author write the article? What can be learned about mathematics as a result of this article? _____

Mathematics Fiction Story

Background Information

The Mathematics Fiction Story is a great way for students to weave mathematical knowledge into everyday life. This strategy has students write narratives in which they develop real or imagined experiences to convey mathematics information. In order for a mathematics fiction story to be believable, it must contain some convincing mathematics. Look for opportunities throughout the mathematics lessons to point out mathematics problems that could be turned into a story.

Grade Levels/Standards Addressed

See page 207 for the standards this strategy addresses, or refer to the Digital Resource CD (standards.pdf) to read the correlating standards in their entirety.

Genre

Narrative

Stages of Writing Process

Prewrite, Draft, Revise, Edit, Publish

Activity

Read a chapter from a mathematics fiction story. Identify with the class the mathematics problem and possible solutions. Discuss the main elements of a story:

- setting
- characters
- problem
- solution

Explain that a story has a beginning, middle, and end. The beginning usually describes the setting and introduces the characters. The reader learns more about the characters and the problem in the middle of the story. The ending tells the solution to the problem. Point out that mathematics facts and details need to be woven into the story and the plot. Work together as a class to write a story outline. Record student ideas on the board or display them using a document camera.

First, discuss the characters. Which characters should be in the story? Remember to limit the number of characters. Too many characters can lead to confusion. Brainstorm with students some settings and problems for their stories. Spend time researching the mathematics topic so students have a clear understanding of the topic and how it could be an issue in everyday life. Write each sentence as a class. Call on one student at a time to add to the story.

Once the story is written, read it to the class. Analyze how well the mathematics elements were handled. Identify any changes or additions that need to be made. Then, have students use the *Mathematics Fiction Story* activity sheet (page 227, mathfiction.pdf) to write their own mathematics fiction story, revising and editing their narratives based on peer and teacher feedback.

Differentiation

Give English language learners resources such as dual-language dictionaries, picture books, and encyclopedias at their reading levels. Hold frequent conferences with English language learner and below-level students throughout the writing process to provide modeling, feedback, and scaffolding. Challenge above-level students to include richer vocabulary, more dynamic language, and more complex sentence structures. Encourage above-level students to conduct research about the mathematics content prior to writing the story.

Mathematics Fiction Story

Directions: Use this story map to help you plan your mathematics fiction story. Follow the arrows to the next step.

Setting (Where and when does the story take place?)

Characters (Who or what are the people, animals, or objects in the story?)

Conflict/Problem (What is the mathematics-related problem?)

Action/Events (What are the attempts to solve the problem?)

Solution (How does the story end?)

Research Report

Background Information

A common writing assignment in the mathematics classroom is the Research Report in which students are expected to research a mathematics concept and write about their findings. Students gather information from print and digital sources to include in their reports.

Grade Levels/Standards Addressed

See page 207 for the standards this strategy addresses, or refer to the Digital Resource CD (standards.pdf) to read the correlating standards in their entirety.

Genre

Expository

Stages of Writing Process

Prewrite, Draft, Revise, Edit, Publish

Activity

Provide a variety of print and digital resources for students on various mathematics topics. Allow time for students to peruse the materials and choose a topic of interest that they would like to research. You may also choose to assign a research topic to students based on your available resources. Demonstrate how to access digital resources or how to use other resources that may be available outside of school, such as magazines, newspaper articles, television specials, etc.

Once students have gathered basic information, they are ready to start the research process. With your guidance and support, instruct students to write the main idea of their research report.

Encourage them to discuss their topics with a partner. Once you have approved the topic, students can begin thoroughly researching it.

Use the *Research Report* activity sheet (page 229, researchreport.pdf) to help students organize their information so that they can produce writing in which the development and organization are appropriate for the research report. The outline lists the main topic and supporting ideas.

Allow plenty of time for students to draft, revise, and edit their reports with partners. Students should develop and strengthen their writing based on their discussions with partners. Consider using the Author's Chair strategy (see pages 182–185) at this stage of the writing process. Group participants can ask questions, anticipate problems, or point out details that have been left out.

Conference individually with students when they have completed the rough draft of their research report. Students can use the tips in the Writing Process section of this book (see pages 16–19) to assist in the revising/editing of these reports. Show students how to cite the resources they used for the report.

Differentiation

Provide English language learners with visuals and extended review on research material to help them gain a clear understanding of the information. Challenge above-level students to research and write about a more complex topic. Require them to cite references. Hold frequent writing conferences with English language learners and below-level students to model, provide feedback, and scaffold the writing process. Also, conduct mini-lessons to preteach the next step of the writing process.

Research Report

Directions: Use this prewriting planner to help you organize your research.

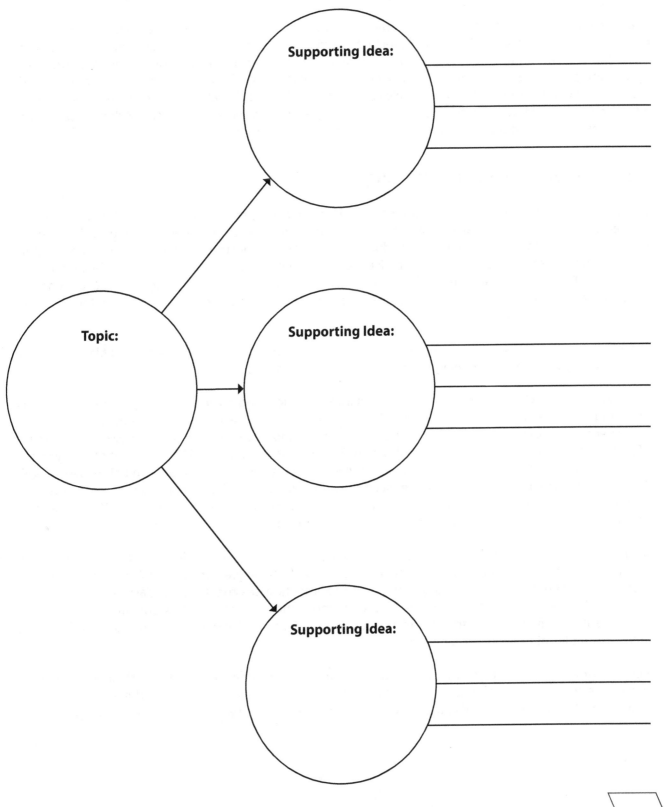

Assessing Writing Overview

Role of Assessment of Writing in the Mathematics Classroom

The role of writing assessment in the mathematics classroom has been another reason mathematics teachers avoid writing (Gahn 1989). However, not all writing assignments or activities in mathematics need to be graded. Writing-to-learn assignments seldom need to be graded. These experiences are to provide opportunities for students to express themselves and what they are learning. The concern for how to grade more formal writing assignments can be alleviated with rubrics and checklists. These two methods can be effective and meaningful ways to assess more formal types of writing in mathematics. Writing assessments will be described and discussed in detail in the last section of this book.

Authentic Assessment of Writing

Views of teaching and learning have changed to include the concept of constructivism—the belief that learners actively and dynamically construct the information they are learning about the world. The learner is not an "empty cup" to be filled with knowledge and information. Constructivism holds a view that learning includes and incorporates a dynamic and active mental process (Jones et al. 1987; Marzano, Pickering, and McTighe 1993; Resnick and Klopfer 1989). Students learn through interactive and integrative experiences in the classroom; the more a student actively listens, speaks, reads, writes, and thinks, the easier the learning and retention of knowledge will be.

There are a variety of ways to construct knowledge and learn (Pressley 1990; Weinstein and Mayer 1986), but one of the key ways to help learning occur is to have students write.

Although many teachers agree with the notion of interactive learning, they feel inadequate when grading or assessing this type of learning. For example, how does a teacher grade writing in mathematics? How does a teacher assign a grade to something that is not formal writing? How does the teacher assess the learning of mathematics skills and concepts through writing? These concerns are valid. Assessment of this type of writing must validate learning, and it must acknowledge the mathematics standards and objectives as well. Authentic assessment reflects back on the meaningful instruction and learning process. There are many different types of authentic assessment of writing done in the classroom (Feuer and Fulton 1993). There is room for authentic assessment in the mathematics classroom, too!

Incorporating authentic assessment in the mathematics classroom requires little time, effort, or experience. It is not uncommon for mathematics teachers to feel uncomfortable grading students' writing, but they may realize that they are already using some types of authentic assessment in their classrooms. The types of authentic assessments that lend themselves to writing in the mathematics classroom include holistic assessment, primary trait assessment, and analytic scoring (Cohen 1994; Herman, Aschbacher, and Winters 1992). Examples of these are included in the following pages.

Self-assessment and peer assessments provide opportunities for students to reflect on their own writing abilities as well as their mathematics understanding. Peer assessment also provides other examples of writing for students to read and compare and contrast with their own writing and understanding.

Assessing Writing Overview *(cont.)*

Standards Addressed

The following chart shows the correlating standards for each strategy in this section. Refer to the Digital Resource CD (standards.pdf) to read the correlating standards in their entirety.

Strategy	McREL Standards	Common Core State Standards
Holistic Assessment	Grades 1–2 (1.4) Grades 3–5 (1.4) Grades 6–8 (1.4) Grades 9–12 (1.4)	Grade 1 (W.1.5) Grade 2 (W.2.5) Grade 3 (W.3.5) Grade 4 (W.4.5) Grade 5 (W.5.5) Grade 6 (W.6.5) Grade 7 (W.7.5) Grade 8 (W.8.5) Grades 9–10 (W.9-10.5) Grades 11–12 (W.11-12.5)
Analytic Assessment	Grades 1–2 (1.4) Grades 3–5 (1.4) Grades 6–8 (1.4) Grades 9–12 (1.4)	Grade 1 (W.1.5) Grade 2 (W.2.5) Grade 3 (W.3.5) Grade 4 (W.4.5) Grade 5 (W.5.5) Grade 6 (W.6.5) Grade 7 (W.7.5) Grade 8 (W.8.5) Grades 9–10 (W.9-10.5) Grades 11–12 (W.11-12.5)
Primary Trait Assessment	Grades 1–2 (1.4) Grades 3–5 (1.4) Grades 6–8 (1.4) Grades 9–12 (1.4)	Grade 1 (W.1.5) Grade 2 (W.2.5) Grade 3 (W.3.5) Grade 4 (W.4.5) Grade 5 (W.5.5) Grade 6 (W.6.5) Grade 7 (W.7.5) Grade 8 (W.8.5) Grades 9–10 (W.9-10.5) Grades 11–12 (W.11-12.5)
Self-Assessment	Grades 1–2 (1.4) Grades 3–5 (1.4) Grades 6–8 (1.4) Grades 9–12 (1.4)	Grade 1 (W.1.5) Grade 2 (W.2.5) Grade 3 (W.3.5) Grade 4 (W.4.5) Grade 5 (W.5.5) Grade 6 (W.6.5) Grade 7 (W.7.5) Grade 8 (W.8.5) Grades 9–10 (W.9-10.5) Grades 11–12 (W.11-12.5)

Assessing Writing Overview *(cont.)*

Strategy	McREL Standards	Common Core State Standards
Peer Assessment	Grades 1–2 (1.4) Grades 3–5 (1.4) Grades 6–8 (1.4) Grades 9–12 (1.4)	Grade 1 (W.1.5) Grade 2 (W.2.5) Grade 3 (W.3.5) Grade 4 (W.4.5) Grade 5 (W.5.5) Grade 6 (W.6.5) Grade 7 (W.7.5) Grade 8 (W.8.5) Grades 9–10 (W.9-10.5) Grades 11–12 (W.11-12.5)
Teacher Conference	Grades 1–2 (1.4) Grades 3–5 (1.4) Grades 6–8 (1.4) Grades 9–12 (1.4)	Grade 1 (W.1.5) Grade 2 (W.2.5) Grade 3 (W.3.5) Grade 4 (W.4.5) Grade 5 (W.5.5) Grade 6 (W.6.5) Grade 7 (W.7.5) Grade 8 (W.8.5) Grades 9–10 (W.9-10.5) Grades 11–12 (W.11-12.5)

Holistic Assessment

Background Information

Holistic Assessment evaluates the overall effectiveness of the writing as opposed to the individual writing components. This assessment uses a list of criteria that are analyzed to produce one score on a scale of 1–6. The criteria, which address both mathematics objectives and writing skills, are determined prior to the assignment, and students are informed of the criteria before writing takes place. The criteria can be adapted to meet students' needs and the objectives of the assignment. The four main criteria are as follows:

- **Idea Development/Organization**—Does the student communicate a central idea or purpose? Has this idea been supported throughout the piece, and is there a conclusion?

- **Fluency/Structure**—Does the student use correct grammar (verb endings, verb tenses, pronouns, etc.) and syntax in the writing?

- **Word Choice**—Does the student incorporate a variety of words and content-specific terms?

- **Mechanics**—Does the student use correct spelling, capitalization, and punctuation?

The objective of this assessment is for students to develop and strengthen their writing by planning, revising, and editing. By implementing this strategy prior to assigning a writing assignment, students can plan and revise their work based on clear expectations and guidelines.

Grade Levels/Standards Addressed

See page 231 for the standards this strategy addresses, or refer to the Digital Resource CD (standards.pdf) to read the correlating standards in their entirety.

Genres

Expository, Summary, Narrative, Persuasive

Stage of Writing Process

Reflection

Activity

Prior to beginning a writing assignment, distribute the *Holistic Assessment* activity sheet (page 234, holistic.pdf); review and discuss it. (Please note that this rubric can be altered to fit the needs of the writing assignment and the age of students.) Be sure that they are clear on the expectations of the writing assignment and on how they will be assessed prior to beginning the writing. You may also choose to include students in creating the criteria. After students complete the writing, pair each student with a partner to exchange the writing and provide suggestions, comments, and feedback. Then, collect students' writing and use the rubric to rate each piece with a score from 1–6.

Differentiation

Adapt the rubric to meet the needs of English language learners and their abilities. They may not be expected to meet the grade-level expectations in grammar and mechanics, for example. Challenge above-level students to create their own criteria and rubric. Help below-level students use the rubric throughout the writing process to meet the expectations.

Name: _____ Date: _____

Holistic Assessment

Title: _____ Topic: _____

Level 6 —Writing conveys clear meaning and ideas.
• organizes the piece with several paragraphs, and develops ideas and a conclusion • incorporates smooth transitions • incorporates necessary mathematics concepts and ideas • uses a variety of vocabulary, including mathematics vocabulary and terms • writing has few or no grammatical or mechanical errors
Level 5—Writing conveys meaning and ideas.
• organizes the piece with several paragraphs, though some portions may not be fully developed • incorporates some smooth transitions • incorporates some mathematics concepts and ideas • uses some mathematics vocabulary and terms • writing has some grammatical or mechanical errors
Level 4—Writing expresses an idea most of the time.
• develops a cohesive paragraph • uses a variety of sentence structures with few transitions • selects some mathematics vocabulary and terms • writing has some grammatical or mechanical errors
Level 3—Begins to write about an idea but fails to support it.
• sometimes develops a cohesive paragraph • uses complete sentences • incorporates few mathematics vocabulary and terms • writing has many grammatical or mechanical errors
Level 2—Attempts to write about an idea.
• there are no cohesive paragraphs • uses complete sentences sometimes • lack of mathematics vocabulary and terms incorporated in writing • writing has multiple grammatical or mechanical errors
Level 1—There is no common theme or idea.
• sentences are written but incomplete • uses sentences with few transitions • mathematics vocabulary and terms are not used • writing has too many grammatical or mechanical errors

#51153—Writing Strategies for Mathematics Second Edition © *Shell Education*

Analytic Assessment

Background Information

With Analytic Assessment, each component of the writing is analyzed independently of the others and given its own score. The writing assignment is given several scores, each representing the different components. The teacher may also choose to weigh one component more heavily than another to add emphasis. Analytic Assessment not only allows the teacher to provide specific feedback to students, but it also helps the teacher target certain areas in planning, instruction, and assessment (Perkins 1983). With any writing rubric, clearly communicate the goals and expectations prior to assigning a writing task.

The objective of this assessment is for students to develop and strengthen their writing by planning, revising, and editing. By implementing this strategy prior to assigning a writing assignment, students can plan and revise their work based on clear expectations and guidelines.

Grade Levels/Standards Addressed

See page 231 for the standards this strategy addresses, or refer to the Digital Resource CD (standards.pdf) to read the correlating standards in their entirety.

Genres

Expository, Summary, Narrative, Persuasive

Stage of Writing Process

Reflection

Activity

Create with students a rubric that scores each component of the writing assignment. The writing components may include composition, mechanics, sentence formation, mathematics content, and usage. Determine if one component of the rubric should receive more emphasis than another. Determine the number of points scored for each component. Review the *Analytic Assessment* activity sheet (page 236, analytic.pdf) with students prior to giving instructions on the writing assignment. Be sure students understand how they will be graded. Show models of writing samples. Allow time for students to complete the writing assignment and then compare it to the designated rubric. Students can then edit their work as they deem necessary. Use the *Analytic Assessment* activity sheet to score students' writing assignments.

Differentiation

Work independently with English language learners to create a rubric that meets their specific needs to ensure a greater chance of success. If desired, include a component of writing in English as part of the rubric. Encourage above-level students to create their own rubrics, score their writing assignments, and compare them with the scores you determined for the writing. You may also weigh certain components more heavily to challenge above-level students. If appropriate, adapt rubrics for below-level students to address their individual needs.

Name: _____ **Date:** _____

Analytic Assessment

Title: _____

Topic: _____

Skill	Excellent (3 points)	Satisfactory (2 points)	Needs Improvement (1 point)
Stays on topic			
Shows a clear purpose (topic sentence)			
Includes supporting details with specific examples			
Has sequential and/or logical development			
Includes a main idea paragraph			
Clearly presents mathematics concepts			
Expresses ideas clearly			
Uses complete sentences			
Uses varied sentence types and structures			
Uses mathematics words correctly			
Uses correct spelling			

Comments: _____

_____

_____

_____

_____

#51153—Writing Strategies for Mathematics Second Edition

Primary Trait Assessment

Background Information

Primary Trait Assessment is a way for the teacher to focus on one specific skill or trait. The teacher determines the skill, trait, or feature that will be analyzed and assessed in a piece of writing. The trait can be writing-based or mathematics-based, depending on the intent of the lesson. In primary trait writing, only the focus or primary trait is scored; the other traits and elements are ignored.

A benefit of using the Primary Trait Assessment is that students may feel more at ease with the primary trait focus because they can focus on one area. Teachers, too, can focus on specific areas of concern. The Primary Trait Assessment also allows the teacher to focus specifically on the mathematics skill or concept while ignoring the mechanics and composition areas of writing. With any writing rubric, clearly communicate the goals and expectations prior to assigning a writing task.

The objective of this assessment is for students to develop and strengthen their writing by planning, revising, and editing. By implementing this strategy prior to assigning a writing assignment, students can plan and revise their work based on clear expectations and guidelines.

Grade Levels/Standards Addressed

See page 231 for the standards this strategy addresses, or refer to the Digital Resource CD (standards.pdf) to read the correlating standards in their entirety.

Genres

Expository, Summary, Narrative, Persuasive

Stage of Writing Process

Reflection

Activity

Determine the writing assignment to be used for the Primary Trait Assessment rubric for scoring. Select the specific trait or skill that you would like students to focus on during the writing assignment. Display the *Primary Trait Assessment* activity sheet (page 238, primarytrait.pdf) for students to see before they begin writing. Tell students the primary trait that is the focus for this writing assignment. Explain that the other areas of writing will be ignored for assessment purposes. Allow time for students to draft and edit their writing before submitting it for assessment. If desired, pair students with partners to edit one another's writing. When using the *Primary Trait Assessment* activity sheet, be sure to give specific feedback on how students can improve in this primary trait. Use this rubric the next time students write so that you can look for progress on the primary trait.

Differentiation

Select a primary trait for English language learners to fit their specific language needs. Challenge above-level students by selecting a primary trait that is not a clear strength, and have above-level students decide how to improve their areas of focus. Give specific feedback to below-level students on what they need to improve, and encourage them to revise and edit their work. Design a specific primary trait focus that will meet their individual needs.

Name: _____ Date: _____

Primary Trait Assessment

Title: _____

Topic: _____

Select the primary trait for focus and use the following rubric (with adjustments, if needed) to assess students' writing. Leave specific feedback.

5 The student demonstrates desired skills throughout the text.

4 Most of the time, the student demonstrates desired skills in the text.

3 Occasionally, the student demonstrates desired skills in the text.

2 Seldom does the student demonstrate desired skills in the text.

1 The student is not using desired skills in the text.

_____ **Content:**
The writer presents a main point and uses a clear organizational structure. The writer presents information logically. The writer anticipates and addresses the concerns and questions of the reader. The writer cites sources of information whenever necessary. The writer uses books and other resources to gather information. The writer conveys an intended purpose in writing. The writer understands and portrays the concepts of mathematics in a meaningful way.   **Comments:** _____
_____ **Writing Conventions:**
The writer has taken time and effort to ensure the writing does not have spelling errors. Each sentence begins with a capital and ends with the correct punctuation. The writing contains clear transitions to convey ideas. Each paragraph of the writing is dedicated to only one idea. The report contains no mechanical errors. The writing is ready to publish.   **Comments:** _____
_____ **Use of Language:**
The writer creates a structure appropriate to the needs of a specific audience. The writer uses descriptive language that clarifies and enhances ideas. The writer engages the reader. The writer expresses an individual, consistent voice. The writer uses an interesting lead.   **Comments:** _____
_____ **Organization/Structure:**
The writing is organized and follows the recommended structure for a report. The parts of a report (title, main idea, examples to support the main idea, and summary or conclusion) are present. The report is at least five paragraphs in length.   **Comments:** _____

Self-Assessment

Background Information

Self-Assessment is a way for students to assess their own work. Students learn to look critically at their own work and analyze it for strengths and weaknesses. A benefit of using Self-Assessment is that students take ownership of the assessment process, which personalizes the learning for them. Some students who are extremely sensitive about receiving feedback may appreciate this method of assessment. Also, teachers can use student reflections as a springboard into developing personal goals for students. Having a personal goal to strive toward will make future writing assignments more meaningful. With any writing assessment, clearly communicate the goals and expectations prior to assigning the task of Self-Assessment.

The objective of this assessment is for students to independently develop and strengthen their writing by planning, revising, and editing. By implementing this strategy prior to assigning a writing assignment, students can plan and revise their work based on clear expectations and guidelines.

Grade Levels/Standards Addressed

See page 231 for the standards this strategy addresses, or refer to the Digital Resource CD (standards.pdf) to read the correlating standards in their entirety.

Genres

Expository, Summary, Narrative, Persuasive

Stage of Writing Process

Reflection

Activity

Determine the writing assignment to be used for Self-Assessment. Display the *Self-Assessment* activity sheets (pages 240–241, selfassessment. pdf) for students to see before they begin writing, using a document camera. Tell students that they will be responsible for evaluating their own writing when they have completed the writing assignment. Encourage students to refer to the checklist and survey throughout the writing process so that they keep the goals in mind as they work. For students who may be unaccustomed to using Self-Assessment, consider allowing them to work in pairs to "practice" completing the checklist and survey before they have officially published their work. This may help them look more critically at their own work before the final evaluation. After students have completed their Self-Assessment checklist and survey, take time to conference individually to provide constructive feedback and set goals for the next writing piece. When work begins on the following assignment, ask students to identify one or two elements on the checklist where they would like to improve.

Differentiation

Consider limiting the elements on the checklist for English language learners and below-level students, while still maintaining a focus on using and applying the grade-appropriate mathematics content. English language learners will need the checklist adapted to meet their specific needs so that the expectations are appropriate for their current levels of language development. Below-level students may focus on one or two elements in each category, so as to not overwhelm them. Challenge above-level students to apply higher-level writing strategies, use more advanced vocabulary, and incorporate more compound, complex, and compound-complex sentence structures. Add to their checklists in areas where they can work on developing their skills so that they are appropriately challenged.

Name: _____ Date: _____

Self-Assessment

Title: _____

Topic: _____

Directions: Answer the questions below to self-assess your writing.

1. **Capitalization**

   _____ Did I capitalize the first word of each sentence?

   _____ Did I capitalize proper nouns such as names and places?

2. **Punctuation**

   _____ Did I put a ., !, or a ? at the end of each sentence?

   _____ Did I use commas in a series?

   _____ Did I use commas in dates?

   _____ Have I been careful not to use the exclamation point too much?

   _____ Have I used quotation marks when I needed them?

3. **Handwriting**

   _____ Did I write neatly?

   _____ Are there missing words that need to be added?

   _____ Are there extra words that need to be deleted?

4. **Spelling**

   _____ Did I check my spelling?

5. **Overall Content**

   _____ Have I been clear about the topic of my writing?

   _____ Is it easy to tell what the main idea is?

   _____ Have I used any special words or phrases that add to my writing?

   _____ Are there any words or phrases that are confusing?

   _____ Have I used an interesting lead?

   _____ Have I considered what would make my writing better?

6. **Mathematics Content**

   _____ Did I use the correct mathematics terms?

   _____ Did I write about the mathematics topic accurately?

   _____ Did I do adequate research on the mathematics topic?

   _____ Did I use my own words?

   _____ Do I clearly understand the mathematics topic I am writing about?

#51153—*Writing Strategies for Mathematics Second Edition*

Self-Assessment *(cont.)*

I think this writing piece shows that I can...

_____

_____

_____

One thing I learned from writing this is...

_____

_____

_____

I have improved my writing in these areas...

_____

_____

_____

The next time I write, I will...

_____

_____

_____

Did I give my best to this writing assignment? Why or why not?

_____

_____

_____

Peer Assessment

Background Information

Peer Assessment is a way for students to practice analyzing the work of others. Students learn to look critically at others' work and analyze it for strengths and weaknesses. They also deepen their understanding of the expectations of each particular writing genre because they must know what a good topic sentence is if they are going to determine if their peers' work have effective topic sentences. As with Self-Assessment, students take ownership of the assessment process—even though they are not assessing their own work—which personalizes the learning for them. This assessment tool can be used in conjunction with another, such as Teacher Conference, or a traditional rubric. Teachers can also ask students to reflect on what they saw in their partners' work and choose an aspect that they might want to include in their own writing in the future. Clearly communicate the goals and expectations of the assignment prior to assigning a writing task. The objective of this assessment is for students to develop and strengthen their writing by planning, revising, and editing. By implementing this strategy prior to assigning a writing assignment, students can plan and revise their work based on clear expectations and guidelines.

Grade Levels/Standards Addressed

See page 232 for the standards this strategy addresses, or refer to the Digital Resource CD (standards.pdf) to read the correlating standards in their entirety.

Genres

Expository, Summary, Narrative, Persuasive

Stage of Writing Process

Reflection

Activity

Determine the writing assignment to be used for Peer Assessment. Display the *Peer Assessment* activity sheet (page 243, peerassessment.pdf) before students begin writing, and model how to complete it with a sample piece of writing. This should be a positive process, so provide explicit examples of feedback and constructive criticism so that students are clear on how they are to evaluate classmates' work. Tell students that they will be responsible for evaluating their peers' writing when they have completed the writing assignment. Encourage students to keep their audience in mind as they work. After all students have completed their writing, distribute the *Peer Assessment* activity sheet and assign partners. Have students read their partners' work and add their comments to the assessment. You may wish to collect the activity sheets to screen the partners' comments or add your own comments before returning them to students with their written work.

Differentiation

Preteach English language learners how to use the activity sheet, as well as the language they will need to respond in this activity. Also consider how to instruct these students' partners about responding to the writing of English language learners so that their comments are directed toward the expectations of their individual language levels. Adjust their response prompts, if needed. Below-level students may not need differentiation to complete the *Peer Assessment* activity sheet, but their partners may need some guidance on how to respond. Consider altering the checklists for these students' writing to address their levels of proficiency. Have above-level students work in small groups to evaluate their writing based on higher-level prompts, and ask them to provide examples to support their feedback and suggestions.

Peer Assessment

Author's Name: _____

Title: _____ Topic: _____

Mark an X under the appropriate column	Very Much	Somewhat
1. I enjoyed reading this piece of writing.		
2. I think this writing is easy to read.		
3. The writing is creative.		
4. The writing made sense to me.		

Finish the following statements as best you can. Remember, your job is to help the writer.

1. One thing I really like about this writing is…

_____

2. One thing I think the author can improve upon is…

_____

3. Something I would like to tell the author is…

_____

4. I think other people that will read this piece will think…

_____

5. One thing that I can learn from the author and this writing is…

_____

Teacher Conference

Background Information

Teachers are often frustrated and disappointed when students' writing assignments are turned in off-topic, disorganized, or lacking the proper amount of information. Teacher Conferences allow teachers to maintain consistent communication with their students throughout the writing process. These opportunities, although brief, can keep students on track and give them the scaffolds and suggestions they need to develop and strengthen their writing. It is important for teachers to also take the time in these conferences to ask questions of students and listen to what challenges they might be facing so that students feel that the conferences are less evaluative and more cooperative.

Grade Levels/Standards Addressed

See page 232 for the standards this strategy addresses, or refer to the Digital Resource CD (standards.pdf) to read the correlating standards in their entirety.

Genres

Expository, Summary, Narrative, Persuasive

Stage of Writing Process

Reflection

Activity

Determine the writing assignment to be used for Teacher Conferences. Display the *Teacher Conference* activity sheet (page 245, teacherconference.pdf) for students to see before they begin writing. Tell students that they will be meeting with you at each stage of the writing process to discuss their writing, share concerns, ask for suggestions, and receive feedback. Students should keep their copy of the activity sheet with them as they write. Encourage them to refer to the form throughout the writing process so that they keep the goals of each phase in mind as they work. As you take students through each phase of the writing process, take time to conference individually to provide constructive feedback and set goals for the next stage. When their writing assignments are complete, be sure to add clear, explicit feedback so that students have a clear understanding of the strengths and weaknesses of their work. When students begin the next assignment, ask them to identify one or two elements on the checklist where they would like to improve.

Differentiation

Consider limiting the elements on the checklist for English language learners and below-level students, while still maintaining a focus of using and applying the grade-appropriate mathematics content. English language learners may need the checklist adapted to meet their specific needs so that the expectations are appropriate for their current levels of language development. Below-level students may focus on one or two elements in each category, so as to not overwhelm them. Above-level students should be challenged to apply higher-level writing strategies, use more advanced vocabulary, and incorporate more compound, complex, and compound-complex sentence structures. Add to their checklists in areas where they can work on developing their skills so that they are appropriately challenged.

Name: _____ **Date:** _____

Teacher Conference

Title: _____

Topic: _____

	Needs Work	Good	Excellent
Brainstorming			
The writing is well thought out.	_____	_____	_____
The writing is easy to follow.	_____	_____	_____
The writing is creative and interesting.	_____	_____	_____
Drafting			
The writing is organized.	_____	_____	_____
The writing uses the correct format.	_____	_____	_____
The writing is complete.	_____	_____	_____
Editing and Revising			
The writing has complete sentences.	_____	_____	_____
The writing uses correct punctuation.	_____	_____	_____
The writing uses capitalization correctly.	_____	_____	_____
The writing uses correct spelling.	_____	_____	_____
The writing uses transition words.	_____	_____	_____
Publishing			
The writing is written or typed neatly.	_____	_____	_____
The writing has a capitalized title.	_____	_____	_____
The writing has been illustrated, if needed.	_____	_____	_____

Teacher Comments

Your writing is very good in these ways: _____

Your writing could be made better by doing these things: _____

_____

© Shell Education   #51153—*Writing Strategies for Mathematics Second Edition*

Name: _____ Date: _____

Internal Text Structure Reference Sheet

Description
The information about a topic (object, person, animal, idea, event) includes facts, characteristics, traits, and features.

Sequence
The facts, events, or concepts are presented in sequential order. The topic is developed in order of importance, or the sequence or steps in a process are given.

Compare and Contrast
The similarities (comparison) and differences (contrast) among facts, people, events, and concepts are presented.

Cause and Effect
The information is presented to make clear that certain things (effects) happen as a result of other things (causes).

Problem and Solution
The development of a problem and possible solutions to it are presented.

References Cited

Adams, Marilyn Jager. 1990. *Beginning to Read: Thinking and Learning about Print*. Cambridge, MA: Massachusetts Institute of Technology.

Allyn, Pam. 2013. *Be Core Ready: Powerful, Effective Steps to Implementing and Achieving the Common Core State Standards*. Upper Saddle River, NJ: Pearson Education.

Anderson, Richard C., and Peter Freebody. 1985. "Vocabulary Knowledge." In *Theoretical Models and Processes of Reading*. 3rd edition. Edited by Harry Singer and Robert B. Ruddell. Newark, DE: International Reading Association, 343–371.

Angelo, Thomas A., and K. Patricia Cross. 1993. *Classroom Assessment Techniques: A Handbook for College Teachers*. 2nd edition. San Francisco: Jossey-Bass.

Atwell, Nancie. 1984. "Writing and Reading Literature from the Inside Out." *Language Arts* 61 (3): 240–252.

Barr, Mary A., and Mary K. Healy. 1988. "School and University Articulation: Different Contexts for Writing Across the Curriculum." *New Directions for Teaching and Learning* 36 (Winter): 43–53.

Bean, John C. 1996. "Helping Students Read Difficult Texts." In *Engaging Ideas: The Professor's Guide to Integrating Writing, Critical Thinking, and Active Learning in the Classroom*. San Francisco: Jossey-Bass, 133–147.

Becker, Wesley C. 1977. "Teaching Reading and Language to the Disadvantaged—What We Have Learned from Field Research." *Harvard Educational Review* 47 (4): 518–543.

Boutwell, Marilyn A. 1983. "Reading and Writing: A Reciprocal Agreement." *Language Arts* 60 (6): 723–730.

Bringle, Robert G., and Julie A. Hatcher. 1996. "Reflection Activities for the College Classroom." Paper presented at the National Gathering on June 21.

Britton, James, Tony Burgess, Nancy Martin, Alex McLeod, and Harold Rosen. 1975. *The Development of Writing Abilities, 11-18*. New York: Macmillan Education.

Brozo, William G., and Michele L. Simpson. 2003. *Readers, Teachers, Learners: Expanding Literacy Across the Content Areas*. 4th edition. Upper Saddle River, NJ: Merrill.

Calkins, Lucy McCormick. 1983. *Lessons from a Child: On the Teaching and Learning of Writing*. Portsmouth, NH: Heinemann.

Calkins, Lucy, Amanda Hartman, and Zoë White. 2005. *One to One: The Art of Conferring with Young Writers*. Portsmouth, NH: Heinemann.

Calkins, Lucy, Mary Ehrenworth, and Christoper Lehman. 2012. *Pathways to the Common Core: Accelerating Achievement*. Portsmouth, NH: Heinemann.

Carey-Webb, Allen. 2001. *Literature and Lives: A Response-Based, Cultural Studies Approach to Teaching English*. Urbana, IL: National Council of Teachers of English.

Chamot, Anna Uhl, and J. Michael O'Malley. 1994. *The CALLA Handbook*. Reading, MA: Addison-Wesley.

References Cited (cont.)

Christen, William L., and Thomas J. Murphy. 1991. "Increasing Comprehension by Activating Prior Knowledge." ERIC Digest. Bloomington, IN: ERIC Clearinghouse on Reading, English, and Communications ERIC Identifier: ED328885.

Cohen, Andrew D. 1994. *Assessing Language Ability in the Classroom.* 2nd edition. Boston, MA: Heinle and Heinle.

Combs, Warren E. 2012. *Writer's Workshop for the Common Core: A Step-by-Step Guide.* Larchmont, NY: Eye on Education.

Corona, Cathy, Sandra Spangenberger, and Iris Venet. 1998. "Improving Student Writing through a Language Rich Environment." M.A. Action Research Project, St. Xavier University and IRI/Skylight, 61 pages.

Dechant, Emerald. 1991. *Understanding and Teaching Reading: An Interactive Model.* Hillsdale, NJ: Lawrence Erlbaum.

Duke, Nell K., and P. David Pearson. 2001. "Developing Comprehension in the Primary Grades." A presentation to the International Reading Association. http://www.ciera.org/library/presos/2001/2001IRA/ira01ddp.pdf.

Dunlap, Carmen Zuñiga, and Evelyn Marino Weisman. 2006. *Helping English Language Learners Succeed.* Huntington Beach, CA: Shell Education.

Eanet, Marilyn G., and Anthony V. Manzo. 1976. "REAP—A Strategy for Improving Reading/Writing/Study Skills." *Journal of Reading* 19 (8): 647–652.

Elbow, Peter. 1973. *Writing without Teachers.* New York: Oxford University Press.

Emig, Janet. 1977. "Writing as a Mode of Learning." *College Composition and Communication* 28 (2): 122–128.

Feuer, Michael J., and Kathleen Fulton. 1993. "The Many Faces of Performance Assessment." *Phi Delta Kappan* 74 (6): 478.

Fink, Rosalie. 2006. *Why Jane and John Couldn't Read—And How They Learned.* Newark, DE: International Reading Association.

Fisher, Douglas, and Gay Ivey. 2005. "Literacy and Language as Learning in Content Area Classes: A Departure from 'Every Teacher a Teacher of Reading.'" *Action in Teacher Education* 27 (2): 3–11.

Fisher, Douglas, and Nancy Frey. 2004. *Improving Adolescent Literacy: Content Area Strategies at Work.* Upper Saddle River, NJ: Pearson Education.

Frayer, Dorothy A., Wayne C. Fredrick, and Herbert J. Klausmeier. 1969. "A Schema for Testing the Level of Concept Mastery. Working Paper No. 16." Madison, WI: Wisconsin Research and Development Center for Cognitive Learning.

Fulwiler, Toby. 1980. "Journals across the Disciplines." *English Journal* 69 (12): 14–19.

Gahn, Shelley Mattson. 1989. "A Practical Guide for Teaching and Writing in the Content Areas." *Journal of Reading* 32 (6): 525–531.

References Cited *(cont.)*

Gentry, J. Richard. 2006. *Breaking the Code: The New Science of Beginning Reading and Writing.* Portsmouth, NH: Heinemann.

Gere, Anne Ruggles, ed. 1985. *Roots in the Sawdust: Writing to Learn across the Disciplines.* Urbana, IL: National Council of Teachers of English.

Goldman, Susan R., Jason L. G. Braasch, Jennifer Wiley, Arthur C. Graesser, and Kamila Brodowinska. 2012. "Comprehending and Learning From Internet Sources: Processing Patterns of Better and Poorer Learners." *Reading Research Quarterly* 47 (4): 356–381.

Graves, Donald H. 1983. *Writing: Teachers & Children at Work.* Portsmouth, NH: Heinemann.

Graves, Donald H., and Jane Hansen. 1983. "The Author's Chair." *Language Arts* 60 (2): 176–83.

Greenberg, Joel, and Christine Rath. 1985. "Empowering Students through Writing." *Educational Leadership* 42 (5): 10–13.

Haggard, Martha Rapp. 1982. "The Vocabulary Self-Collection Strategy: An Active Approach to Word Learning." *Journal of Reading* 26 (3): 203–207.

Haggard, Martha Rapp. 1986. "The Vocabulary Self-Collection Strategy: Using Student Interest and World Knowledge to Enhance Vocabulary Growth." *Journal of Reading* 29 (7): 634–642.

Hamilton-Wieler, Sharon. 1988. "Writing as a Thought Process: Site of a Struggle." *Journal of Teaching Writing* 7 (2): 167–180.

Hamilton-Wieler, Sharon. 1989. "Awkward Compromises and Eloquent Achievements." *English Education* 21 (3): 152–169.

Hamp-Lyons, Elizabeth. 1983. "Developing a Course to Teach Extensive Reading Skills to University-Bound ESL Learners." *System* 11 (3): 303–312.

Harste, Jerome C., Kathy G. Short, and Carolyn Burke. 1988. *Creating Classrooms for Authors: The Reading-Writing Connection.* Portsmouth, NH: Heinemann.

Harvey, Stephanie. 1998. *Nonfiction Matters: Reading, Writing, and Research in Grades 3–8.* Portland, ME: Stenhouse Publishers.

Hefflin, Bena R., and Douglas K. Hartman. 2002. "Using Writing to Improve Comprehension: A Review of the Writing-to-Reading Research." In *Improving Comprehension Instruction: Rethinking Research, Theory, and Classroom Practice*, edited by Cathy Collins Block, Linda B. Gambrell, and Michael Pressley. San Francisco: Jossey-Bass, 199–228.

Herman, Joan L., Pamela R. Aschbacher, and Lynn Winters. 1992. *A Practical Guide to Alternative Assessment.* Alexandria, VA: Association for Supervision and Curriculum Development.

Hightshue, Deborah, Dott Ryan, Sally McKenna, Joe Tower, and Brenda Brumley. 1988. "Writing in Junior and Senior High Schools." *Phi Delta Kappan* 69 (10): 725–728.

Hoyt, Jeff E. 1999. "Remedial Education and Student Attrition." *Community College Review* 27 (2): 51–73.

References Cited (cont.)

Huba, Mary E., and Jann E. Freed. 2000. "Using Rubrics to Provide Feedback to Students. In *Learner-Centered Assessment on College Campuses: Shifting the Focus from Teaching to Learning.* Needham Heights, MA: Allyn & Bacon, 151–200.

Jones, Beau Fly, Annemarie Sullivan Palincsar, Donna Sederburg Ogle, and Eileen Glynn Carr, eds. 1987. *Strategic Teaching and Learning: Cognitive Instruction in the Content Areas.* Alexandria, VA: Association of Supervision and Curriculum Development.

Karelitz, Ellen Blackburn. 1982. "The Rhythm of Writing Development." In *Understanding Writing: Ways of Observing, Learning, and Teaching*, edited by Nancie Atwell and Thomas Newkirk. Chelmsford, MA: Northeast Regional Exchange.

Koedinger, Kenneth R., and Hermina J. M. Tabachneck. 1994. "Two Strategies Are Better Than One: Multiple Strategy Use in Word Problem Solving." Paper presented at the Annual Meeting of the American Educational Research Association in New Orleans, April 4–8.

Laflamme, John G. 1997. "The Effect of Multiple Exposure Vocabulary Method and the Target Reading/Writing Strategy on Test Scores." *Journal of Adolescent & Adult Literacy* 40 (5): 372–384.

Lenski, Susan Davis, Mary Ann Wham, and Jerry L. Johns. 1999. *Reading & Learning Strategies for Middle & High School Students.* Dubuque, IA: Kendall/Hunt.

Marzano, Robert J., Debra J. Pickering, and Jay McTighe. 1993. *Assessing Student Outcomes: Performance Assessment Using the Dimensions of Learning Model.* Alexandria, VA: Association for Supervision and Curriculum Development.

Moore, David W., and Sharon Arthur Moore. 1986. "Possible Sentences." In *Reading in the Content Areas: Improving Classroom Instruction.* 2nd edition. Edited by Ernest K. Dishner, Thomas W. Bean, and John E. Readence, and David W. Moore. Dubuque, IA: Kendall/Hunt.

Moore, David W., Sharon Arthur Moore, Patricia M. Cunningham, and James W. Cunningham. 1994. *Developing Readers and Writers in the Content Areas. K–12.* 2nd edition. White Plains, NY: Longman.

Nagy, William E., and Judith A. Scott. 2000. "Vocabulary Processes." In *Handbook of Reading Research, Volume III*, edited by Michael L. Kamil and Rebecca Barr. Mahwah, NJ: Lawrence Erlbaum Associates, Inc., 269–284.

National Center for Education Statistics. 2013. "120 Years of Literacy." National Assessment of Adult Literacy. http://nces.ed.gov/naal/lit_history.asp.

National Governors Association Center for Best Practices, Council of Chief State School Officers. 2010. *Common Core State Standards: English Language Arts Standards.* Washington, DC: National Governors Association Center for Best Practices, Council of Chief State School Officers.

Ogle, Donna M. 1986. "K-W-L: A Teaching Model that Develops Active Reading of Expository Text." *Reading Teacher* 39 (6): 564–70.

Palmatier, Robert A. 1973. "A Notetaking System for Learning." *Journal of Reading* 17 (1): 36–39.

Pauk, Walter. 1988. *A User's Guide to College: Making Notes and Taking Tests.* Lincolnwood, IL: Jamestown Publishers.

References Cited *(cont.)*

Peregoy, Suzanne F., and Owen F. Boyle. 2005. *Reading, Writing, and Learning in ESL: A Resource Book for K–12 Teachers*. 4th edition. Upper Saddle River, NJ: Pearson Education.

Perkins, David N., and Gavriel Salomon. 1988. "Teaching for Transfer." *Educational Leadership* 46 (1): 22–32.

Perkins, Kyle. 1983. "On the Use of Composition Scoring Techniques, Objective Measures, and Objective Tests to Evaluate ESL Writing Ability. *TESOL Quarterly* 17 (4): 651–671.

Pinnell, Gay Su. 1988 (January). "Success of Children at Risk in a Program That Combines Writing and Reading. Technical Report No. 417." In *Reading and Writing Connections*, edited by Jana M. Mason. Boston, MA: Allyn & Bacon.

Pressley, Michael. 1990. *Cognitive Strategy Instruction That Really Improves Children's Academic Performance*. Cambridge, MA: Brookline Books.

Readence, John E., Thomas W. Bean, and R. Scott Baldwin. 1981. *Content Area Literacy: An Integrated Approach*. Dubuque, IA: Kendall Hunt Publishing.

Resnick, Lauren B., and Leopold Klopfer, eds. 1989. *Toward the Thinking Curriculum: Current Cognitive Research*. Alexandria, VA: Association for Supervision and Curriculum Development.

Ryder, Randall J., and Michael F. Graves. 2003. *Reading and Learning in Content Areas*. 3rd ed. New York: John Wiley & Sons, Inc.

Santa, Carol Minnick, Lynn Havens, and Shirley Harrison. 1996. "Teaching Secondary Science through Reading, Writing, Studying, and Problem Solving." In *Content Area Reading and Learning: Instructional Strategies*, edited by Diane Lapp, James Flood, and Nancy Farnan. Needham Heights, MA: Allyn & Bacon, 165–179.

Schwartz, Robert M., and Taffy E. Raphael. 1985. "Concept of Definition: A Key to Improving Students' Vocabulary." *The Reading Teacher* 39 (2): 198–205.

Self, Judy, ed. 1987. *Plain Talk About Learning and Writing Across the Curriculum*. Richmond, VA: Virginia Department of Education.

Sloan, Megan S. 1996. "Encouraging Young Students to Use Interesting Words in Their Writing." *The Reading Teacher* 50 (3): 268–269.

Smith, Christine C., and Thomas W. Bean. 1980. "The Guided Writing Procedure: Integrating Content Reading and Writing Improvement." *Reading World* 19 (3): 290–294.

Sorenson, Sharon. 1989. *Webster's New World High School Writer's Handbook: A Complete Guide for Writing Across the Curriculum*. Englewood Cliffs, NJ: Prentice Hall.

Staton, Jana. 1980. "Writing and Counseling: Using a Dialogue Journal." *Language Arts* 57 (5): 514–518.

Steffens, Henry. 1988. "The Value and Difficulties of Teaching the History of Science and Technology in Secondary Schools." Paper presented at the Annual Meeting of the American Historical Association. Cincinnati, OH: ED 306182.

Sullo, Bob. 2007. *Activating the Desire to Learn*. Alexandria, VA: Association for Supervision and Curriculum Development.

References Cited *(cont.)*

Taba, Hilda. 1967. *Teacher's Handbook for Elementary Social Studies.* Palo Alto, CA: Addison-Wesley.

Tierney, Robert J., Rebekah Caplan, Linnea Ehri, Mary K. Healy, and Mary Hurdlow. 1989. "Writing and Reading Working Together." In *Collaboration through Writing and Reading: Exploring Possibilities,* edited by Anne Haas Dyson. Urbana, IL: National Council of Teachers of English, 169–209.

Tileston, Donna Walker. 2004. *What Every Educator Should Know About Student Motivation.* Thousand Oaks, CA: Corwin Press.

University of Nebraska–Lincoln Writing Center. 2013. "Assessing Student Writing." University of Nebraska–Lincoln. Accessed June 20. http://www.unl.edu/writing/assessing-student-writing.

Vacca, Richard T., and Jo Anne L. Vacca. 2005. *Content Area Reading: Literacy and Learning Across the Curriculum.* 8th ed. Boston: Pearson Education, Inc.

Venn, John. 1880. "On the Diagrammatic and Mechanical Representation of Propositions and Reasonings." *Philosophical Magazine and Journal of Science* 9 (59): 1–18.

Wagner, Tony. 2008. *The Global Achievement Gap.* New York: Basic Books.

Walker, Anne. 1988. "Writing-across-the-Curriculum: The Second Decade." *English Quarterly* 21 (2): 93–103.

Weinstein, Claire E., and Richard E. Mayer. 1986. "The Teaching of Learning Strategies." In *Handbook of Research on Teaching and Learning,* edited by Merlin C. Wittrock. New York: MacMillan, 315–327.

West, Charles K., James A. Farmer, and Phillip M. Wolff. 1991. *Instructional Design: Implications from Cognitive Science.* Upper Saddle River, NJ: Prentice Hall.

Widmayer, Sharon, Elena Collins, Holly Gray, Laurie Miller, and Gray Rossen. 2004. "Technology that Reaches and Teaches Every Student." TESOL Pre-Convention Institute.

Willis, Scott. 1992. "Interdisciplinary Learning: Movement to Link the Disciplines Gains Momentum." *ASCD Curriculum Update* 34 (2): 1–8.

Winchester School District. 1987. "*Winchester High School Excellence in Education Grant: Reading and Writing Across the Curriculum Final Report.*" Washington, DC: Office of Educational Research and Improvement. ERIC Identifier: ED305589.

Wolk, Ronald A. 2011. *Wasting Minds: Why Our Education System Is Failing and What We Can Do About It.* Alexandria, VA: Association for Supervision and Curriculum Development.

Wood, Karen D. 1984. "Probable Passages: A Writing Strategy." *The Reading Teacher* 37 (6): 496–499.

Worsley, Dale, and Bernadette Mayer. 1989. *The Art of Science Writing.* New York: Teachers and Writers Collaborative.

Yinger, Robert. 1985. "Journal Writing as a Learning Tool." *Volta Review* 87 (5): 21–33.

Suggestions for Further Reading

Cunningham, James W., Patricia M. Cunningham, and Sharon V. Arthur. 1981. *Middle and Secondary School Reading*. New York: Longman.

Fulwiler, Toby. 1982. "Writing: An Act of Cognition." In *Teaching Writing in All Disciplines*, edited by C. Williams Griffin. San Fransisco: Jossey-Bass, 15–23.

Gagne, Ellen D., Carol Walker Yekovich, and Frank R. Yekovich. 1993. *The Cognitive Psychology of School Learning*. New York: Addison-Wesley.

Kamil, Michael L., Peter B. Mosenthal, P. David Pearson, and Rebecca Barr, eds. 1984. *Handbook of Reading Research, Volume III*. Mahwah, NJ: Lawrence Erlbaum Associates, Inc.

McGinley, William J., and Peter R. Denner. 1987. "Story Impressions: A Prereading/Writing Activity." *The Journal of Reading* 31 (3): 248–253.

McNeil, John D., and John Wiles. 1990. *The Essentials of Teaching*. Farmington Hills, MI: Macmillan.

O'Malley, J. Michael, and Anna Uhl Charmot. 1990. *Learning Strategies in Second Language Acquisition*. New York: Cambridge University Press.

Pearson, P. David, and Linda Fielding. 1991. "Comprehension Instruction." In *Handbook of Reading Research, Volume II*, edited by Rebecca Barr, Michael L. Kamil, Peter Mosenthal, and P. David Pearson. Mahwah, NJ: Lawrence Erlbaum Associates, Inc., 815–860.

Pearson, P. David, and Dale D. Johnson. 1978. *Teaching Reading Comprehension*. New York: Holt, Rinehart, and Winston.

Poplin, Mary S. 1988. "Holistic/Constructivist Principles of the Teaching/Learning Process: Implications for the Field of Learning Disabilities." *Journal of Learning Disabilities* 21 (7): 401–416.

Contents of the Digital Resource CD

Pages	Resource	Filename
N/A	Correlation to Standards	standards.pdf
42	Frayer Model	frayermodel.pdf frayermodel.doc
47	Concept of Definition Map	conceptdefinition.pdf conceptdefinition.doc
52	List-Group-Label	listgrouplabel.pdf listgrouplabel.doc
62	Word Trails	wordtrails.pdf wordtrails.doc
71	KWL Chart	kwlchart.pdf kwlchart.doc
75	Think Sheet	thinksheet.pdf thinksheet.doc
79	Free-Association Brainstorming	freeassociation.pdf freeassociation.doc
84	Probable Passages	probablepassages.pdf probablepassages.doc
95	Reader-Response Writing Chart	readerresponse.pdf readerresponse.doc
115	Double-Entry Journal	doubleentry.pdf doubleentry.doc
122	Three-Part Journal	threepartjournal.pdf threepartjournal.doc
128	Cornell Note-Taking System	cornellsystem.pdf cornellsystem.doc
132	Note-Taking System for Learning	notesystemlearning.pdf notesystemlearning.doc
136	T-List	tlist.pdf tlist.doc
142	Frame	frame.pdf frame.doc

Contents of the Digital Resource CD *(cont.)*

Pages	Resource	Filename
146	Venn Diagram	venndiagram.pdf venndiagram.doc
150	Triangular Venn Diagram	triangularvenn.pdf triangularvenn.doc
154	Cause-and-Effect Map	causeeffect.pdf causeeffect.doc
158	Semantic Word Map	semanticwordmap.pdf
167	Problem-Solution Map	problemsolution.pdf problemsolution.doc
171–172	Time Order Map	timeorder.pdf timeorder.doc
181	Reading-Writing Workbench	readwriteworkbench.pdf readwriteworkbench.doc
190	Read, Encode, Annotate, Ponder	reap.pdf reap.doc
196	GIST	gist.pdf gist.doc
203	Guided Reading and Summarizing Procedure	grasp.pdf grasp.doc
209	Summary-Writing Microtheme	summarywriting.pdf summarywriting.doc
211	Thesis-Support Microtheme	thesissupport.pdf thesissupport.doc
213	Data-Provided Microtheme	dataprovided.pdf dataprovided.doc
215	Quandary-Posing Microtheme	quandaryposing.pdf quandaryposing.doc
217	RAFT Assignment	raft.pdf raft.doc
219	Business Letter	businessletter.pdf businessletter.doc
221	Friendly Letter	friendlyletter.pdf friendlyletter.doc
223	Data Report	datareport.pdf datareport.doc
225	Newspaper Article	newspaperarticle.pdf newspaperarticle.doc

Contents of the Digital Resource CD *(cont.)*

Pages	Resource	Filename
227	Mathematics Fiction Story	mathfiction.pdf mathfiction.doc
229	Research Report	researchreport.pdf researchreport.doc
234	Holistic Assessment	holistic.pdf holistic.doc
236	Analytic Assessment	analytic.pdf analytic.doc
238	Primary Trait Assessment	primarytrait.pdf primarytrait.doc
240–241	Self-Assessment	selfassessment.pdf selfassessment.doc
243	Peer Assessment	peerassessment.pdf peerassessment.doc
245	Teacher Conference	teacherconference.pdf teacherconference.doc
246	Internal Text Structure Reference Sheet	internaltextstructure.pdf